With the creativity and communication skills we have come to expect from Thaddeus Williams, this outstanding, engaging, and interactive volume guides readers to think deeply about the greatness and grace of God in fresh and thoughtful ways. With Scripture, readings, stories, art, and the reflections of other key thinkers, Williams invites us to worship, trust, love, adore, follow, and enjoy the eternal triune God, who is our creator, providential sustainer, and redeemer. Encouraging prayerful response and application, the book prioritizes reverence over relevance, with the hope of bringing renewal to our lives and reform to our churches. It is a genuine joy to heartily recommend *Revering God*.

DAVID S. DOCKERY, president, Southwestern Baptist Theological Seminary

One can never read too many books that revel in the awesome attributes of God, and Thaddeus Williams's *Revering God* is a worthy addition to the genre. Deftly weaving timely cultural analysis with timeless theological truth, the book is a valuable reminder to the contemporary church: reverence to God is a far more pressing priority than relevance to the culture.

BRETT MCCRACKEN, senior editor at The Gospel Coalition; author, *The Wisdom Pyramid: Feeding Your Soul in a Post-Truth World*

Combining great writing with great theology, Williams uses everything from The Joker to the Sistine Chapel to a civil rights hero to a "rolling saint" to reveal the true nature and aims of God. Williams guides readers through readings, rhythms, reflections, repentance, and resources, and the inevitable result is a renewed reverence for the Great Seeker.

KATY FAUST, founder and president of Them Before Us

Thaddeus Williams doesn't just want us to know God; he wants us to love him. In this book, he skillfully works toward that goal by weaving together theology, apologetics, and personal accounts of seasoned Christians in a way that is both emotionally satisfying and intensely practical. The result is a multifaceted presentation of our infinitely deep, loving, wise, gracious, creative, awe-inspiring God that moved me to worship. My hope is that many who have never before encountered a God-centered view of all reality—not to mention the God who is worthy of it—will read *Revering God* and be changed forever.

AMY K. HALL, writer, editor, and podcaster at Stand to Reason

T0315528

The best place to begin the study of God is with worship. As my colleague Thaddeus Williams writes compellingly in *Revering God*, "Human beings are designed for awe." Beginning with reverence, Williams mines deeply into who God is, who we are, and how to know and worship him. This book is a rare find among theologians as it is both deep and wide, filled with truth and approachable for the believer hungry to know and worship our awesome God.

ED STETZER, dean of Talbot School of Theology, Biola University

For many reasons, this is an important, carefully argued book but is especially important in that it undertakes to creatively discuss the essential, even difficult, elements of the Reformed and scriptural doctrine of God, with an extensive knowledge and use of popular culture. It is thus hopefully able to capture a youthful readership with a subject long considered appropriate only for scholars. For this reason, I wish the book great success.

REV. DR. PETER R. JONES, executive director, TruthXChange; associate pastor, New Life Presbyterian Church, Escondido, CA

If your God is small, his character, attributes, and Word will mean little to you. If he is big, however, these will make all the difference in the world. Thaddeus Williams shows us the bigness of God.

JOANNE JUNG, associate dean and professor of Theology and Biblical Studies, Talbot School of Theology, Biola University

REVERING GOD

REVERING
GOD

HOW TO MARVEL AT YOUR MAKER

THADDEUS J. WILLIAMS

with the voices of Vishal Mangalwadi,
John Perkins, Michael Horton, Fred Sanders,
Erik Thoennes, and Joni Eareckson Tada

ZONDERVAN
REFLECTIVE

ZONDERVAN REFLECTIVE

Revering God
Copyright © 2024 by Thaddeus J. Williams

Published in Grand Rapids, Michigan, by Zondervan. Zondervan is a registered trademark of The Zondervan Corporation, L.L.C., a wholly owned subsidiary of HarperCollins Christian Publishing, Inc.

Requests for information should be addressed to customercare@harpercollins.com.

Zondervan titles may be purchased in bulk for educational, business, fundraising, or sales promotional use. For information, please email SpecialMarkets@Zondervan.com.

ISBN 978-0-310-16042-1 (audio)

Library of Congress Cataloging-in-Publication Data

Names: Williams, Thaddeus J., author.
Title: Revering God : how to marvel at your maker / Thaddeus J. Williams.
Description: Grand Rapids, Michigan : Zondervan Reflective, [2024] | Includes bibliographical references and index.
Identifiers: LCCN 2024007637 (print) | LCCN 2024007638 (ebook) | ISBN 9780310160403 (softcover) | ISBN 9780310160427 (audio) | ISBN 9780310160410 (ebook)
Subjects: LCSH: God (Christianity) | Creation. | Christian life. | BISAC: RELIGION / Christian Living / Spiritual Growth | RELIGION / Christian Living / Personal Growth
Classification: LCC BT103 .W5548 2024 (print) | LCC BT103 (ebook) | DDC 248.3—dc23/ eng/20240326
LC record available at https://lccn.loc.gov/2024007637
LC ebook record available at https://lccn.loc.gov/2024007638

Cover design: Emily Weigel
Cover photos: © Vlad Ra27 / Shutterstock; Emily Weigel
Interior design: Sara Colley

Printed in the United States of America
24 25 26 27 28 LBC 5 4 3 2 1

*To my father, Russ, who modeled and taught
me so much about the Father.*

CONTENTS

PART 3 – VICTORIOUS: GOD RULES

PART 4 – ETERNALLY LOVING: GOD IS FATHER, SON, AND HOLY SPIRIT

PART 5 – REDEMPTIVE: GOD SAVES SINNERS

PART 6 – EXPRESSIVE: GOD MAKES BEAUTY

HOW TO READ THIS BOOK

THE BOOK YOU ARE NOW HOLDING WAS BUILT ON THE COUNTERCULTURAL PREMISE that you, for all your best qualities, are nowhere near as interesting, awesome, or worthy of worship as the Creator of the universe. You find your true self not by trying to figure yourself out but by seeking God. I don't mean the god of the televangelists who serves as a kind of cosmic Santa Claus to shower prosperity on faithful donors. I don't mean the Republican or Democrat god, a god saddled on an elephant or donkey, who exists primarily to give a supernatural endorsement of your political convictions. I don't mean god as an abstract *x* at the end of a philosopher's neat syllogism. I mean the God who actually exists, "the King of the ages, immortal, invisible, the only God, [to whom is due] honor and glory forever and ever" (1 Tim. 1:17).

A brief word about the structure and flow of this book: after a short introduction on the qualifications of a theologian—in which I build the unflattering but biblical case that the good theologian is an idiotic, fanatical, nerdy, violent slave—we embark on our study of six divine truths. Structured around the word *revere*, we will behold our Maker as . . .

Reliable: God tells the truth.
Enjoyable: God satisfies.
Victorious: God rules.
Eternally loving: God is Father, Son, and Holy Spirit.
Redemptive: God saves sinners.
Expressive: God makes beauty.

Notice that each of these divine attributes corresponds to an aspect of our God-given humanness. How does the reliability of God shape our intellectual lives? How does the enjoyability of God impact our emotional lives? How does the victory of God effect our actions? How does his eternal love deepen our relational lives? How does his redemptive grace liberate our moral lives? How does his expressive artistry inspire our creative lives and spark our imaginations? You see, God is to be God over the *whole human person*. God is God over all or no God at all. He wants to redeem, enhance, and glorify every facet of our humanness. No more half measures. No more dabbling with your Maker. No more shivering on the shore and toe dipping. Let us plunge our whole selves into the ocean of his infinite goodness. Let us revere him as Lord over our minds, our feelings, our actions, our relationships, our morals, our imaginations—all of us.

We begin our study of each of the six divine attributes with "Readings," in which we ponder select passages of Scripture to prime our souls to better internalize the truth about God. I recommend you choose one of the passages, whichever resonates with you most profoundly, and commit it to memory.

After "Readings" comes "Rhythms," which offers down-to-earth suggestions for living out the truth of a given divine attribute in your daily life. Take me up on one or two suggestions so the truth about God migrates from your head and heart to your hands. The best theology is not merely believed but also lived, not merely contemplated but also habituated into our actions.

Next come five concise chapters blending philosophy, psychology, apologetics, church history, pop culture, personal stories, and, most importantly, Scripture to deepen our understanding and reverence for God. Unlike some theology books, which hold all the thrill of a PowerPoint presentation on integer mass values in Java coding, these chapters aim to describe the least boring Being in existence in a way that is, well, not boring.

Then comes a personal account from one of six brilliant living theologians of how a particular attribute of God has impacted their life. This includes such luminaries as "India's foremost Christian intellectual"[1] Vishal Mangalwadi, civil rights pioneer John Perkins, world-class systematic theologians Michael Horton, Fred Sanders, and Erik Thoennes, along with disability rights advocate and artist Joni Eareckson Tada. Each of the six parts then closes with a prayer, a set of "Reflect" questions for personal or small group study, and a "Repent" guide to help you identify areas of your life that are out of sync with God's attributes. Last comes a "Resources" section to point you toward helpful books to deepen your awe of God.

It has taken a while, but the science is slowly catching up to the Scriptures that human beings are designed for awe, captured in the frequent biblical command to have *yirah*—awe, fear, reverence—for our Maker. Recent studies have found that being awestruck makes people more generous, altruistic, environmentally responsible, and intellectually discerning while less depressed and less anxious.[2] No wonder more than thirty-five thousand people make the trek to Mount Everest each year, 3.5 million to Yosemite, 4.5 million to the Grand Canyon, and 30 million to Niagara Falls.[3] We crave awesomeness and the joyous self-forgetfulness it brings. It is my prayer that this book gives you a much-needed break from the burden of self. I pray that it evokes awe, that it inspires you to marvel at your Maker, that you find yourself revering the reliable, enjoyable, victorious, eternally loving, redemptive, and expressive God of the Bible, and thereby fulfill the chief end of your existence, to glorify and enjoy him forever.[4]

THADDEUS WILLIAMS
Rancho Mission Viejo, California

WHAT IS A THEOLOGIAN?

HE RANKS AS ONE OF *TIME* MAGAZINE'S TOP FIFTY LIVING THINKERS. HE HAS BEEN my personal mentor for over twenty years. His free will, metaphysics, and philosophy of mind graduate classes trained me how to think. He is a die-hard Chiefs fan. He has been a sage through seasons of deep doubt and a friend through bouts of deep anxiety.

His name is J. P. Moreland, and he thinks I'm an idiot.

How do I know he thinks I'm an idiot? Because he regularly reminds me. Our office doors are about a first down apart, and we cross paths often. Before you conclude that J. P. belongs on *Time* magazine's Top 50 Living Insensitive Jerks list, let me tell you what he means and why it's a blessing I'd like to pass along. It has something to do with taking God so seriously we can take ourselves unseriously. It's what G. K. Chesterton was after when he said, "Angels can fly because they take themselves so lightly."[1]

If you set out to do the sacred task of theology—which I can safely assume since you are holding this book—then you are an idiot like me. A biologist can achieve a certain level of expertise in the field of biology to merit the title. The same goes for arithmetic, chemistry, cardiology, and a host of other studies. But there's something unique about theology—the study of God—on account of the sheer magnitude and infinity of its subject.

A good definition of a theologian, then, is one who realizes what a total idiot he or she is about the deepest things of God, yet seeks to mitigate his or her idiocy as much as possible by bringing it often to the sacred Scriptures. (Perhaps theology conferences should be called idiot conventions.) The man history remembers as the "prince of preachers"—Charles Spurgeon—made the point in a sermon in Southwark, UK, on January 7, 1855, when he was just twenty years old.

[Theology] is a subject so vast, that all our thoughts are lost in its immensity; so deep, that our pride is drowned in its infinity. Other subjects we can compass and grapple with; in them we feel a kind of self-content, and go our way with the thought, "Behold I am wise." But when we come to this master-science, finding that our plumb-line cannot sound its depth, and that our eagle eye cannot see its height, we turn away with the thought that vain man would be wise, but he is like a wild ass's colt; and with solemn exclamation, "I am but of yesterday, and know nothing." No subject of contemplation will tend more to humble the mind than thoughts of God.[2]

Far too few preachers today preach like that, and far too few theologians think like that anymore. What fills stadium-sized sanctuaries, catapults books to the *New York Times* bestseller lists, and turns average Joes (along with Joels and Joyces) into celebrity super-pastor rock stars are messages about being "stronger than we think," "ruling our day," "unleashing the power of go," and "achieving our best life now." If that God-is-merely-a-means-to-my-own-power-and-prosperity propaganda irks or exhausts you, then you are reading the right book.

Beyond the church, we have mainstream messages about being true to ourselves, following our hearts, living our truths, and other junior-high-yearbook-worthy advice masquerading as wisdom. All this self-centered, pseudo-profundity amounts to so much unnecessary and impossible pressure on ourselves. If you can see the writing on the wall, the numbered days of this self-obsession, then this is the book for you.

There's something unique about theology—the study of God—given the sheer magnitude and infinity of its subject.

We need more Spurgeons today, people so unconcerned with their own likability that they can tell it to us straight. Our pride needs a good drowning. A healthy serving of humble pie would do us all a lot of good, especially in our age that so brazenly markets pride as a virtue. There's nothing more pride-killing than pondering a Being who is infinitely more interesting, good, powerful, just, wise, and glorious than we are. We could all use a five-foot-seven mustachioed *Time* magazine Top 50 philosopher hobbling toward us in the morning to remind us, ever so kindly, of our idiocy.

So, consider this your formal invitation to be a theologian. The only qualification is that you're an idiot, willing to study alongside another idiot. Congratulations!

FIVE MARKS OF A THEOLOGIAN

Every time I enter a lecture hall at my university, I commence the class with the same two words: "Greetings, theologians!" In the chairs sit art, film, communications, psychology, business, computer science, engineering, and sociology majors among others, always outnumbering the Bible and theology majors. Yet I greet *all* of them as theologians. It's not a gimmick or catchphrase. I want every student who comes through my classroom to walk out with a sense that, as R. C. Sproul loved to say, "everyone is a theologian." From the Greek *theos* for "God" and *logos* for "study," anyone who seeks to study and learn more about their Creator is a theologian. When my seven-year-old son asks, "Is Jesus God?" or "Why did God make broccoli?" he is a miniature theologian.

Of course not everyone will sport a corduroy blazer with elbow patches, learn Greek and Hebrew, cite Augustine or Aquinas, or explain how Platonism inspired the docetic heresies in the first to fourth centuries. But regardless of your major, how you earn a paycheck, how much (or how little) you've read, or whether you can say *hypostatic union* ten times fast whilst puffing Captain Black through a briar pipe, if you seek to better understand your Maker, then you, too, are a theologian. So let us begin.

· · ·

Greetings, theologian!

We have already established that the first requirement of a theologian is to be an idiot. But what else goes into this sacred task? Five hundred years ago, Martin Luther famously listed six requirements. In one of his famous Table Talks (number 3425, to be exact), delivered around his long wooden kitchen table (I've seen it at his Wittenberg home), flanked by young theologians in training, the stout German Reformer highlighted the following:

1. The grace of the Spirit.
2. *Anfechtung*, a German term for terrible dread or agonizing struggle as we realize our utter helplessness without God.[3]

3. Experience—not just abstract pondering but real-life, transformative personal encounters with God in his Word and in a local flesh-and-blood community of fellow believers.
4. Opportunity—spotting and taking daily moments to share gospel truths with others.
5. Consistent reading and study of sacred Scripture.
6. Broad engagement with other academic disciplines.

Two hundred years ago, former slave, Revolutionary War veteran, and theologian Lemuel Haynes, also the first black man ordained as a minister in the United States, offered five marks of a theologian:[4]

1. Love for Christ.
2. Wisdom, including knowing "the deceit in his own heart" and "the intrigues of the enemy."
3. Patience to withstand "the storms of temptation" and "all the fatigues and sufferings to which his work exposes him."
4. Courage and fearlessness in the face of opposition.
5. Vigilance not to fall asleep on the job but "to watch for the first motion of the enemy and give the alarm, lest souls perish through his drowsiness and inattention."[5]

Solid lists no doubt. Allow me to build on Luther and Haynes. A theologian should also be marked by these characteristics:

1. IDIOCY

We covered this above, but some clear scriptural support is in order. One of history's seminal theologians, the apostle Paul, said, "Never be wise in your own sight" (Rom. 12:16). He added, "'Knowledge' puffs up, but love builds up. If anyone imagines that he knows something, he does not yet know as he ought to know" (1 Cor. 8:1–2). Good theologians have the humility to acknowledge that on this side of eternity, we see in a "mirror dimly" (1 Cor. 13:12). If God is what Herman Bavinck called "an ocean of essence, unbounded and immeasurable,"[6] then the theologian knows he or she only offers mere drops from that infinite ocean—precious, soul-hydrating, life-giving drops, but drops nonetheless.

After celebrating Christmas Mass in 1273, and after writing an estimated eight million words of theology (including classics like *Summa Contra Gentiles* and the unfinished *Summa Theologiae*), Thomas Aquinas told a close friend, "All that I have written appears to be so much straw." Aquinas, like all good theologians, was smart enough to realize his own idiocy before an infinite God. Charles Octavius Boothe concurred:

> Before the charge "know thyself," ought to come the far greater charge, "know thy God." But, though the study of the being and character of God is a duty which we dare not disregard, still, let us not be unmindful of the fact that we vile, short-sighted worms should approach the solemn task of studying God with feelings of humility and awe. God is found of the lowly, but hides himself from the proud and self-sufficient man.[7]

2. FANATICISM

For our second mark, let us eavesdrop on the prayers of some of history's great theological minds:

> "Please show me your glory."
>
> —Moses (Ex. 33:18)

> O God, you are my God; earnestly I seek you; my soul thirsts for you; my flesh faints for you.
>
> —David (Ps. 63:1)

> Oh, the depth of the riches and wisdom and knowledge of God! How unsearchable are his judgments and how inscrutable his ways! . . . To him be glory forever. Amen.
>
> —Paul (Rom. 11:33, 36)

> Lord my God, my sole hope, help me to believe and never to cease seeking you. Grant that I may always and ardently seek out your countenance. Give me the strength to seek you, for you help me to find you.
>
> —Augustine[8]

> O my God, teach my heart where and how to seek you, where and how to find you. . . . Let me seek you in my desire, let me desire you in my seeking. Let me find you by loving you, let me love you when I find you.
>
> —Anselm[9]

We taste Thee, O Thou Living Bread, and long to feast upon Thee still:
We drink of Thee, the Fountainhead, and thirst our souls from Thee to fill.

—Bernard of Clairvaux[10]

It is a joy of heart to us that you are what you are, that you are so gloriously
exalted at the right hand of God. We long more fully and clearly to behold
that glory.

—John Owen[11]

Give me . . . the passion that will burn like fire, Let me not sink to be a
clod; Make me Thy fuel, Flame of God.

—Amy Carmichael[12]

May it be my sleep, my food and drink, to do the will of my Heavenly
Father.

—George Whitefield[13]

Lord, help us to worship Thee in life as well as lip. May our whole being be
taken up with Thee. . . . Our hearts are weary for Thee, thou King.

—Charles Spurgeon[14]

What is a man without Thee! What is all that he knows, vast accumulation
though it be, but a chipped fragment if he does not know Thee!

—Søren Kierkegaard[15]

O God, the Triune God, I want to want thee; I long to be filled with longing; I thirst to be made more thirsty still.

—A. W. Tozer[16]

Such are the prayers of fanatics (in the original sixteenth-century Latin
sense of *fanaticus*, "one inspired by a God," and the seventeenth-century
"zealous person, person affected by enthusiasm," or the dictionary definition
of "someone with excessive and single-minded zeal."[17]). These are prayers
from men and women who surveyed the universe and found that, of all
things to spend our calories and willpower to seek, nothing compares to
the one who made the universe. Without God, the universe itself is an
expanding, dying void.

In a self-obsessed world, a world that champions creature worship over

Creator worship, the theologian may very well come across as a madman. Yet the theologian can stomach ridicule because he or she recognizes God as the *summum bonum*, Anselm's "something than which nothing greater can be thought,"[18] Augustine's "good of all things,"[19] Edwards's "only happiness with which our souls can be satisfied,"[20] Bavinck's "overflowing fountain of all goods."[21] God is the Good behind every good, the Truth behind every truth, and the Beauty behind every beauty. The obsession, the fanatical longing, the insatiable thirst to enjoy more of our Maker, the stubborn refusal to settle for finite fixes are marks of good theologians. They echo the psalmist, "How precious to me are your thoughts, O God" (Ps. 139:17). They heed Paul's command, "Do not be slothful in zeal, be fervent in spirit" (Rom. 12:11).

Of all things to spend our calories and willpower to seek, nothing compares to the one who made the universe.

In all the zealous seeking after God, it is never about book knowledge for book knowledge's sake. It is to *know about* God, yes, but for the chief aim of *knowing* God. J. I. Packer said it best:

> To be preoccupied with getting theological knowledge as an end in itself, to approach Bible study with no higher a motive than a desire to know all the answers, is the direct route to a state of self-satisfied self-deception. . . . Our concern must be to enlarge our acquaintance, not simply with the doctrine of God's attributes, but with the living God whose attributes they are. . . . We must seek in studying God, to be led to God.[22]

3. NERDINESS

As fanatics seeking to know God, good theologians immerse themselves in God's words. They "nerd out" to Scripture. Jamie Love implores us to "go hard after the word of God . . . to devote yourselves to the study of God's word for all your days, to labor to know the mind of God and to be conformed to it, to be bold in proclaiming God's testimonies, to delight in the word of God, and to pursue obedience to the word of God for the sake of our character and conduct."[23]

A good *Lord of the Rings* nerd spends so much time in Tolkien's text. They can name the five Maiar (or wizards) sent to Middle-earth by the Valar, pontificate for hours about the mysterious Tom Bombadil, or lull you into deep REM sleep with facts about the origin and fate of all 20 Rings of Power. They love the story so dearly that they enjoy probing ever deeper into the text. So it is with those who love God's story. They become holy nerds. In an age in which 12 percent of Americans think Joan of Arc was Noah's wife and 75 percent can't name the four gospels,[24] we need legions of holy nerds who love the inspired text.

Psalm 119 is our credo here. "Teach me your statutes!" (v. 12); "Open my eyes, that I may behold wondrous things out of your law" (v. 18); "Give me life according to your word" (v. 25); "Give me understanding, that I may keep your law and observe it with my whole heart" (v. 34); "I trust in your word" (v. 42); "I will meditate on your statutes" (v. 48); "I delight in your law" (v. 70); "The law of your mouth is better to me than thousands of gold and silver pieces" (v. 72); "I hope in your word" (v. 81); "Forever, O LORD, your word is firmly fixed in the heavens" (v. 89); "How sweet are your words to my taste, sweeter than honey to my mouth!" (v. 103); "The sum of your word is truth" (v. 160); "Deliver me according to your word" (v. 170). Quina Aragon (not to be confused with Aragorn) comments on this psalm,

> Motivated by God's self-revealing character, the psalmist humbly asks for understanding, but not just any kind of understanding. He wants the intimate, experiential, and transformative knowledge of God that can only come from an encounter with God. Like Moses, the psalmist is essentially praying, "Please show me your glory" (Exod. 33:18) and he looks in the right place to see it: God's word.[25]

The verses of Psalm 119—all 176 of them—are addressed to God. They are prayers. As Helmut Thielicke counseled aspiring theologians, "A theological thought can breathe only in the atmosphere of dialogue with God."[26] Good theologians converse with their Creator often. If you feel burned out, unmoved, jaded, or bored with the Bible, then ask its Divine Author to open your eyes to behold wondrous things in the text. Then read it; then pray some more; then read it again and pray some more; then read. . . . Rinse and repeat all the days of your life.

4. VIOLENCE

We discover the aim of all this prayerful study of God's Word in Psalm 119: "I have stored up your word in my heart, *that I might not sin against you*" (v. 11, emphasis added). The true theologian is not content with biblical insights until those insights make their way from the head and heart to the hands. Holy living to the glory of God is the end game of good theology.

In June 2010 I passed a marble bust of Abraham Kuyper and entered a hall of learned men in medieval robes, each one seeking to publicly tear my research on free will to shreds.[27] I took my place at the podium in my tuxedo and white bow tie, with theological titans like Herman Bavinck and Herman Dooyeweerd looking on from their oil portraits behind me. To my right sat my paranymph, my bride, Jocelyn. The Free University of Amsterdam has maintained a centuries-old tradition for their doctoral defenses. Each defender is required to have at least one paranymph by his or her side during the dispute. In European history, paranymphs were, at times, armed to physically defend the doctoral candidate in the event that the theological dispute erupted into physical violence. (Thankfully, my wife's fearsome presence kept my examiners in check.)

When I say violence is a mark of a theologian, I do not mean physical violence or any form of violence against others. I mean, rather, what Paul spoke of when he said, "By the Spirit you *put to death* the deeds of the body" (Rom. 8:13, emphasis added), "*Put to death* therefore what is earthly in you" (Col. 3:5, emphasis added), and "Those who belong to Christ Jesus have *crucified the flesh* with its passions and desires" (Gal. 5:24, emphasis added). Good theologians are not perfect, but they do engage in what the Puritans called "mortification," the Holy Spirit-powered effort to kill whatever sins haunt and terrorize their hearts.

I know of no faster way to sever your head from your heart, no surer path to a dead orthodoxy, no quicker route to a spiritually barren, nihilistic wasteland, than to allow sin to go unchallenged and unmortified in one's daily life. English puritan John Owen said it better: "The life, vigour, and comfort of our spiritual life depend much on our mortification of sin. . . . [Unmortified sin] intercepts all the beams of God's love and favour. It takes away all sense of the privilege of our adoption. . . . Kill sin or sin will be killing you."[28]

5. SLAVERY

One of the most slickly advertised lies of our day is that there is such a thing as absolute freedom, that an individual can be lord of their own universe, servant to none. Self-glory, not servanthood, is the name of the game.

Not serving, however, is simply not an option. "It may be the devil or it may be the Lord, but you're gonna have to serve somebody,"[29] sang the great troubadour-theologian Bob Dylan. The people most convinced they are being their most authentic selves have a way of unwittingly bowing to ideologues and influencers. Consider the twentysomething who says, "To hell with the prison of traditional sexual morality. I'm going to embrace and express all my sexual desires!" (Never mind the fact that study after study shows that those in monogamous male-female marriage covenants enjoy the most satisfying sex lives.[30]) Our sexual revolutionary is hardly as liberated and courageous as he, she, they, or ze may think. They are faithfully living out the dogmas of men like Alfred Kinsey, Wilhelm Reich, Michel Foucault, John Money, and other ideologues they've likely never heard of,[31] not to mention their tragic, secret bondage to a certain dark lord (2 Tim. 2:26).

When the delusion of self-lordship makes its way into the theological world, we end up with prima donna theologians chasing celebrity status. They gradually stop speaking hard truths from God's Word for fear of upsetting their growing fan base. They become chameleons taking on the colors of mainstream culture. The spirit of the age eventually holds more sway in their hearts than the Spirit of truth. They catch the waves of the *zeitgeist*, which, like all other waves, will crash and leave them wiped out and irrelevant on the sand.

True theologians know both *that* they are servants and *who* it is they serve. They are mastered not by the *zeitgeist*—the spirit of the age—but *Gottgeist*—the Spirit of God. They can say with Paul, "For am I now seeking the approval of man, or of God? Or am I trying to please man? If I were still trying to please man, I would not be a servant of Christ" (Gal. 1:10). Like Paul, they think of themselves as God's slaves (Rom. 1:1; Titus 1:1), pouring themselves out for the church (Phil. 2:17), and servants to all (1 Cor. 9:19).

When the apostles trained as *talmudim* (the ancient equivalent of seminary students) in the school of Rabbi Jesus (read: ancient Jewish theology professor), they began jockeying for power and a prized spot at his right hand. The Great Teacher set his students straight: "Whoever would be great among you must be your servant, and whoever would be first among you must be your slave, even as the Son of Man came not to be served but to serve, and to give his life as a ransom for many" (Matt. 20:26–28).

The New Testament makes a clear connection between being a theologian and being enslaved (the Greek word *doulos*, often translated "servant," is often better rendered "slave," though not in the American antebellum South's sense of the word). "You will be *a good servant* of Christ Jesus, being *trained in the words of the faith* and of *the good doctrine* that you have followed" (1 Tim. 4:6, emphasis added). God raises theologians within the church "to equip the saints for the work of ministry . . . until we all attain . . . the knowledge of the Son of God . . . that we may no longer be children, tossed to and fro by the waves and carried about by every wind of doctrine . . . speaking the truth in love . . . [to make] the body grow so that it builds itself up in love" (Eph. 4:12–16). The lone ranger theologian is simply not a category within New Testament Christianity. Theologians serve local flesh-and-blood gatherings of believers.

The lone ranger theologian is simply not a category within New Testament Christianity.

Oh, dear theologian, how desperately the church needs your bold and humble service! Heretics are no longer in the streets trying to breach the church doors; they are in our pulpits, as more and more churches hire pastors for on-stage charisma rather than biblical fidelity. The Cultural Research Center found that a mere 41 percent of senior pastors, 28 percent of associate pastors, 13 percent of teaching pastors, and a dismal 4 percent of executive pastors adhere to a basic Christian worldview.[32] "From a worldview perspective," George Barna states, "a church's most important ministers are the Children's Pastor and the Youth Pastor." Why? Because "a person's worldview primarily develops before the age of 13."[33] Yet a meager 12 percent of children's and youth pastors consistently uphold biblical beliefs.

With sermons often resembling stand-up comic routines and self-help pep talks, lightly peppered with proof texts rather than serious theological exposition of the inspired text, it is little wonder that those in the pews are in a sad state:

- Half of evangelicals agree that "God learns." Sixty-five percent believe "everyone is born innocent." Forty-three percent agree that "Jesus was a great teacher, but he was not God."[34]
- Two-thirds of parents of preteens in America identify as "Christian," yet only 2 percent meet a minimal criteria of possessing a biblical worldview.[35]
- Roughly one in four parents of preteens believe in objective moral truth, the personal agency of the Holy Spirit, and that life is sacred.[36]
- Millennials, who now make up a majority of today's parents, have become the generation least likely to ascribe to a biblical worldview, with just 4 percent meeting the basic criteria.[37]

- Nearly half of "practicing Christian Millennials" believe that "it is wrong to share one's personal beliefs with someone of a different faith in hopes that they will one day share the same faith."[38] (Thankfully, the Jim and Elisabeth Elliots, the Lottie Moons, Amy Carmichaels, Hudson Taylors, David Brainerds, William Careys, and other great missionaries of church history did not share this opinion.)
- Forty percent of millennials have bought into the false notion that "if someone says they disagree with you, it means that they're judging you."[39]

Calling all theologians: The church is in dire need of your humble service. Let's get to work.

REVERE GOD

What, then, is a theologian? A theologian should be an enslaved, violent, nerdy, fanatical idiot.[40] When we serve our own egos and platforms, when we forget our moment-by-moment need for God's grace, when we tolerate indwelling sin, when our Bibles get dusty, when we settle for knowing about God without knowing and enjoying him, when we become puffed up know-it-alls, we fail at the sacred task of theology.

Perhaps we can sum it all up in a single word—*reverence*. The theologian is one who *reveres* God. How much reverence is there in a man who loves his own mind rather than loving God with his mind? How much does a man revere God if he merely dabbles in God's inspired words, if he allows his sin to go unmortified, if he takes his reputation more seriously than his Maker's? Not much. He breaks one of the most repeated commands in Scripture, the command to *yirah YHWH*, that is, to fear / revere / be awestruck before the Lord (appearing more than three hundred times).

There is truly no more pride-crushing, joyous, and life-giving pursuit than the reverent study of your Maker. As we set out to marvel at the God who tells the truth, satisfies, rules, loves, saves sinners, and makes beauty, let us begin with a prayer from Augustine:

Great are you, O Lord, and exceedingly worthy of praise; your power is immense, and your wisdom beyond reckoning. And so we men, who are a due part of your creation, long to praise you—we also carry our mortality about with us, carry the evidence of our sin and with it the proof that you thwart the proud. You arouse us so that praising you may bring us joy, because you have made us and drawn us to yourself, and our heart is restless until it rests in you.[41]

REFLECT

1. Of the five marks of a theologian, what are the top two or three where you need the most growth? Idiocy (having the humility to recognize that God is always bigger and better than your finite intellect can comprehend), fanaticism (fervency and zeal to know God), violence (fighting the sins in your heart by the Holy Spirit's indwelling power), nerdiness (studying the text of Scripture often and deeply), or slavery (putting one's whole self in the service of God, his church, and his image bearers)? Ask God to make a better theologian out of you.

2. We have seen that the fastest way to reduce theology to a set of cold, joyless propositions is to allow sin to go unchallenged and unmortified in our lives. As the psalmist prayed, "Search me, O God, and know my heart! Try me and know my thoughts! And see if there be any grievous way in me, and lead me in the way everlasting!" (Ps. 139:23–24). Echo that prayer. Ask the Holy Spirit to expose any grievous ways, any besetting sins that are hindering your understanding and enjoyment of God. Ask the Holy Spirit to kill those sins.

3. Is there anything in you that may want to study theology for the wrong reasons? Do you want to make a name for yourself, be the next C. S. Lewis, have a big public platform, dazzle people with big words, own people in debates, feel intellectually or spiritually superior to others, please the masses, grace the big conference stages with your presence, or any reason other than knowing God and making him known? Take those wrong reasons to the cross of Christ.

PART 1

RELIABLE

GOD TELLS THE TRUTH

OVER THE COMING CHAPTERS, WE WILL EXPLORE THE RELIABILITY OF GOD AND ITS impact on our intellectual lives together. We will be asking and seeking answers to questions like these:

Just how trustworthy is God?

What if God did *not* speak; what would become of our quest for the meaning of life?

What are the benefits—psychologically, spiritually, intellectually, and relationally—to reading our Bibles often?

How do our God-given intellects fit into our spiritual lives?

What exactly was the serpent's temptation to Adam and Eve at the Tree of the Knowledge of Good and Evil, and how do we face that same temptation today?

How can we have security and meaning when God and his plan go beyond our finite reasoning powers?

How can we revere God with our minds?

READINGS

Set aside a few minutes to read, really read—slowly, prayerfully, thoughtfully—through the following texts on the reliability of God. Ask God to open your heart and mind to what he is saying to you about himself and how you can best respond to that truth about him with reverence. Choose one of the following passages to commit to memory over the coming week.

NUMBERS 23:19

"God is not man, that he should lie,
   or a son of man, that he should change his mind.
Has he said, and will he not do it?
   Or has he spoken, and will he not fulfill it?"

PSALM 119:89-96, 127-130 (NIV)

Your word, LORD, is eternal;
   it stands firm in the heavens.
Your faithfulness continues through all generations;
   you established the earth, and it endures.
Your laws endure to this day,
   for all things serve you.
If your law had not been my delight,
   I would have perished in my affliction.
I will never forget your precepts,
   for by them you have preserved my life.
Save me, for I am yours;
   I have sought out your precepts.
The wicked are waiting to destroy me,
   but I will ponder your statutes.
To all perfection I see a limit,
   but your commands are boundless.

Because I love your commands
   more than gold, more than pure gold,
and because I consider all your precepts right,
   I hate every wrong path.

Your statutes are wonderful;
   therefore I obey them.
The unfolding of your words gives light;
   it gives understanding to the simple.

2 TIMOTHY 3:14-17 (NIV)

But as for you, continue in what you have learned and have become convinced of, because you know those from whom you learned it, and how from infancy you have known the Holy Scriptures, which are able to make you wise for salvation through faith in Christ Jesus. All Scripture is God-breathed and is useful for teaching, rebuking, correcting and training in righteousness, so that the servant of God may be thoroughly equipped for every good work.

HEBREWS 6:17-18

So when God desired to show more convincingly to the heirs of the promise the unchangeable character of his purpose, he guaranteed it with an oath, so that by two unchangeable things, in which it is impossible for God to lie, we who have fled for refuge might have strong encouragement to hold fast to the hope set before us.

2 PETER 1:19-21 (NIV)

We also have the prophetic message as something completely reliable, and you will do well to pay attention to it, as to a light shining in a dark place, until the day dawns and the morning star rises in your hearts. Above all, you must understand that no prophecy of Scripture came about by the prophet's own interpretation of things. For prophecy never had its origin in the human will, but prophets, though human, spoke from God as they were carried along by the Holy Spirit.

RHYTHMS

Revering God isn't just a matter of filling our heads with new information. It includes forming habits. Choose two or more of the following suggestions this week to help you as you read to better internalize the truth we will explore and to better revere the supremely reliable God:

1. Although God has spoken in Scripture, we can often fall into patterns of disregard and neglect of his Word. Reading the Bible one to three times a week manifests little to no different outcomes compared with those who don't read at all. At four-plus times a

week, we become less lonely, less angry, less addicted to alcohol or pornography, less spiritually stagnant, more evangelistic, better disciples. Set aside four or five days this week, no distractions, and read the inspired text.

2. This Sunday sit under the faithful teaching and preaching of God's Word at a local church. Take notes.

3. The way we consume information in the age of the smartphone has a tendency to reduce our attention spans. Our brains become rewired for snappy bite-sized bits of information, and we begin to lose the mental stamina to do the long reading required to grow as theologians and use our God-given minds the way he intended. Spend no fewer than twenty uninterrupted minutes reading and thinking deeply about what you read. The subject matter can be anything. See how many consecutive days you can build the habit of extended reading and thinking.

OUT OF THE
SILENT UNIVERSE

WHAT DO YOU THINK IS THE MOST REPEATED PHRASE IN THE ENTIRE BIBLE? IF YOU said, "Thus says the Lord," you would be correct. It appears more than four hundred times. The God of the Bible is not the stone-cold silent god of the ancient Greeks. He is not the Stoic or Epicurean Zeus, too busy enjoying the amenities of divine bliss to bother with humanity, shaving a few strokes off his short game on some distant galactic golf course. No. The God who exists is the God who speaks.

It is all too easy to take the fact that God speaks for granted. We need help from one of the most famous atheists of the twentieth century, the French existentialist Albert Camus (pronounced Ka-me-you).

Camus did not believe in a speaking God. Yet he is one of my personal favorite atheists. He did what so few atheists have been willing or able to do. He reckoned honestly with the implications for the human race if no speaking God exists. "When it comes to man's most basic questions of meaning and purpose," Camus said, "the universe is silent."[1] We shout, "Why are we here?" to the night sky, and the answer is crickets.

The implication is that "all human attempts to answer the questions of meaning are futile. . . . In a word, our very existence is absurd."[2] That absurdity of life in a silent cosmos was precisely the tough pill Camus offered us in his best novels. *The Plague* showed us the nobility yet utter futility of fighting death and despair in a godless universe as a pandemic strikes a

French colony in 1940s Algeria. *The Stranger* chronicles a post-Christian drifter killing an Arab on a beach, yet seeking no redemption because the categories of good, evil, guilt, and grace are nonsense in the absence of God. In *The Myth of Sisyphus*, Camus rebooted the Greek tragedy of a man condemned to roll a boulder up a hill only to watch it roll back down again and again and again forever. Camus offers a helpful, albeit depressing metaphor for modern man, the kind of ennui and unbearable absurdity that sets the protagonists of Mike Judge's *Office Space*, David Fincher's *Fight Club*, and Vince Gilligan's *Breaking Bad* on their respective antihero paths to cyber fraud, corporate terrorism, and meth cooking.

Something astounding happened to Camus, something that has everything to do with a God who speaks. In the 1950s a New York Methodist pastor named Howard Mumma was guest preaching at a church in Paris. Mumma noticed a mysterious figure in a dark trench coat circled by admirers. It was none other than Albert Camus, mid-twentieth-century international atheist celebrity, and a self-described "disillusioned and exhausted man."[3] He confessed that he had never read the Bible himself, and Mumma agreed to be his tour guide through the text. What followed was a friendship that lasted five years, Mumma visiting Paris and Camus visiting New York City to explore the possibility that God has spoken. Camus confided in Mumma,

> [When] I wrote the *Myth of Sisyphus* . . . [and] my first novel, *The Stranger*, I tried to show that all human attempts to answer the questions of meaning are futile. . . . In a word, our very existence is absurd. . . . So, what do you do? For me, the only response was . . . to commit suicide, intellectual suicide or physical suicide. . . . To lose one's life is only a little thing. But, to lose the meaning of life, to see our reasoning disappear, is unbearable. It's impossible to live a life without meaning.[4]

Then came a moment no one saw coming. Camus, famed atheist, asked Mumma if he could be baptized. Given his celebrity status, Camus had only one condition. The baptism must be private, behind closed doors. That way no paparazzi, no protesting atheists, no opportunist Christians could exploit Camus's sacred sprinkling. Mumma kindly explained that the very concept of a private baptism was a contradiction in terms, an oxymoron like "jumbo shrimp," "crash landing," or "soft rock." Baptism is a public sacrament, a visible declaration of one's new identity in the death and resurrection of Jesus.

Camus said he would consider it. They parted ways. Camus died a couple of weeks later in a car crash. His final words to Mumma were, "I am going to keep striving for the Faith."[5] The man who wrestled so desperately with the silence of the universe saw a ray of hope that the God who made the universe is not silent.

"Thus says the Lord." Dear friends, do not take those four words lightly. Don't miss their life-or-death profundity. Run the depressing thought experiment. If there is no speaking God, then what have you got? How would you begin to answer the existential questions that seize us in our most sober (and often in our least sober) moments? Science can answer questions about *how* the universe works. But science cannot answer a single *why* question. Thank God for science, but no amount of science, much less entertainment, alcohol, orgasms, income, or obsessive self-analysis can extinguish the burning *why* questions.

We might be tempted to delegate the answers to *why* questions to the politicians. Yet the twentieth century's hundred-million-plus casualties of totalitarian megalomaniacs unite like a chorus of ghosts to shout, "Resist! Don't sell your soul!" We might then be tempted to take the inward turn. The universe may be silent and the ideologues may lie, but our hearts can show us the way. "The answers are within" is the kind of advice offered either by those selling something by stroking your ego or those who have never plunged deep enough within to behold the contradictions and corruptions that lurk in our depths. The human heart is "deceitful above all things and beyond cure. Who can understand it?" (Jer. 17:9 NIV).

Thankfully, "God is not man, that he should lie" (Num. 23:19). "Your word, LORD, is eternal; it stands firm in the heavens. Your faithfulness continues through all generations" (Ps. 119:89–90 NIV). Because God exists and God speaks our quest to answer *why* questions does not leave us cosmically alienated and pondering a noose in Camus's silent universe. Deep trust becomes possible, a trust in something or rather *Someone*

> **Because God exists and God speaks, deep trust becomes possible.**

infinitely more trustworthy than scientists, politicians, and everyone else, including ourselves. Camus was right that "human attempts to answer the questions of meaning are futile." Yet, your existence is not absurd. Your quest is not doomed. You *have purpose* because you were created *on purpose* by a *purpose-driven God.* "All things," which would include you, "were created through him and for him" (Col. 1:16).

God's purpose-illuminating words can be accessed whenever you want and with greater ease than anytime in human history. Bibles are no longer under lock and key in the Latin Vulgate that average folks couldn't understand. Today at least some Scripture can be found in 3,589 languages.[6] A ten-second app download can put hundreds of translations at our fingertips.

We revere God when we take his word seriously. Such reverence has a proven positive impact. When researchers Arnold Cole and Pamela Caudill Ovwigho polled forty thousand people ranging from eight to eighty years old, they made some unexpected discoveries. People who read their Bibles once or twice a week experienced no benefit over those who never read their Bibles. At three times a week, some minor gains were detected. But with at least four times of reading Scripture per week, everything seemed to spike.

- Sharing their faith skyrocketed 200 percent.
- Discipling others jumped a whopping 230 percent.
- Feelings of loneliness dropped 30 percent.
- Anger issues dropped 32 percent.
- Relationship bitterness dropped 40 percent.
- Alcoholism plummeted by 57 percent.
- Feelings of spiritual stagnancy fell 60 percent.
- Viewing pornography decreased 61 percent.[7]

Do you battle a sense of purposelessness as Camus did in his silent universe? Do you feel lonely, lost, or stuck? Thankfully, God is not silent. Open a Bible and hear your Maker speak.

THE SOURCE OF REASON

WE HAVE SEEN HOW THE FACT THAT GOD SPEAKS PULLS US FROM THE PIT OF existential despair. But how can we revere with our minds the God who reveals himself? How might the existence of a revelatory and reliable God shape our intellectual lives? To answer these questions, let us set our gaze on the world's most famous ceiling, that of the Sistine Chapel. It took Michelangelo four years (1508–12) of his midthirties to plaster and paint his five-thousand-square-foot masterpiece. He worked sixty feet off the ground on splintered planks, his neck cricked upward, brush overhead, fighting mold and the "crazy, perfidious tripe"[1] of his own thoughts. For a man who said, rather hilariously, "I am not a painter," it was, in a word, "torture."[2] In the following pages, we will look at four of the nine Sistine frescoes and, more importantly, the Scriptures behind them. There we will find four profound changes that occur in our minds when we revere Someone infinitely more brilliant than ourselves.

To see the first way that revering an omniscient God impacts our intellectual lives, let us focus on *The Creation of Adam*, the fourth of nine frescoes. It is by far the most iconic. You know the one. God's outstretched arm reaches down to Adam's. Their fingertips are centimeters apart. It is Michelangelo's creative rendering of the moment just a few seconds before Genesis 1:26: "Then God said, 'Let us make man in our image, after our likeness.'"

A nonchalant Adam reaches out. He is listless and dim-witted. There is no spark, no inspiration, no focused, mindful determination like we see in

The Creation of Adam. Michelangelo, ca. 1511. Sistine Chapel.
Public domain

God's face. Michelangelo's God is suspended in space by a maroon shroud painted with impressive anatomical precision to resemble a massive brain. God extends his finger to infuse the powers of consciousness into humanity.

Despite its theological untruths (i.e., the God of the Bible is transcendent spirit, not a bearded white dude with bulging biceps), there are some important theological truths in Michelangelo's most famous fresco. God made a rationally structured cosmos. He also populated his cosmos with an extraordinary species that reflects his power of rational thought. To be an image bearer of the God of the Bible is to image the one who thought up astrophysics, thermodynamics, biology, and the periodic table. You are not a dead-eyed automaton. You and I are post-fingertip-touch beings who exhibit the extraordinary gift of consciousness, the gift we are using this very moment.

It follows from this that neglect for the life of the mind is disregard for the God who sparks our minds to life in the first place. Apathy toward truth seeking is antipathy toward the God of truth. If we revere God and believe that our intellects are indeed gifts from him, then we will never be content with a glossy-eyed, mindless faith. Reverence will inspire us to think deeply about God and the world God made. Something inside of us will recoil when charismatics and televangelists say things like, "God offends the mind to reveal the heart,"[3] or "Don't give me that doctrinal doo-doo! I don't care about it,"[4] or "The Lord is saying, 'I'm bypassing your mind and going straight to your heart,' [because] the heart is what matters to the Lord."[5]

Such claims imply that your mind doesn't matter to God. (Of course, name-it-claim-it televangelists have a vested interest in discouraging thought. If their audience were thinking, then no one would reach into their wallets or purses to fund the televangelists' opulent lifestyles.) An anti-intellectual god is not the God we meet in the Bible who commands (not suggests) that we love him with all our minds.

An anti-intellectual god is not the God we meet in the Bible.

Galileo was far more reverent than today's televangelists when he declared, "I don't believe that the God who endowed us with sense, reason, and intellect intends for us to forego their use."[6] God gave you a mind, so don't waste it. It was this notion of thinking as a God-glorifying action that helped spark the scientific revolution some four hundred years ago.[7]

Sadly, much of today's Christian world has lost the chronic curiosity and truth-seeking vision of Galileo, Brahe, Newton, Boyle, Kepler, and Bacon. Far too many have retreated into a purely subjective faith of chasing the next Jesus buzz. Os Guinness exposes the root problem: "Most evangelicals simply don't think. . . . It has always been a sin not to love the Lord our God with our minds as well as our hearts and our souls. . . . We have excused this with a degree of pietism and pretend that this is something other than what it is—that is, sin."[8]

If you took an anonymous survey to discover which sins Christians believe they struggle with, you would likely find a long list of vices—pride, lust, gossip, selfishness, laziness, lying, and so on. One vice that probably would not but, based on a biblical viewpoint, definitely *should* make the list is intellectual sloth. It is a failure to revere the God who could have made us with rocks in our skulls but instead chose to make us in his own rational image.

If there is no thinking God[9] who made us to think, then we face a very real problem.[10] In a personal letter to a friend, Charles Darwin saw the problem centuries ago: "The horrid doubt always arises whether the convictions of man's mind, which has been developed from the mind of the lower animals, are of any value or at all trustworthy. Would any one trust in the convictions of a monkey's mind, if there are any convictions in such a mind?"[11]

Because Michelangelo and the Bible's authors before him traced our origin not to unthinking matter, but to a Mind with a capital *M*, they never suffered such a "horrid doubt." They didn't reduce reason to an untrustworthy survival mechanism. They embraced it as a truth-knowing mechanism gifted to us by the transcendent God of truth. It comes as no surprise, then, that the Bible's first and greatest commandment is that we love God not only with our hearts and strength but also our minds. A biblical worldview gives us a reason to reason, namely, to glorify the God whom we have to thank for the fact that we are more than biological robots or meaningless clusters of chemical reactions.[12] Our intellects are no longer denounced as unspiritual or explained out of existence for being too spiritual. Rather, our intellects are nourished and expanded as we obey the Great Commandment to "love God with all our minds."

THE STANDARD
OF REASON

GOD IS NOT ONLY THE SOURCE OF REASON; HE IS ALSO THE STANDARD OF REASON. TO see this second way in which reverence for God inspires our intellectual lives, we move through the Sistine Chapel to the sixth fresco, *The Fall of Man*. In the center of the painting stands the Tree of the Knowledge of Good and Evil. Here is the original text that inspired Michelangelo: "The Lord God commanded the man, saying, 'You may surely eat of every tree of the garden, but of the tree of the knowledge of good and evil you shall not eat, for in the day that you eat of it you shall surely die'" (Gen. 2:16–17).

What are we to make of this mysterious, deadly tree? Was it like the poisonous manchineel that grows in Florida and the Caribbean today, with toxic green fruits that Christopher Columbus branded "death apples"? Was the Tree of the Knowledge of Good and Evil God's great scare tactic to keep us stupid, submissive, and superstitious? If you reach up to take a juicy bite of knowledge, just look at all the hell and terror you will unleash!

This has become the unquestioned favorite reading of the text by people who haven't read it.[1] "See, you worship an anti-knowledge God! Biblical faith will turn you into a thick-headed, drooling moron!" The problem with interpreting the tree as a knowledge deterrent is how laughably out of place it becomes when we superimpose it on the actual biblical narrative. We have already seen that the God of the Bible cares much about our intellectual lives. He is more enthusiastically pro-knowledge than all the Nobel Prize

The Fall of Man. Michelangelo, 1508–1512. Sistine Chapel.
savcoco/stock.adobe.com

winners combined. He created and sustains the elegant laws of physics, biology, chemistry, and astronomy that humanity's brightest minds have taken millennia to discover. One of God's first commands to his image bearers was to carry on his creative vision in making something of his universe, to nurture and enhance rather than ransack and exploit it (see Gen. 1:26–28; 2:15). Keeping God's command to take care of the world requires us to understand it well.[2]

If the tree is not a scare tactic to keep us in eternal Dark Ages, then what is it? Look at the actual words of the ancient text. To eat from "the tree of knowledge of good and evil"[3] would make Adam and Eve "*like God* in knowing good and evil." How does God *know* good and evil?

God *knowing* is Hebrew shorthand for God *choosing*—creating, determining, crafting, defining what is good and evil.[4] "Good and evil" is a Hebrew idiom, an ancient way of speaking that names polar opposites to include everything in between. It would be like saying "black and white" to refer to every color, or saying "the Beatles and Nickelback" to refer to every rock band. "Good and evil" is Hebrew shorthand for *everything.*[5]

God is the supreme knowing Maker of everything.

Simply put, God is the supreme knowing Maker of everything. He determines the nature of reality. He defines the scope and meaning of the cosmos. He "made all things" (Isa. 44:24). He "laid the foundation of the earth" and "determined its measurements" (Job 38:4–5). He "bind[s] the chains of the Pleiades" and "loose[s] the cords of Orion" (Job 38:31). He "know[s] the ordinances of the heavens" and "establish[ed] their rule on the earth" (Job 38:33). "Knowing good and evil," then, is a compact Hebrew way of saying that God is *the* Creator. He and he alone is the originator, the determiner, the authority, the boundary setter, the ultimate meaning maker of the universe.

Our brief foray into ancient Hebrew makes sense of our original question. What was the "tree of the knowledge of good and evil"? It was the truth, expressed in wood and chlorophyll, that God is God, the supreme knowing Maker and Creator of the universe, and we are not. He is the Creator; we are the created.[6] What Michelangelo painted at the center of his sixth fresco is a poignant visible symbol of this all-important distinction. The command not to eat its fruit was a command to acknowledge the utterly unique godhood of God. It was a command to be authentic, that is, to be true to who God is as Creator and to be true to who we are as creatures rather than pretending that we are the ultimate standard of what is true, good, and beautiful.

This also makes sense of the first temptation from the serpent to be "like God," and it makes sense of all temptations ever since: "Instead of letting God be the ultimate knowing Maker of the world, take that knowledge for yourselves![7] You are the standard of what's true. You are the source of what's good. You get to say what's beautiful. Why settle for being creatures when you can be Creators? Believe in yoursssselves."

Again, we must be careful here to avoid the televangelists' trap of projecting an anti-knowledge God into the sky. God commands us to love him with our minds and to seek truth. God wants us to know. He made us to know. He does not want us to know *autonomously* as our own smug standards of truth. He wants us to discover truth, not define it for ourselves. He is the standard, not us. That is the point of the Tree of the Knowledge of Good and Evil. God wants us to know within the context of loving relationship, which is how we know truth most truly.

God's love motivated him to ban the fruit and save us from "knowing good and evil." He didn't want us to become our own autonomous meaning-makers.

I offer two reasons why God opposes such autonomy. First, because God loves us, he wants us to grow deep in knowledge. To know something independent of him is to limit the depth of our knowledge. It prevents us from seeing the ultimate significance and nature of things as defined by their Maker. For example, I can know many facts about my next-door neighbor, Paul. He is six feet tall, about 160 pounds. He is a professional cycling coach in far better shape than me, a good father, a helpful neighbor, a spiritual seeker, a prankster, a punk rock enthusiast, and so on. My mental list of Paul facts could grow and grow. But until I know Paul as God defines him—Paul the divine image bearer, created to enjoy and reflect his Creator who loves him infinitely—then I don't know Paul in the truest sense. To know Paul autonomously, independent of God's authoritative verdict about him, would make it all too easy for me to stereotype, judge, and exploit my neighbor. The attitude that says, *My own limited view of you is the authoritative view of you, and I will treat you accordingly*, is the source of untold drama, strife, and prejudice in society. When God is my standard of truth rather than my own limited perspective, I come to know and treat my neighbors, and indeed the whole world, better.

This points to the second reason God reserves "knowing good and evil" for himself. God is well aware of all the havoc and heartache we unleash when we mistake our own reasoning as the sacred and authoritative word on reality. Imagine yourself living in California at the brink of the twentieth century. If you were among California's elite few who considered themselves on the cutting edge of knowledge and progress, you would find yourself a card-carrying member of the eugenics movement. What did the highly educated California eugenicists "know"? They "knew" that humans emerged through an unguided process of random variation and natural selection. They "knew" that the fit survive and the weak are eaten alive. They "knew" that this Darwinian process was nature's engine for driving the progress of our species. They "knew" that able-bodied white, educated Westerners were natural selection's most glorious production to date, the chosen few perched happily upon the highest branches of the evolutionary tree. They "knew" that sterilizing "undesirables" would free future generations from their contaminated bloodlines, catapulting our species to new levels of evolutionary glory.

In places like Auschwitz and Dachau, a German leader with a funny mustache and his highly educated accomplice, Dr. Josef Mengele, began implementing this cutting-edge "knowledge" from the California eugenicists. They defined for themselves what was good—a thousand-year reich—and what was evil. They became the final authorities on what was true—anything they, the pure-blooded supermen declared—and what was false. They became the dictators over who was beautiful—the Aryans—and who was ugly and should be exterminated—Jews, gypsies, and homosexuals.

The Nazis' problem was not that they were uneducated. They were highly educated. Their problem was autonomy. They took the serpent up on his ancient offer to "be like God, knowing good and evil." They crossed the Creator-creature divide. They pretended to be God over the whole earth. They made themselves the standard of the true, the good, and the beautiful. In doing so, they did what every creature does when it plays God; they brought lies, evil, and ugliness.

Think of any vice in your life. Follow any rotten fruit down to its deepest root. There you will find, in some form, the same ancient lie: *I can be like God, sovereign over my own world.* This is God's lesson of the tree: *Adam and Eve, I have sprawled a vast cosmos around you. Explore it. Unravel its mysteries. Use the intellects I gave you to multiply the net beauty and life in the world. But in the whole expansive universe, I have fenced off one single tree as a testament to the fact* **Reason. Learn. Innovate. But be humble.** *that, for all the knowledge you may achieve, I am forever the one true omniscient God and you are not. This trunk, these branches, leaves, and fruit stand as my monument to the Creator-creature distinction, a reminder that, in all the unique genius I have gifted to you and your species, you still answer to Someone.* Reason. Learn. Innovate. But be humble. *You are not the standard. I am. Rely on me and live. Try to replace me and you will perish.*

THE SAVIOR OF REASON

IN *THE CREATION OF ADAM* AND *THE FALL OF MAN*, WE HAVE SEEN GOD AS BOTH THE source and standard of reason. We revere him by exercising our minds not with hubris but with humility.[1] We turn next to Michelangelo's ninth fresco on the Sistine ceiling, *The Drunkenness of Noah*. Here is the Genesis text that inspired it: "Noah began to be a man of the soil, and he planted a vineyard. He drank of the wine and became drunk and lay uncovered in his tent" (Gen. 9:20–21).

There is something revealing in how Michelangelo chose to paint Noah. The drunk old man is reclining in virtually the same position as Adam in the famous finger-touch painting. This makes for a striking visual contrast. In *The Creation of Adam*, man receives the gift of rational consciousness. In *The Drunkenness of Noah*, man lays unconscious in an irrational stupor. In *The Creation of Adam*, a new man with open eyes extends his hand upward before the penetrating gaze of God. In *The Drunkenness of Noah*, an old man's wrist is limp and his eyes are closed as he lays sprawled before his sons, who turn their heads in shame.

What happened between the fourth and the ninth fresco, between Adam receiving the gift of reason and a blackout drunk Noah? The sixth fresco, *The Fall of Man*, happened. When humanity tried to become "like God, knowing good and evil"—that is, when we tried to make ourselves the ultimate standard over all of reality—something went terribly wrong with the human psyche. Gifted by God to do intelligent, noble, and creative things, our minds now do stupid, shameful, and self-destructive things.

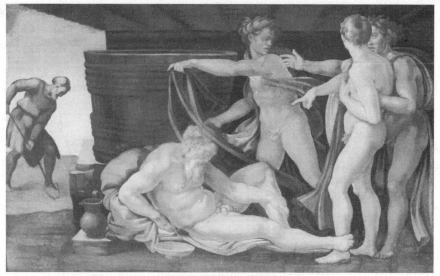

The Drunkenness of Noah. Michelangelo, 1508–1512. Sistine Chapel.
Richard Mortel/CC BY 2.0

The human mind becomes its own worst enemy. Our post-fall minds "suppress the truth by their wickedness" (Rom. 1:18 NIV). Our "thinking became futile." "Although they claimed to be wise, they became fools" (vv. 21–22 NIV).

What did Michelangelo have to say about this? Did the great Italian artist leave us in our self-imposed irrationality? Has Noah of the ninth fresco become the final symbol of humanity? Are we left in an eternal stupor? No. Michelangelo not only painted a solution; he painted the Bible's solution. He did so, like all great artists, without being patronizingly obvious. He painted the solution in three ways.

The first is through a singular light source that illuminates the entire ceiling. That light source is God himself, from *The Separation of Light and Darkness.* It was the last fresco painted and the first from the book of Genesis.[2] Michelangelo's God is the God who said, "'Let there be light,' and there was light" (Gen. 1:3). God beams. He reveals. When our minds are in the oblivion of the ninth fresco Noah, God shines into our darkness.

How does God shine true knowledge to blackout drunks? He speaks. He exhales Scripture (2 Tim. 3:16). This is the second way Michelangelo painted the solution to human ignorance. Everything to which Michelangelo gave shape and color in his nine frescoes came from the Word of God. God spoke through human prophets (seven of whom Michelangelo painted around his nine frescoes) to illuminate who he is,[3] and how to live because of who he is. As the psalmist said, "Your word is a lamp to my feet and a light to my path" (Ps. 119:105). Michelangelo's God "is not man, that he should lie" (Num. 23:19).

What if such a trustworthy God remained silent? We would be forever stuck in the ninth fresco with Noah, oblivious to our Creator, ourselves, and the world around us. We would find ourselves in a hopeless epistemological plight. If you shout your pressing existential questions to the universe—"Who am I? Why am I here? Is there any point to all this?"—the answer is a yawning, chilling, intolerable silence. Remove the light-shining God of the first fresco, take away his Word, and the whole beautiful ceiling turns black.

Thankfully, God is there, and he is not silent!

Thankfully, God is there, and he is not silent![4] Unlike all the mute idols of the ancient Near East, unlike the silent lightyears of space all around us, God speaks. Only a speaking God can save our minds from epistemological despair.

This leads us to the third way Michelangelo painted the solution to our blackout drunken state. He framed all nine frescoes with twelve squares. In seven sit Jewish prophets. In five sit non-Jewish prophetesses called "Sibyls." Michelangelo believed that all twelve foretold the coming of one particular person. Zigzagging between twelve squares are eight triangles, each one featuring the ancestors of that same special someone. At the four corners of the entire ceiling are four large Bible scenes, each one foreshadowing what this special someone would do for a world in darkness. We also have multiple symbols of this person and his saving work in the nine frescos themselves. We find more than three hundred figures on the more than five-thousand-square-foot ceiling. But the ceiling is not about three hundred figures. The Sistine ceiling is about *one* figure. He is nowhere to be seen on the ceiling, and yet he is everywhere. (It would take another twenty-two years after completing the chapel ceiling for Michelangelo to return and paint him on the wall behind the Sistine altar.[5])

This singular figure is God's ultimate solution to our ninth-fresco stupor. In the words of Scripture, "For God, who said, 'Let light shine out of darkness,' has shone in our hearts to give the light of the knowledge of the glory of God in the face of Jesus Christ" (2 Cor. 4:6). We "reach all the riches of full assurance of understanding and the knowledge of God's mystery, which is Christ, in whom are hidden all the treasures of wisdom and knowledge" (Col. 2:2–3). The Father sent "the light of the world" (John 8:12), "the true light" (John 1:9), "the radiance of the glory of God and the exact imprint of his nature" (Heb. 1:3).[6] Jesus launched his public ministry by quoting the prophet Isaiah, "The people dwelling in darkness have seen a great light, and for those dwelling in the region and shadow of death, on them a light has dawned" (Matt. 4:16).[7] Yes, Jesus came to save not only our broken bodies from death and our broken souls from sin. Thankfully, he also came to save our blackout drunk minds from ignorance.[8]

THE SHADOW OF REASON

THE GOD OF SCRIPTURE IS THE SOURCE, THE STANDARD, AND THE SAVIOR OF REASON. This leads to our fourth and final lesson from Genesis and the Sistine ceiling. We turn to the last of the nine frescoes that Michelangelo painted and the first from the book of Genesis, *The Separation of Light and Darkness*. We have already seen that the God of this fresco is the light source for the entire ceiling. But the title of the fresco is *The Separation of Light* and *Darkness*. God creates day *and night*. He reveals *and conceals*. The God who shines is also the God who hides, filling his universe with shadows and mystery.[1] God sees everything in vivid Technicolor—"Even the darkness is not dark to you; the night is bright as the day" (Ps. 139:12), but that same Bible says, "Truly, you are a God who hides himself" (Isa. 45:15), "His greatness no one can fathom" (Ps. 145:3 NIV), "His understanding has no limit" (Ps. 147:5 NIV), his knowledge is "too wonderful for me, too lofty for me to attain" (Ps. 139:6 NIV).[2]

Every good systematic theology book includes "incomprehensibility" among God's attributes.[3] Thanks to his self-revelation in Scripture and in Jesus, our finite minds can articulate true things about God. But for every true thing we might say about him, there remains an infinite unknown. You can't drink in the Pacific Ocean through a soda straw. The God whom Herman Bavinck described as "an ocean of essence, unbounded and immeasurable"[4] is too expansive to fit through the tiny cylinder of the human mind.[5]

Since God is infinitely bigger and brighter than us, it stands to reason that much of who he is and what he does will be utterly baffling.[6] Years ago, while teaching a philosophy elective called History of Atheism in the Western World, I pointed to the rectangular whiteboard behind me. "Pretend that big white rectangle represents all possible knowledge." I offered my marker to students. "Come and draw a shape whatever size you want inside that box to represent how much you think you know out of everything that can be known." Each semester that box would be speckled up with tiny dots scattered in the white expanse.

The Separation of Light and Darkness.
Michelangelo, 1508–1512. Sistine Chapel.
Public domain

God comprehends and works throughout the entire whiteboard. He is omniscient; we are speckles.[7] What is light to his mind is usually dark to ours. Paul put it poetically: "The foolishness of God is wiser than human wisdom" (1 Cor. 1:25 NIV). When we don't *believe* in this omniscient being, we often try to *be* an omniscient being,[8] and that is a recipe for anxiety and despair. This is a crucial plot point throughout the Bible.

When we don't believe in this omniscient being, we often try to be an omniscient being.

When God promised Abraham and Sarah a son (see Gen. 17:15–16), Abraham was a year shy of triple digits and his wife had recently celebrated her ninetieth birthday. They were hardly hot and heavy newlyweds in their baby-making primes. A sensible doctor would have written the geriatric couple a referral not to an ob-gyn but to a good psychiatrist. Human calculated probability of successful pregnancy? Nil.

God promised Moses, "You will liberate Israel from her Egyptian oppressors" (see Ex 3:10). The whitewash of the Red Sea foamed at Moses' toes while Pharaoh's troops approached from the horizon. Death by drowning or death by Pharaoh's swords. Human-calculated chance of survival? Zero.

Jesus promised that he was the living, breathing fulfillment of the messianic hopes of the Old Testament. The disciples watched in horror as that Promise let out an earth-shaking moan and breathed his last. Reason to hope on a scale of one to ten? Negative one.

Examples abound.[9] In each scenario, human reason drew perfectly reasonable conclusions—infertility, annihilation, and despair. Yet each conclusion was wrong, and what was "perfectly reasonable" turned out to be hilariously false.

This is the problem with a human mind left to itself. It often draws conclusions that are totally depressing, totally logical, and yet totally false. If you catch me on a bad day, I could lay out a great case for cynicism, as I have heard so many students build that case in my office over the years. You would have a hard time poking a logical hole in our case. There is a certain ironclad and smothering logic to depression.[10] We cannot reason our way out of the straitjacket; we can only rely on someone else. We cannot rationalize our way out, but we can be loved out of an otherwise impossible conundrum.[11]

This cuts to the heart of what the Bible means by "faith." Faith means trusting Someone smarter than you are, relying on God and his glowing vision when everything goes dark for you. Faith is the Bible's answer to what J. I. Packer called the "York-signal-box mistake."[12] Packer invited readers to join him on the end of the platform at York station in the eastern United Kingdom to watch the trains come and go. We "will only be able to form a very rough and general idea of the overall plan." There is, however, a "magnificent electrical signal box that lies athwart platforms 7 and 8 . . . with little glow-worm lights moving or stationary on different tracks to show the signalmen at a glance exactly where every engine and train is." God has that sweeping York-signal-box view. We do not. We are down on the platform where life events come at us in unpredictable, often head-spinning succession.

From the platform we have three options. First, we may think, *Since I can see no elegant master plan from where I sit, there must be no master plan and no master to plan it. Life, therefore, is meaningless.* Call this "Platform Pessimism." The Platform Pessimist has made a basic philosophical blunder. He has reasoned falsely to the conclusion "*There is* no grand meaning to it all" from the premise "*I see* no grand meaning to it all." He has mistaken epistemological nonsense with metaphysical nonsense.

A second option is Signal-Box Seeking. "Sure, it looks meaningless. But it only *looks* that way. If I read enough philosophy and physics books, if I collide enough quantum particles, if I sit with my fist on my chin long enough, peer through enough telescopes, fill enough blackboards with enough chalky symbols, then I can find my Theory of Everything. I can explain everything from dark energy and the New York Stock Exchange to how to become irresistible to the opposite sex."[13] Packer commented, "The harder you try to understand the divine purpose in the ordinary providential course of events, the more obsessed and oppressed you grow with the apparent aimlessness of everything, and the more you are tempted to conclude that life really is as pointless as it looks."[14]

The most motivated and zealous Signal-Box Seekers, in other words, will often, after much mental exhaustion, find themselves among the Platform Pessimists. They may find some philosophical or scientific breakthrough and declare, "I made it! I've made it to the signal box!" But before too long, it will dawn on them, with horrifying clarity, that the grand unified theory still eludes them. Life throws too many anomalies at them.

There is a third way, what I believe is the only way to a lasting and joyous sanity. It is not to join the Platform Pessimists in denying the signal box's existence. It is not with the Signal-Box Seekers trying to break into the signal box. It is to trust him who, in the UK, used to be called "the stationmaster." He sees the big picture. He knows the blinking interweaving route of every glowworm in all its orchestrated elegance. In trusting the man behind the signal box, we are freed from the neurotic obsession to behold the entire signal box ourselves. He beholds it all, and we can take him at his word. We can trust that our itineraries will be posted precisely when they should and with precisely what we need to know when we need to know it.

In short, happiness and security don't come from knowing everything, but from knowing the one who does. As the psalmist said, "Our heart is glad in him, because we trust in his holy name" (Ps. 33:21).[15] Don't despair on the platform. Don't make a mad scramble for the signal box. Trust the Stationmaster. Exactly what you need to know will come exactly when you need to know it. At his command and in his timing, board the train and enjoy the ride. Packer concluded, "We can be sure that the God who made this marvelously complex world-order . . . knows what He is doing and 'doeth all things well,' even if for the moment He hides His hand. We can trust and rejoice in Him, even when we cannot discern His path."[16]

This ends our tour of the Sistine Chapel. We have walked the full 133 feet from one end to the other, necks cricked, following the Genesis narrative that inspired Michelangelo. What have we learned, other than the fact that

Michelangelo was either the king of sarcasm or delusional when he said, "I am not a painter"? What does it mean, in conclusion, to revere the infinitely intelligent God?

Reverence means that we rely on him as the *source* of our minds so that we don't waste them. Thinking deeply becomes an act of worship. This is our lesson from Genesis 2 and *The Creation of Adam*. How can we live it? Let's not bombard our minds with anything, whether it be too many glowing images, too much internet garbage, or an overdose of chemicals that might shut down such an awesome gift. Let's get a good night's sleep. Overtired minds don't work well. Let's pick up a good book and then pick up another. Let's pick up *the* Good Book, then pick it up again and again. Let's study God's Word, and let's study God's world. Let's take our education seriously. Become an expert on something and a curious student of everything. Let's not limit ourselves to weather and sports; let's talk big ideas. And let us reject the mindless faith of the televangelists for the irreverence to God that it is.

Reverence means that we rely on him as the *standard* of reason. We do not pretend that our own minds are the authoritative and defining standard of reality. We think with humility. This is the lesson of Genesis 3 and *The Fall of Man*. Let's remind ourselves often that we've been wrong before and will be wrong again. Let's surround ourselves with people who lovingly take us down a peg. And let's do the number one thing that takes us down a peg. Let us read the Father's words with an open mind that says, "What you say is infinitely more trustworthy than anything my own finite mind tells me." Let us read his words so frequently that his voice becomes the voice in our heads.

Reverence means that we rely on him as the *Savior* of reason. We look to his Word, the light he sheds in Scripture and most radiantly in his Son, Jesus. This is the lesson of Genesis 9 and *The Drunkenness of Noah*. Let's be honest with ourselves about how often we, left to ourselves, look just like Michelangelo's Noah in a blackout state, oblivious to God. Let's snap out of it by meeting Jesus in the Bible every day. Let's read the gospel accounts of Jesus's life often so that we get to know him who is the "radiance" of God and "exact imprint of his nature" (Heb. 1:3).[17] Let us ask him not only to be "the light of the world" but also the light of our own thought lives.

Reverence means that we rely on God as the *shadow* of reason. This is the lesson of Genesis 1 and *The Separation of Light and Darkness*. Life is confusing. Rather than freak out when nothing makes sense, let's look at the unknown as an opportunity to trust our loving Father. Let's learn to distrust the logic of depression, to know that the God who sees the big picture loves us and works all things, the understandable and the totally baffling, for our good and his glory. Let's talk to him often to unload our doubts and fears. Take Paul's advice to "take captive every thought to make it obedient to Christ" (2 Cor. 10:5 NIV) and Peter's advice to "Cast all your anxiety on him because he cares for you" (1 Peter 5:7).

Rather than freak out when nothing makes sense, let's look at the unknown as an opportunity to trust our loving Father.

We've seen four Scriptures, four frescoes, and four lessons for our intellectual lives that follow from the infinite brilliance and reliability of the Father. "The fear of the LORD is the beginning of wisdom" (Prov. 9:10).[18] As the Jewish rabbis of the Mishnaic period said, "Where there is no wisdom, there is no awe; where there is no awe, there is no wisdom."[19] Ayanna Thomas Mathis echoes, "If we claim to be wise but do not reverence the One from whom wisdom and knowledge both come, then we are kidding ourselves."[20] We display reverence for God and find wisdom when we rely on him as the Source, the Standard, the Savior, and the Shadow of our minds.

VISHAL MANGALWADI ON THE RELIABILITY OF GOD

Vishal Mangalwadi has been hailed by *Christianity Today* as "India's foremost Christian intellectual." He is the author of *The Book That Changed Everything: The Bible's Amazing Impact on Our World*, and the founder-president of Revelation Movement (www.revelationmovement.com) and Truth Matters (www.truthmatters.tv). He is also a man who reveres God. This is his story of how the reliability of God has impacted his life.

Learning philosophy from learned professors made it very difficult for me to believe that God speaks and that the Bible is his Word. As a young man committed to pursue truth, where was I to turn?

I decided to believe what the modern thought leaders believed to be true. French philosopher Rene Descartes (1596–1650) launched the modern project of Rationalism, in which *a priori* logic independent of divine revelation could get us to certain truth. Scottish philosopher David Hume (1711–1776) punctured Cartesian confidence in logic and proposed an alternative philosophy—Empiricism, in which truth could be attained through the five senses alone. German philosopher Immanuel Kant (1724–1804) demolished Hume's faith in the empirical, arguing that we can never touch the actual world of objective truth because we are forever trapped in the phenomenal world of our minds. Friedrich Nietzsche (1844–1900) took Kant's philosophical pessimism to the next step. Truth only pretends to describe reality, but is just "a noble army of metaphors" enlisted to advance "the Will to Power."

The modern project of seeking truth independent of God ushered us into a post-truth era. Anti-philosophies, including Marxism, Fascism, Existentialism, Deconstructionism,

Relativism, and Critical Theories filled the void. Philosophy was a dead end.

Modern philosophy failed because it followed Renè Descartes's fundamental mistake, which was to rule out revelation and trust only human reason. In *The Book That Made Your World: How the Bible Created the Soul of Western Civilization* (Thomas Nelson, 2011), I have explained that the Bible inspired the West to institutionalize the life of the mind in monasteries and universities. It was the Bible that taught the West that to be godly or God-like required human beings to cultivate their minds, because the mind is made in God's likeness. God commanded us to love him with all our minds because he wants his children to know him and the truth he has hidden in his words and works.

Without the oxygen of divine revelation, the flame of Western thought turned to ash. In a cosmos without *Logos*, logic, reason, and our other truth-seeking faculties were reduced to what atheist Bertrand Russell called "the accidental collocations of atoms," mere by-products of nonrational chemistry. Without revelation, the Western mind is mostly confused. Its universities, media, politicians, scientists, and even the courts no longer know what is male or female, sex or gender, love and marriage, family and divorce, right and wrong, rule of law, justice, human dignity, equality, rights, liberty, history, or story. Ideas of nation and sanctity of national borders no longer make sense because Europe had learned them from the Bible.

The sun is setting on the West. Lamentation is necessary, but returning to the revealed Light can begin a new reformation. Therefore, let me pick up the thread of my journey again:

I turned to books claiming to be divine revelation, beginning with Hinduism's most sacred texts—the Vedas. I went to the Gita Press, Gorakhpur, to procure a copy of the Vedas in my native tongue. The manager said, "We don't translate or publish the Vedas. They are not texts to be studied and interpreted. They are mantras to be recited to give you powers. "It will be nice to have some power," I said to the gentleman, "but right now I am looking for truth, not for power." My quest for truth in the Qur'an hit a similar dead end.

My older sister asked me to read the Bible.

"I've read the Bible," I said to her. "It is a collection of childish stories."

"No!' She retorted firmly. "You were a child when you read it. Now you think that you are a philosopher. Reread it critically and see if it has the truth that you are seeking."

I reluctantly followed her advice. Genesis and Exodus were interesting, but Leviticus, the third book of the Bible, bored me. By the time I came to the books of Judges and Ruth, I found the Bible morally repulsive. The next six books of Samuel, Kings, and Chronicles tired me with lists of kings who did evil in the sight of the Lord and God killed them. "What does it have anything to do with my life or my philosophical questions?"

I was ready to close the Bible once and for all when something intrigued me. Our elders had always told us how good, great, and glorious our ancient leaders and rulers had been. Why then was this Jewish book telling me how wicked their rulers were? It couldn't be court history. Kings wouldn't have paid historians to describe their ancestors' misdeeds. Who then wrote and preserved this horrible history of the Jews? And why?

The priests must have been the authors was my next guess, because in Hinduism priests and kings come from rival castes—Brahmins and Kshatriyas. The priests must have penned these unflattering portraits of political leaders.

I took another look at those historical books to confirm my opinion. The third reading made matters worse. Those books were describing the corruption of Israel's religious leaders! God hated their religious rituals and ceremonies. Then it must be written from the point of view of the common man, exploited by political and religious leaders. A fourth look became essential. I wasn't prepared for what I read. The Jewish Bible accused ordinary Jews as wicked adulterers, idolatrous, liars, thieves, murderers, cheats, exploiters.

The Jewish Bible's focus on the corruption of politicians, priests, and people suggested that those historical books must have been written by prophets because they love to condemn everyone. So there I was, well aware that these books seemed irrelevant, yet reading them for the fifth time within two or three months. Why? Just to be sure that my view was correct: these books were written by prophets who love criticizing everyone.

The text refuted my interpretation. The books said that the majority of the prophets were "false prophets." The good ones were the losers. They tried to save their nation but could not save even their own lives. They were beaten, imprisoned, thrown into dungeons, and killed. Their nation was destroyed.

The good ones were acknowledged as God's prophets not because of a blind belief but because their words came true. They denounced their people, priests, and kings, but their interpretations of Jewish history inspired hope. The generations that came after them believed their words, returned to their homeland, and risked their lives to rebuild God's temple, Jerusalem, and their ruined nation.

Reading and rereading those books made one thing clear: right or wrong, the text was claiming to be God's word—*his* interpretation of Jewish history. As my mentor Francis Schaeffer loved to say, "God is there, and he is not silent." God spoke and acted in Israel's history to reveal himself and to reform the nation, to make her a light to the nations, including to their enemies—Assyrians, Babylonians, Persians.

The more I read the more I came to grasp that doom and destruction are not the end of God's message. The God who speaks is also the God who saves. One of the Bible's recurring and overarching plot points is that God wants a personal relationship with us. He called Abraham to leave his household and culture to walk with him. God promised, "Fear not, Abram, I am your shield; your reward shall be very great" (Gen. 15:1). In August 1969 I asked God to confirm to me within the next twenty-four hours that he is my shield. Is God's word to me for my life? Can I step out on life's adventure counting on his protection? Will he be my reward? The details of how he confirmed those truths deep in my soul must be left for another book. Once I was convinced that God tells the truth and is a shield and reward to me, my next question was, Are you, Lord, calling me to trust and follow you?

The next morning came God's Word: "I am God Almighty; walk

before me, and be blameless, that I may make my covenant between me and you, and may multiply you greatly" (Gen. 17:1–2). God's promise that is he is *my* shield has made the Bible a living book for me. That made it possible for me to take God's Word at face value and follow him on unusually risky roads. I've walked with him for over five decades—mostly without a salary or financial security and faced serious threats to my life. The God who has spoken to me in his Word and given my life truth and purpose is the same God who speaks to you in his Word. Take time to listen.

A PRAYER TO REVERE THE RELIABLE GOD

Father, your mind is infinitely bigger and brighter than ours. You are the omniscient Creator. We are not. We confess our intellectual sloth and ask you to help us to use the minds you gifted us with to better understand you and your universe. We confess the times we have tried to be the sovereign lords of the universe, and we ask for humility. Save our minds, Lord. Help us to read your Word and to find your Word there, Jesus, in whom are hidden all mysteries and treasures of knowledge. And when we are in the dark, when nothing makes sense, when you hide, help us to trust in you, the omniscient God who sees the big picture and orchestrates it for our good and your glory. Amen.

REFLECT

Ponder these questions for personal study or group discussion:

1. Imagine either that God does not exist or that God was silent, never revealing himself to humankind. Imagine that there was no such thing as God's Word, the Bible. Try to list five differences it would make in your life had God never spoken.

2. When people don't rely on God as the source and standard of truth, what are some other alternatives people often turn to as their new authorities?

3. When we don't trust God as supremely reliable, we can easily turn to our own understanding, trying to rationalistically rule out worst-case scenarios. The ironic result is that such chronic overanalysis often leaves us deeply anxious if not panicked. Because we are not omniscient like God, we are stuck with uncertainties. How can living out the trustworthiness of God in our thought lives help to relieve such anxiety?

REPENT

In the left column, write down ways that you revere God in his supreme reliability and love him with the mind he gave you. In the right column, list ways that your life does *not* revere him. We often wear rose-colored glasses when we introspect, so pray with the psalmist, "Search me, O God, and know my heart! Try me and know my thoughts! And see if there be any grievous way in me, and lead me in the way everlasting!" (Ps. 139:23–24). Ask yourself honestly: *Do I trust God? Do I make the most of the mind he gifted to me, or am I intellectually lazy in my faith?*

HOW I AM REVERING	HOW I AM *NOT* REVERING

HOW I AM REVERING	HOW I AM *NOT* REVERING

Pray your way down the left column. Thank God for any ways that you are living out his supreme reliability. Recognize that any ways in which you actually revere him are not from your own willpower but from his grace, so he gets the praise and thanks. Then pray down the right column, confessing any ways in which you are not trusting him or serving him with the intellect he gave you. Ask him for a supernatural dose of faith.

RESOURCES

Here are great theological resources to take your reverence for the reliable God to the next level:

G. K. Beale, *The Erosion of Inerrancy in Evangelicalism* (Crossway, 2008).
John Frame, *The Doctrine of the Word of God* (P&R, 2010).
J. P. Moreland, *Love Your God with All Your Mind: The Role of Reason in the Life of the Soul* (NavPress, 2012).
Mark Noll, *The Scandal of the Evangelical Mind* (Eerdmans, 1995).
John Owen, *The Divine Original: Authority, Self-Evidencing Light, and Power of the Scriptures* (Banner of Truth, 1988).
John Piper, *Think: The Life of the Mind and the Love of God* (Crossway, 2011).
Vern Poythress, *Inerrancy and Worldview* (Crossway, 2012).
Francis Schaeffer, *He Is There and He Is Not Silent* (Tyndale Elevate, 2001).
Rodney Stark, *The Victory of Reason: How Christianity Led to Freedom, Capitalism, and Western Success* (Random House, 2006).
B. B. Warfield, *The Inspiration and Authority of the Bible* (Benediction Classics, 2019).

PART 2

ENJOYABLE

GOD SATISFIES

OVER THE COMING CHAPTERS, WE WILL EXPLORE THE ENJOYABILITY OF GOD AND ITS impact on our emotional lives together. We will be asking and seeking answers to questions like these:

Why do we often enjoy finite sins more than we enjoy God, the
infinite source of all true joy and satisfaction?
Why are the doctrines of the fatherhood of God and our adoption into
God's family so vital to experiencing real joy in the Christian life?
What if, instead of joy, our emotional lives are ravaged by anxiety,
depression, panic, and a worrisome sense that God is hiding from
us? Does that make us spiritual freaks?
Scripture is clear *that* God hides, but *why* does he hide? How can we
reconcile God's hiddenness with his commitment to our happiness?
Culture tells us to follow our hearts if we want real authenticity and
fulfillment. Why is "Follow your heart" terrible advice, and why
is following God's heart a more joyous pursuit?

READINGS

To prepare your soul for the coming chapters, set aside a few minutes to read, really read—slowly, prayerfully, thoughtfully—through the following texts on the enjoyability of God. Ask God to open your heart and mind to

what he is saying to you about himself and how you can best respond to him
with reverence.

PSALM 16:9-11

> Therefore my heart is glad, and my whole being rejoices;
>> my flesh also dwells secure.
> For you will not abandon my soul to Sheol,
>> or let your holy one see corruption.
>
> You make known to me the path of life;
>> in your presence there is fullness of joy;
>> at your right hand are pleasures forevermore.

PSALM 34:8

> Oh, taste and see that the LORD is good!

PSALM 37:4

> Delight yourself in the LORD,
>> and he will give you the desires of your heart.

JOHN 10:10

> "The thief comes only to steal and kill and destroy. I came that they may
> have life and have it abundantly."

PHILIPPIANS 4:4

> Rejoice in the Lord always; again I will say, rejoice.

RHYTHMS

Revering God isn't just a matter of filling our heads with new information. It
includes forming habits. Choose two or more of the following suggestions this
week to help you better enjoy God as you read through the following chapters:

1. In Galatians 5:22 joy is pictured as a fruit produced in us by the Holy
   Spirit. Set aside five minutes to ask the Holy Spirit to do precisely
   that. Offer up to his indwelling presence any spaces inside of you that
   are joyless, anxious, fearful, depressed, lonesome, angry, or empty.

2. Attend church this week with this prayer: "God help me enjoy you as Father here in the presence of my fellow adopted brothers and sisters in Christ."

3. God surrounds us with pointers to himself, good things in the universe that signal the goodness of its Creator. Get out in God's creation: take a walk, hike, ride a bike, stroll by trees, water, or whatever other nature you can find. Spend meaningful time with family or friends. Eat good unprocessed food. Ask God to intensify your enjoyment of him as you enjoy his creations.

BE BORING

I DON'T MEAN TO BRAG, BUT I HAPPEN TO BE BOTH A PROFESSOR AND ALUMNUS OF what has been "officially" ranked as the most boring university in all of California—Biola University.[1] Okay, I *do* mean to brag. The Biola Eagles secured the silver medal as the second-most boring university in the entire United States, trailing only behind Liberty University in Lynchburg, Virginia. I staunchly dispute the results, however, because compared with Lynchburg, it's far more difficult to rank nationally for boredom when your university is fifteen minutes from Disneyland, twenty minutes from the Pacific Ocean, and thirty minutes from Hollywood (or three hours, depending on LA traffic). According to Tripadvisor, first on the list of "Things to Do in Lynchburg"[2] is visit the Old City Cemetery. Either way, look out, Flames, the Biola Eagles are going for national boring gold. (I note, only in passing, that Liberty chose an Eagle named Sparky to represent their school at athletic events. Mascot envy? A case could be made.)

Why proudly brandish an award for boringness? "Boringness" may very well be a measure of those most radically committed to joy. What case could be built for such an outlandish claim? The criteria for fun/happiness/excitement used in the national rankings had to do not with anything resembling Christian joy but with partying. Presumably, the pollsters did not measure the mirthful, biblical sense of partying, such as the exuberant and eternal wedding fiesta to which Jesus invites us (see Matt. 22:1–10). Instead, the survey focused on "partying" in the more bacchanalian, *Animal House*, keg stand, and anonymous hookup sense of partying. Even the ancient Greek philosopher Epicurus, from whom we get the term *Epicurean* to capture a lifestyle of pursuing pleasure, saw such partying as hopelessly nearsighted, its painful hangovers and regrets counterbalancing its momentary pleasures.[3]

C. S. Lewis captured the insight in an oft-quoted passage from *The Weight of Glory*: "We are half-hearted creatures, fooling about with drink and sex and ambition when infinite joy is offered us. Like an ignorant child who wants to go on making mud pies in a slum because he cannot imagine what is meant by the offer of a holiday at the sea. We are far too easily pleased."[4]

When offered infinite joy, we must be severe anti-hedonists to settle for tequila shots, one night stands, pill popping, or any other short-lived fix. In fact, the very word *joy* seems too noble for such fleeting rushes. I have known many who have thrown themselves into such rushes, and *joyful* is not the word I (or they) would use to describe their lives.

Nevertheless, there is a stereotype about the Christian life that I hope to debunk. It is the stereotype that while the world out there is having all the fun, throwing itself headlong into happiness, the church is for those who say no to pleasure. Churched folks, it is alleged, say no to the world's pleasures by saying no to pleasure. Nothing could be further from the truth. Here is a sentence worth committing to memory. *True Christianity does not say no to the world's pleasures by saying no to pleasure but by saying yes to superior pleasure, namely, pleasure in God himself.* Scripture repeats the call to superior pleasure often. I offer a dozen brief examples:

> *True Christianity does not say no to the world's pleasures by saying no to pleasure but by saying yes to superior pleasure, namely, pleasure in God himself.*

"The joy of the LORD is your strength." (Neh. 8:10)

In your presence there is fullness of joy;
at your right hand are pleasures forevermore. (Ps. 16:11)

Oh, taste and see that the LORD is good! (Ps. 34:8)

Delight yourself in the LORD. (Ps. 37:4)

Satisfy us in the morning with your steadfast love,
that we may rejoice and be glad all our days. (Ps. 90:14)

Be glad in the LORD, and rejoice, O righteous,
and shout for joy, all you upright in heart! (Ps. 32:11)

Your words became to me a joy
and the delight of my heart,
for I am called by your name,
O LORD, God of hosts. (Jer. 15:16)

"These things I have spoken to you, that my joy may be in you, and that your joy may be full." (John 15:11)

"Ask, and you will receive, that your joy may be full." (John 16:24)

May the God of hope fill you with all joy. (Rom. 15:13)

But the fruit of the Spirit is . . . joy. (Gal. 5:22)

Rejoice in the Lord always; again I will say, rejoice. (Phil. 4:4)

Why, then, do finite fixes often seem sweet and irresistible while God may seem bland? Is it that, objectively, sin is more satisfying than God? No. The problem is not that God is not sweet and savory; it is with the warped taste buds of our hearts, taste buds that register sin as delicious and infinite glory as dull.

How, then, do we become boring in the world's sense? How do we become more radical joy seekers, refusing to settle for the next fleeting fix? How do we enjoy more of God? A good place to start is simply by asking for more. Trillia Newbell counsels, "Today, you and I can ask the Lord to enlarge our hearts, so that we would no longer cling to the dust which leads to death and sorrow, but instead run towards life and receive enlarged hearts filled with truth. God, who delights in giving us good things, and who is faithful beyond measure, will surely do it."[5]

Ask God to supernaturally recalibrate the taste buds of your soul so that God begins to taste as sweet and satisfying and nourishing and joyful as he truly is. Ask that your favorite sins begin to taste as vomit-worthy as they truly are. Open your heart to the Holy Spirit, the third person of the Trinity, and invite him to go to work reordering your affections, intensifying your delight of Jesus and your disgust of sin. That is your first step to becoming admirably boring in the world's eyes and, therefore, truly joyous. Go, Eagles!

IN AN ELEVATOR
WITH A SOCIOPATH

IN WHAT DOES THIS JOY CONSIST, THE JOY THAT MAKES THE WORLD'S HALF-HEARTED and hungover "hedonism" seem so intolerably dull? Is it the joy of being forgiven, declared not guilty by God the Judge, living free of shame and free from the fear of death, having the promise of life everlasting? Certainly there is joy to be found there. Revel in those gospel truths! Shout them from the rooftops. But what if there is something deeper still to which all those joys point?

Our chief excavator to those depths is one of the great theologians of the last century, J. I. Packer. With more than seventy years of studying theology, Packer summed up the New Testament in three words—"Adoption through propitiation," adding, "I do not expect to ever meet a richer and more pregnant summary of the gospel than that."[1] Packer makes his case that the point of Jesus bearing our sins wasn't merely that we could be declared "not guilty," although that is incredibly good news. The goal of Jesus's death also wasn't merely that you or I get to go to heaven when we die, although that, too, is stupendous news. What Jesus accomplished on the cross had an even more profound, intimate, and joyous effect: it made us children of God. "To be right with God the Judge is a great thing, but to be loved and cared for by God the Father is greater."[2] We enjoy God as justifier that we might enjoy him more profoundly still as Father.

Consider the breakthrough Blair Linne experienced:

I had been forgiven by a holy Judge. I'm grateful for that forgiveness, but I almost felt like God was just tolerating me. It was this transaction like, "I saved you. Now you need to keep this thing going, so work hard." . . . It took me a while to get to, "God is also my Father." It took a couple years to realize that he's more than a judge. He wants to be my loving Heavenly Father. . . . He's a God who's filled with mercy, who loved me when I was still in my sin, who chose me before the foundation of this world to be His, realizing that fatherhood didn't originate with my earthly father. It doesn't originate with even the best earthly father. Fatherhood originates with God. He is the essence and the truth of that concept. He was a father before this world began.[3]

To better make sense of Packer and Linne's insights, let us begin in a most unlikely spot, a busted elevator with one of the greatest comic villains of all time, the Joker from Batman lore. Of the twenty-five plus actors who have taken on the Joker role over the last fifty years—including such celebrated talents as Cesar Romero, Jack Nicholson, and Heath Ledger—there is one particular version of the Joker best suited to shed light on Packer's theological insight into the joy of calling God Father. That is the Joker of Todd Phillips's feature-length film, *Joker*, starring an emaciated and unhinged Joaquin Phoenix as the caped crusader's rising nemesis, while the Batman gets only a combined twenty-nine seconds of screentime and that as an adolescent.

If we watch *Joker* from within a closed universe, sealed off from supernatural reality, then our explanations of Arthur Fleck's actions are limited to factors like physical abuse, mental illness, and broken social systems. Such explanations are enlightening but incomplete. What if we watch *Joker* within an open, theologically charged universe? As Christians we have the awesome and underappreciated privilege of adoption, calling the Creator our *Abba*. Whether we translate the Aramaic as "Father," "Daddy," or "Papa," the truth it conveys is what J. I. Packer calls "the highest privilege that the gospel offers."[4] From this perspective we come to see Arthur more profoundly as a man tragically seeking Abba. Arthur's descent into the Joker offers a chilling exposition of what happens without adoption, that is, when our deep existential need to be chosen, protected, embraced, and

> As Christians we have the awesome and underappreciated privilege of adoption, calling the Creator our Abba.

heard goes unmet. To grasp this, let us imagine ourselves stuck in a busted elevator with the Joker. Here are five truths we could tell Arthur.

1. You Were Abandoned, but There Is a Father Who Chooses

From the paperwork Arthur steals from the Arkham mental ward, we read, "Child was abandoned." It was not only his biological father who abandoned him. Arthur asks, "What do you get when you cross a mentally ill loner with a society that abandons him and treats him like trash?"

Many first-century Christians also knew what it was to be abandoned by their biological fathers and treated like trash by society. Many cities in the Roman Empire had literal human dumps outside their gates, a place where unwanted infants could be tossed away like garbage. They were often taken in by slave masters and exploited. They would have been among the first to read Paul's letter to Ephesus: "Blessed be the God and Father of our Lord Jesus Christ, who has blessed us in Christ with every spiritual blessing in the heavenly places, even as he chose us in him before the foundation of the world, that we should be holy and blameless before him. In love he predestined us for adoption to himself as sons through Jesus Christ" (Eph. 1:3–5).

Your lowercase *f* fathers gave you nothing. Your capital *F* Father has blessed you with every spiritual blessing. Your fathers tossed you on the human dump. Your Father chose you before the world began and deems you unblemished. Your fathers abandoned you. Your Father predestined you for adoption into the divine family.

Dear Arthurs of the world, there is a Father who takes those treated like trash and chooses them to be his beloved sons. Through Christ, you can step into a new identity from abandonment to adoption.

2. You Were Brutalized, but There Is a Father Who Protects

After being abandoned, Arthur is adopted by a woman who subjects him to his next failed father figures. The authorities find young Arthur chained to a radiator, covered in bruises, with a massive head injury. All this trauma came at the hands of his mother's abusive boyfriends. There are lowercase *f* father figures who brutalize rather than protect. The doctrine of adoption means that we have a better father, a Father we can count on as "a shield," "a hiding place," and "a refuge" (Pss. 3:3; 32:7; 46:1). Romans 8 tells us, "For you did not receive the spirit of slavery to fall back into fear, but you have received the Spirit of adoption as sons, by whom we cry, "Abba! Father!" (v. 15). For all the tribulation, distress, persecution, famine, nakedness, danger, and swords the world throws our way, nothing can separate us from the Father's love (vv. 35–39).

Dear Arthurs of the world, you were brutalized, but through Christ there is a Father who vows to protect and preserve us, and nothing can separate us from his love.

3. You Were Rejected, but There Is a Father Who Embraces

Next comes Arthur's relationship with Murray Franklin, the late-night television host played by Robert De Niro. While watching from his drab Gotham apartment, Arthur's imagination transports him into the studio audience. He shouts, "I love you Murray!" Murray returns an "I love you too." Arthur basks in the spotlight, with the glowing smirk of a seven-year-old being praised. Then comes one of the most important lines of the film. Murray pulls Arthur close and confides, "You see all this: the lights, the show, the audience? All that stuff, I'd give it all up in a heartbeat to have a kid like you."[5] Murray wraps his arms around Arthur in a fatherly hug. We don't see the iconic red makeup smile. We see unpainted, teary-eyed joy on Arthur's face.

There is a Father who embraces us, even at our worst.

But it is only a fantasy of Arthur's imagination. In reality Murray rolls a clip of Arthur's standup routine to mock him. He sets up the clip with the line "Take a look at this joker," and behold, the moniker of the iconic villain is born. He wasn't embraced as a son. He was humiliated as a "joker." Later in the green room, Arthur asks, "Murray, when you bring me out, could you introduce me as the Joker? I mean, that's what you called me isn't it?"[6] Fleck assumes his new identity of mockery and rejection.

Instead of an imaginary hug from someone who in reality makes fun of us, the doctrine of adoption tells us that there is a Father who embraces us, even at our worst. Think of the parable of the prodigal son. "But while he was still a long way off, his father saw him and felt compassion, and ran and embraced him and kissed him" (Luke 15:20).

Dear Arthurs of the world, you were rejected as a joker, but through Christ we find a Father who races toward us and hugs and kisses us as his celebrated sons.

4. You Were Unheard, but There Is a Father Who Listens

Then Arthur discovers that Thomas Wayne may be his father. Arthur contrives a bathroom break encounter with Wayne. "I don't want anything from you. Maybe a little bit of warmth. Maybe a hug, Dad!" Wayne responds by punching Arthur in the nose, threatening to kill him, and storming away. It's brutality, rejection, and abandonment all over again. Later Arthur emotes, "If it was me dying on the sidewalk you'd walk right over me. I pass you every day and you don't notice me. . . . You think men like Thomas Wayne ever think what it's like to be someone like me? To be someone but themselves. They don't."[7]

Instead of being invisible, the doctrine of adoption tells us that we are "known by God" (Gal. 4:9). "Your Father knows what you need before you ask him" (Matt. 6:8). We can approach him "with confidence" and "receive mercy and find grace and help in time of need" (Heb. 4:16). "We know that he hears us in whatever we ask" (1 John 5:15).

Dear Arthurs of the world, you have spent your whole life feeling like you don't exist, unheard and unloved, but through Christ we have a Father who meets us not with fists but with open arms.

5. You're Inspiring a Movement of Destruction; Instead, Join a Family of Redemption

We not only need a Father. We need brothers and sisters. When we grasp the awesome privilege of calling God "Father," we begin to understand the meaning of calling one another "brother" and "sister." Church becomes a family gathering. We learn what it means to honor our Father as we reflect his only begotten Son together, adding to the net hope, beauty, and life in the world. Without Abba, those deep relational needs don't magically vanish. Instead of church, we form an anti-church, seeking accomplices and comrades in our mission of destruction. Like Heath Ledger's Joker, we "want to watch the world burn."[8] Like Joaquin Phoenix's Joker, we want others around us in clown masks to join us in unleashing rage and chaos.

Dear Arthurs of the world, you have sparked a movement to burn an already smoldering world. Through Christ you can join brothers and sisters on a mission of bringing beauty, life, and redemption to the world.

Instead of seeing Phillips's Joker as senseless gore, we may see it as a timely reminder of just how necessary and precious the doctrine of adoption is. The truth is that we are surrounded by Arthurs every day. Let's be honest. We are all Arthurs seeking Abbas. We all want someone to love us at our worst and our weirdest. Who doesn't want to be chosen, protected, embraced, heard, and enlisted on a redemptive mission? We all want Abba. The glorious truth of adoption is that we have Abba thanks to Christ. "See what kind of love the Father has given to us, that we should be called children of God; and so we are" (1 John 3:1). We must preach that joyous truth to the Arthurs inside of us and to those around us. Otherwise, we, too, become agents of mayhem and destruction. Instead, let us rejoice in our adoption and the fatherhood of God, as described in the *Westminster Confession*:

> All those that are justified, God vouchsafeth, in and for his only Son Jesus Christ, to make partakers of the grace of adoption: by which they are taken into the number, and enjoy the liberties and privileges of the children of God; have his name put upon them, receive the Spirit of adoption; have access to the throne of grace with boldness; are enabled to cry, Abba, Father; are pitied, protected, provided for, and chastened by him, as by a father; yet never cast off, but sealed to the last day of redemption, and inherit the promises, as heirs of everlasting salvation.[9]

NO, YOU ARE
NOT A FREAK

I APPRECIATE THE CHRISTIAN TRADITION OF HEDONISM[1] AS CELEBRATED BY PAUL, Augustine, the Westminster divines, Pascal, Edwards, Lewis, Piper, and others who identify joy at the center of the Christian emotional life.[2] What happens, however, when we can't emotionally access the joy of God as our Father?

Over the years, I have spoken with thousands of Christians who harbor a totally unnecessary amount of shame, doubt, and self-worry over that particular issue. They don't *feel* God anymore. God seems distant and unthrilling. The joy has vanished. The honeymoon is over. They no longer sense the life-giving embrace of God's presence and worry that they've done Christianity wrong and God has hit the road. Many would gladly give up a limb if only to feel God's love again. Many overanalyze themselves trying to pinpoint where things went wrong. *If only I read more, pray harder, do more, then I can conjure up my old spiritual euphoria. But nothing works. What am I, some kind of spiritual freak?*

To make matters worse, they may attend a church service with happy-clappy major-chord worship anthems, surrounded by fellow believers who all seem swept up in divine romance. Everyone else seems to be basking blissfully in the warmth of God's goodness, while troubled believers shiver in the cold. They now feel not only disconnected from God but from brothers and sisters who appear more connected to God. Christianity seems to work for everyone but them. It can be dreadfully lonesome. I know from experience.

Here is where the spiritual and social expectations of today's church can generate an idyllic, spit-shined version of what it means to know God that does not match the muddy complexity of Scripture. Perhaps those whom church culture makes to feel most freakish are actually those who would be most at home sipping beverages with the often brooding authors of Scripture. Isaiah 45:15 says, "Truly, you are a God who hides himself."[3] That is a Holy Spirit–inspired author of Scripture speaking.[4]

If you feel like God is hiding from you and you no longer feel his presence, then be assured that has been a *normal* experience of people seeking to know God from time immemorial. You are far from alone. There is nothing freakish about feeling like you are forsaken or abandoned by God.

There is nothing freakish about feeling like you are forsaken or abandoned by God.

Recently, there has been an effort to take the stigma out of mental illness in society. We must advance a Christian version of this phenomenon.

It is a sweet grace of God that he included Psalm 88 in Scripture to be read by millions to normalize what they have misidentified as their spiritual freakery. It is normal to feel "my soul is full of troubles" (v. 3), like "a man who has no strength" (v. 4), "cut off from [God's] hand" (v. 5), "in the depths of the pit in the regions dark and deep" (v. 6), "overwhelm[ed]" (v. 7), shunned by friends (v. 8), eyes "dim through sorrow" (v. 9). It is not freakish to ask, "O Lord, why do you cast my soul away? Why do you hide your face from me?" (v. 14).

These are the words of Heman the Ezrahite. We know very little about him other than that he was a musician in David's royal court. These are his only preserved lyrics. It is a grace of God that Heman's psalm does not end on a high note of hope but with the dismal words "my companions have become darkness" (v. 18), or as the NIV puts it, "Darkness is my closest friend." Sometimes life feels like there is no light at the end of the tunnel, just more dark tunnel. Psalm 88 grants us permission to acknowledge that feeling of doom and gloom.

Join the club with biblical characters. In the oldest book of the Bible, Job said of God, "He passes by me, and I see him not; he moves on, but I do not perceive him" (9:11). In Job 30:16–20 (NLT) he said,

Depression haunts my days.
At night my bones are filled with pain,
    which gnaws at me relentlessly. . . .
    I'm nothing more than dust and ashes.

I cry to you, O God, but you don't answer.
    I stand before you, but you don't even look.

Elijah cried out in 1 Kings 19:4, "I have had enough, LORD. . . . Take my life, for I am no better than my ancestors who have already died." Jeremiah literally wrote a book called Lamentations in which he said, "I have cried until the tears no longer come; my heart is broken" (2:11; cf. Jer. 20:14, 18). Jonah sat sun-blistered under a scorched tree, wishing for death, "It is better for me to die than to live" (Jonah 4:8). Habakkuk felt like God had broken his promises as the prophet watched his beloved city Jerusalem smoldering under the heat of Chaldean conquest and cried, "O LORD, how long shall I cry for help, and you will not hear?" (Hab. 1:2).

Throughout Psalms, David described himself as distressed (4:11; 25:17; 31:9; 69:17; 116:13; 118:5; 120:1), greatly troubled (6:3; 71:20; 77:4; 86:7; 88:3; 119:143; 138:7), weary with moaning (6:6; 77:3), forgotten (13:1; 31:12; 42:9; 88:5), forsaken (22:1), lonely and afflicted (25:16), like those who go down to the pit (28:1; 88:4, 6), dismayed (30:7; 90:7), wasted (31:9; 32:3), brokenhearted and crushed in spirit (34:18; 143:3), feeble and crushed (38:8), poor and needy (40:17; 70:5; 74:21; 86:1; 109:22), panting, thirsty, cast down (42:1, 2, 5, 6, 11; 43:5; 63:1; 74:1; 143:6), in turmoil (42:5, 11; 43:5), rejected, disgraced, shamed, bowed down to the dust (44:9, 15, 25; 89:45), restless, anguished, terrified, fearful, trembling, horrified, overwhelmed (55:2, 4, 5; 88:7; 116:3), faint (63:1; 77:3; 84:2; 142:3), sinking, weary, parched, (69:2, 3, 14; 143:6), stricken, rebuked, failing (73:14, 26; 109:22), downtrodden (74:21), thrown down, withered (102:10, 11), encompassed by death (116:3), consumed with longing (119:20), afflicted from youth (129:1–2), brought very low (142:6), and appalled (143:4). And we're supposed to believe that a relationship with God is all cotton candy and sunshine?

Paul said that he and his ministry companions found themselves "so utterly burdened beyond our strength that we despaired of life itself" (2 Cor. 1:8). Even Jesus is described as "a man of sorrows and acquainted with grief" (Isa. 53:3). He described his soul as "overwhelmed with sorrow to the point of death" (Mark 14:34 NIV). "His sweat became like great drops of blood," (Luke 22:44) and he cried out "My God, my God, why have you forsaken me?" (Matt. 27:46).

You are also in good company with many historic heroes of the faith. The Protestant Reformer Martin Luther confessed, "For more than a week I was close to the gates of death and hell. I trembled in all my members. Christ was wholly lost. I was shaken by desperation and blasphemy of God."[5]

We hear the prayers of the Puritans. "My soul feels alienated from you," Philip Doddridge complained. "Why can I not just come to you with the affection of a child, as I once did? Why do I avoid serving you? It was once my greatest pleasure. Now it seems like a burden."[6] William Bridge lamented, "I am done, Lord, I am done. I have questioned and questioned my condition these many years. And I see there is no end of such questioning. I get nothing by it. I am a poor weak creature, and I fear I will never be able to bear testimony of the truth of Jesus Christ."[7] David Clarkson begged, "Lord, hear me! Bring my soul out of this mire and clay, out of unbelief, out of the pit where there is no comfort, no refreshment, and no relief."[8]

David Brainerd, evangelist to the Native Americans, whose journals inspired multiple generations of missionaries, longed for death at least twenty-two places throughout his diary. For example, on Sunday, February 3, 1745, he wrote, "My soul remembered 'the wormwood and the gall' (I might almost say hell) of Friday last; and I was greatly afraid I should be obliged again to drink of that 'cup of trembling,' which was inconceivably more bitter than death, and made me long for the grave more, unspeakably more, than for hid treasures."[9]

God never wastes an ounce of our angst.

William Cowper (pronounced Cooper), the great Christian poet and hymn composer, was haunted throughout his life with the thought, "It is all over with you; you are lost."[10] Charles Spurgeon, hailed as the "Prince of Preachers," spoke frankly about his recurring battles with seemingly "causeless depression" as "a shapeless, undefinable, yet all-beclouding hopelessness."[11] C. S. Lewis, likely the most quoted and influential apologist of the twentieth century, said "Go to [God] when your need is desperate, when all other help is vain, and what do you find? A door slammed in your face, and a sound of bolting and double-bolting from the inside. After that, silence."[12]

The list could go on and on—Abraham Kuyper, Lottie Moon, Henri Nouwen, Corrie ten Boom, Francis Schaeffer, Joni Eareckson Tada, J. P.

Moreland, Louie Giglio, and more. If you feel distant from God, you are not a freak. You are in good company. God never wastes an ounce of our angst. He uses *all* of it for our good and his glory. No need to pretend your Christianity is all smiles. True Christianity is far more profound, realistic, messy, character forming, and sanctifying. It always has been.

THE HIDING CHEF

WE HAVE ESTABLISHED *THAT* GOD HIDES. THIS LEAVES US WITH THE MORE PRESSING existential question of *why* God hides. The same Bible that says, "Truly, you are a God who hides himself" (Isa. 45:15), also says, "Rejoice in the Lord *always*; again I will say, rejoice" (Phil. 4:4, emphasis added). Anyone who has been a Christian for long knows both Isaiah's "Where's God?" angst and Paul's "Here's God!" euphoria. There is tension between God's hiddenness and our happiness that self-aware saints know well.

The six-letter word "always" in Paul's passage pushes the tension. How can we "rejoice in the Lord always" when that same Lord "hides himself"? How can joy be constant when God's detectable presence is not? Are we to force a smile in those inevitable seasons of the spiritual life when prayers seemingly bounce off the ceiling, when Scripture reading is more like studying algebra than savoring the Almighty, when everyday anxieties feel real and consuming and God does not? How then are we to be satisfied in God in the dissatisfactions of life? The ancient psalmist offered several clues.

> Oh God, you are my God; earnestly I seek you;
> > my soul thirsts for you;
> my flesh faints for you,
> > as in a dry and weary land where there is no water.
> So I have looked upon you in the sanctuary,
> > beholding your power and glory.
> Because your steadfast love is better than life,

my lips will praise you.
So I will bless you as long as I live;
in your name I will lift up my hands.

My soul will be satisfied as with fat and rich food,
and my mouth will praise you with joyful lips. (Ps. 63:1–5)[1]

David started his prayer, "O God, you are my God" (63:1). If everything was going his way, David might have written, "O Self, you are my God." It is far easier to live under the delusion of our own deity when everything is going our way. When things go wrong and we end up in a wilderness, we learn that our attempts to play God lead only to chaos and wandering. God often hides to help us realize how terrible we are at being sovereign lords of the universe.

After acknowledging the godhood of God, David said, "Earnestly I seek you" (63:1). By earnestly seeking God, we worship him in a way that we would not if his presence was always detectable. Sometimes God plays hide-and-seek, because when he hides, we seek him, and often the longer he hides the more "earnestly" we need to seek.

In the wilderness where he was panting for more of God, David said, "So I will bless you as long as I live; I will lift up my hands to Your name." God was hiding, and David was still worshiping! He was not worshiping with the "Here's God!" happy part of his heart but with the "Where's God?" hungry part of his heart. The greatest commandment, according to Jesus, includes loving God with *all* of our hearts, not "Love the Lord your God with only the happy parts of your heart." *All* means all. There is something profoundly mature and noble and beautiful about Christians who learn by bitter experience to love God with the sad, angry, anxious, bored, panicked, lonesome, broken, and grief-stricken parts of their hearts. God is God over the full scope of human feelings.

The greatest commandment, according to Jesus, includes loving God with all of our hearts.

Next David expressed from his state of spiritual hunger, "I *will be fully satisfied* [future tense] as with the richest of foods; with singing lips my mouth *will praise* [future tense] you" (63:5 NIV, emphasis added). David expressed hope that out of his present tense spiritual starvation, God would in the future tense bring deep satisfaction. Sometimes God hides just to make his detectable presence that much more awe inspiring when he does eventually make himself detectably present again.

The greatest commandment includes loving God with *all* of our hearts, not merely the happy parts.

Allow me to tie these insights together with a thought experiment inspired by the psalmist's hope that "My soul will be satisfied as with fat and rich food." Imagine the existence of a Master Chef who makes infinitely satisfying food. He is a culinary god in the kitchen. Chicken divan crepes, lobster mashed potatoes, marbled Wagyu sizzled to perfection. This Master Chef has committed himself to your infinite satisfaction in his manifold delicacies.

You sit starving, rummaging through the couch cushions for potato chip shrapnel and fallen Cheetos. The Master Chef is sizzling away in his kitchen. He could push through the swinging doors any second, arms stacked with heavenly creations. But he doesn't. There are no swinging doors, no smiling chefs, no savory morsels from where you sit—just whatever old, stale Cheetos you discover between couch cushions. You wonder, *Where's my satisfaction now? Where is this Master Chef committed to my joy? What if life is all just stale Cheetos?* The Chef, while cooking in his exquisite glory, can hear you growl from the stomach of your soul. You growl, he waits. You starve, he tarries. You're dissatisfied, and he hides away in his kitchen, committed to your joy. What?! How could he possibly be committed to your joy if he has platter after platter of pure eating pleasure at his disposal and knows you are munching on expired snacks?

Aah, the Master Chef knows something you do not. He knows just how satisfying his mouthwatering meal really is because he made it. Moreover, he knows just what will satisfy you and when it will satisfy you most because he made *you* (we're obviously talking about the Divine Chef). He knows just what state your soul's stomach must be in to find its maximum satisfaction in his many dishes. He knows that the more starved your soul, the more satisfying the long-awaited five-star meal. He knows what it takes to show you how unfulfilling old Cheetos are compared to his eternal feast. And as the omniscient Chef, he knows how certain sweets now would spoil your satisfaction later.

It is not because God has neglected your joy in those times that he makes you feel dissatisfied and distant from him. On the contrary, it is precisely because he is so unfailingly committed to your satisfaction that he makes you feel dissatisfied and distant. I will say it again: God hides precisely *because* he wants to maximize your fulfillment and joy. God's hiddenness and your enduring happiness are not at odds. The former is one of God's many sovereign means to the latter. As a God who is happy in your happiness (Isa. 43:6–7; Zeph. 3:17) and who cannot fail in his own happiness (Isa. 46:9–10; 48:9–11), he cannot fail in making you infinitely happy (Ps. 115:3; John 6:44; Rom. 8:30). As an all-knowing God, he knows exactly what will make you happy—namely, himself. He knows exactly when it will make you most happy—namely, after intense hunger. He knows exactly how to show you how unsatisfying the stale Cheetos God-substitutes of sin really are.

At last we reach our conclusion: *God hides for our happiness. (And we must be careful not to confuse this God-given happiness with fleeting hits of dopamine in the brain's pleasure receptors.)* We can be satisfyingly dissatisfied knowing that God can and does bring about lasting satisfaction through our temporary dissatisfactions. John Piper concludes,

> God is worshipped, honored and savored both when we faint for him and when we feast on him. Fainting is the form of worship when God is distant, and feasting is the form of worship when he is near. The heart that savors God above all things will experience yearning and longing and thirsting and panting and fainting when the vision of God is distant and dim. And that same heart will experience feasting and satisfaction when the vision draws near and becomes clear.[2]

THE WISDOM OF A NINE-YEAR-OLD

OUR STUDY OF THE ENJOYABILITY OF GOD WOULD BE INCOMPLETE WITHOUT EXPOSING what I believe to be one of biggest obstacles to enjoying him in our age.[1]

For years my children and I have played a game together called Spot the Lie. If they can identify a false idea in whatever we happen to be watching and explain why it was false, they earn a dollar. When she was nine years old, my daughter Holland ("Dutch" for short) came cheerfully bounding down the stairs, saying, "You owe me another dollar!" "What did you find this time, Dutch?" She had just seen an ad for a new pink pixie fairy princess unicorn doll or whatever. "The commercial told me I should follow my heart." "Okay, so where's the lie?" I asked. Her answer will forever live in the file in my mind marked "Ultimate Parenting Wins." Her answer, and I recall it verbatim, was, "Daddy, I don't want to follow my own heart. My heart is fallen. I'd way rather follow God's heart. It's way better!" Cue the proud daddy tears. Let's just say she earned five dollars for that one.

Some may think, *What a shame—he's indoctrinating that poor girl.* The opposite is true. I'm trying to make a heretic out of her. I want her to question and ultimately rebel against the doctrines of our day. Indeed, we need an entire generation of heretics, iconoclasts, renegades, mavericks, and rebels who refuse to march like good little cows, mooing in unison with the herd. When advertisers, TikTok influencers, singing princesses, pop star divas, animated potatoes, and university professors tell them to be true to themselves, find the answers within, and follow their hearts, they say, "To hell with your dogma!"

It was Apple cofounder, black turtleneck enthusiast, and former Pixar chairman Steve Jobs who publicly declared, "There is no reason not to follow your heart."[2] For most of human history, feelings could be embraced, resisted, ignored, celebrated, chastened, silenced, trained, or challenged. Our ancestors could do a whole lot with their emotions. The "freedom" of our day is far more limiting. You have one option when it comes to your heart—follow it.

Today 84 percent of Americans believe the "highest goal of life is to enjoy it as much as possible,"[3] 86 percent believe that to be fulfilled requires you to "pursue the things you desire most," while 91 percent affirm that "the best way to find yourself is by looking within yourself." How is this trendy follow-your-heart orthodoxy of expressive individualism working out for us, really?

Out of adolescents between the ages of thirteen and eighteen, a generation raised on a steady diet of follow-your-heart propaganda, a record-breaking one-third now suffer from anxiety disorders.[4] In *The American Paradox*, psychologist David Myers carefully documents how from 1960 to the turn of the twenty-first century, as America increasingly embraced expressive individualism, America doubled the divorce rate, tripled the teen suicide rate, quadrupled the violent crime rate, quintupled the prison population, sextupled out-of-wedlock births, and septupled the rate of cohabitation without marriage (which is a significant predictor of eventual divorce).[5] The truth is that following our hearts is making us miserable. Answering Steve Jobs who saw no good reason not to follow our hearts, let me offer five reasons autocardiac obedience makes people so paradoxically miserable.

The truth is that following our hearts is making us miserable.

1. Our Hearts Are Too Dull

Validating our every feeling seems exhilarating, at least at first. Yet we end up trapped inside our own mental constructs. We become what David Foster Wallace called "lords of our tiny skull-sized kingdoms, alone at the center of all creation."[6] Looking inside our hearts does not give us limitless freedom so much as a bad case of claustrophobia. Don't get me wrong, I have no doubt that your heart is fascinating. But compared with following the heart of God our hearts hold all the thrill of a mossy fishbowl.

2. Our Hearts Are Too Dithering

The Greek philosopher Heraclitus famously said you never step in the same river twice because it is always flowing. Our hearts, too, are in constant flux. Some hearts may be as turbulent as the Ganges in monsoon season, and others move like molasses on a cold day, but all human hearts are in motion. The truth is that what God says is true about you is infinitely more trustworthy than whatever your fallen feelings say from one moment to the next. If you don't want to end up in a chronic identity crisis, don't take your flowing feelings at their word; take God at his. His joyous verdict about you is trustworthy and solid as stone.

3. Our Hearts Are Too Divided

The follow-your-heart dogma naively assumes that our hearts are like a choir, with each of our emotions harmonizing with all other emotions. The truth is, our hearts are less like a choir and more like a Guitar Center storefront in which fifty guitarists on fifty different guitars and amps are all trying to out-shred one another. In *The Abolition of Man*, C. S. Lewis captures the point using the language of "instinct." "Telling us to obey instinct is like telling us to obey 'people.' People say different things: so do instincts. . . . Each instinct, if you listen to it, will claim to be gratified at the expense of all the rest."[7] Even Buddy Pine, the supervillain Syndrome from *The Incredibles*, gets the point. "You always say, 'Be true to yourself,'" Pine complains to his former idol, Mr. Incredible, "but you never say which part of yourself to be true to!"[8]

4. Our Hearts Are Too Depraved

The call to autocardiac obedience makes sense only if we follow French revolutionary Jean Jacques Rousseau in his dogma that "there is no original perversity in the human heart,"[9] the great philosopher Celine Dion in her belief that "I don't think you can go wrong if you follow your heart,"[10] or great theologian Joel Osteen in his teaching that the "heart is right."[11] The Bible offers us a humbling dose of realism. "The heart is deceitful above all things, and desperately sick; who can understand it?" (Jer. 17:9), asked the Jewish prophet. "The hearts of the children of man are full of evil, and madness is in their hearts while they live" (Eccl. 9:3), said the Jewish philosopher. "Out of the heart come evil thoughts, murder, adultery, sexual immorality, theft, false witness, slander" (Matt. 15:19–20), said the Jewish Messiah. Proverbs 28:26 sums it up bluntly: "One who trusts in his own heart is a fool" (NASB).

5. Our Hearts Are Too Delusional

A phenomenon known as the "self-serving bias" stands as one of the best documented findings in the social sciences. Psychologist David Meyers documents that most Americans view themselves as more intelligent, more ethical, and less prejudiced than their neighbors and peers.[12] The science is catching up with the Scriptures. "Every way of a man is right in his own eyes" (Prov. 21:2). This self-serving bias helps explain why the call to follow our hearts does not strike us as absurd as it actually is. The evidence, however, is stacked against us.

In a Yale University basement in 1961, Stanley Milgram found that a majority of everyday folks would be willing to jolt the bodies of strangers with potentially lethal voltage. (Thankfully, the shock victims were actors and not actually fried alive by strangers.) Ten years later came the controversial Stanford Prison Experiment. Philip Zimbardo selected two dozen psychologically fit young men for a two-week study of behavior in a simulated prison environment. Within twenty-four hours, the "guards" sprayed "prisoners" with fire extinguishers, stripped them nude, took their mattresses away, and threw unruly prisoners into solitary confinement. Coming days brought so much brutality that authorities had to stop the experiment.

If you still doubt the human capacity for inhumanity, attend a Black Friday blowout sale the midnight after Thanksgiving. Human hearts can flip from gratitude to greed in a matter of milliseconds. Still not convinced? Watch an episode of *Dance Moms*. Attend a church-sponsored Easter egg hunt. Introspect for ten honest seconds.

Become a heretic against today's trending cult of self-worship.

Become a heretic against today's trending cult of self-worship and expressive individualism.[13] Want to be miserable? Follow your dull, dithering, divided, depraved, and delusional heart. Want to find real joy? Take the wise advice of a nine-year-old and follow God's heart instead.

JOHN M. PERKINS ON THE
ENJOYABILITY OF GOD

John M. Perkins is a hero of the civil rights movement, president emeritus of the John and Vera Mae Perkins Foundation, and author of the trilogy *One Blood*, *He Calls Me Friend*, and *Count It All Joy*. Most important, he is a man who reveres God. This is his story of how the enjoyability of God has impacted his life.[1]

My family were sharecroppers in rural Mississippi during the Great Depression and the height of Jim Crow segregation. When I was seven months old, my mother died of starvation. I was sixteen years old when a racist officer shot my brother dead as we left a theater together. My oldest sister was killed by her boyfriend. Two of my beloved sons died long before I was prepared to let them go. After a civil rights protest in 1970, I was tortured and nearly beaten to death in the Rankin County Jail in Mississippi along with nineteen Tougaloo College students. My head was battered, bludgeoned, and bloodied by a mob of policemen, whose rage had no limits. God released me from that prison of torture, but that was just the beginning of how he intended to set me free.

I had learned to hate white folks early in life. And learning forgiveness and love took time. But God got me there. Our enemies may never change, but it's in our new God-given nature to love, forgive, suffer for and with hurting souls, to model the heart of Christ. When we do that—fighting back our fleshly desires for revenge and submitting to the Holy Spirit in us to love—*that's joy*!

Now, at age ninety-three, I am in my third bout with cancer, which sometimes leaves me asking, "Why does God allow so much suffering?" Maybe that's your question too. "Why, God? Why did this terrible thing happen to me?" I'm grateful that God allows us to ask why. We don't have to pray pretty prayers when we are suffering. We don't have to cross all the *t*'s and dot all the *i*'s when we are in agony. We can just cry out! When I'm in deep pain, I cry out, "God, have mercy on me!" God offers himself. He is there. He is present. The God who knows about suffering is there. The God who loves me—he is there. He is there as my Father with awesome power to keep me. And he hears my feeble cry. That's what lament is. It's crying out to God, and there's something about a child of God crying out to his heavenly Father that gets his attention. To have a loving Father who always hears us—*that's joy*!

Some suffering is so ugly and so heinous that it's hard even to talk about it. It's something to be able to say, "After all I've been through, I still have joy." I pray that you are able to say that. That's a testimony of God's faithfulness and goodness. God redeems our suffering. He reclaims it for his purposes. It was trust in the sovereignty of God that kept my ancestors going through the pain, ugliness, and degradation of slavery. They sang songs like "We'll Understand It Better By and By" and "Swing low, sweet chariot, coming for to carry me home." These songs were born out of a struggle and the pain-refined trust in the sovereignty of an almighty God.

God uses the things that set us apart and make us unique to prepare us for the work he intends for us to do. And he especially uses the ways in which we are broken. He can use that brokenness to develop a tender heart for others who are suffering like we are. And in that I do rejoice. There is no waste of tears or suffering. God brings it all together in service to his purposes because of his great love for us. And there is no greater joy in this life than knowing that every tear matters. Somehow God works it all together in his master plan to produce beauty from ashes—*that's joy*!

God shows up in all his glory at our moments of great despair. The fact that we have not lost our minds or destroyed ourselves or utterly given up is proof of his awesome power to keep us! We don't serve a dead God. He is real. Real in the world. Real in my soul. At ninety-three years of age, I can finally say, like David and like the apostle Paul, "Thank You, Lord, for my suffering. Thank You for the storms You brought me through. Thank You for every tear that has been shed. Thank You for Your watchful eye that knew just how much I could bear. I rejoice in all that You have done. Thank You, Lord, for my hurting."

I have been blessed to live long enough to be able to look back and see how the Lord was able to use the very things that the enemy intended to cripple me to make me useless for the kingdom. Instead of being the end of me, the Lord used those things to open doors of service and strengthen my faith. And oh, the doors he has opened over the course of my lifetime! We are not limited by what we can do or by who we know. His sufficiency becomes more than enough— *that's joy!*

So, my friend, I count it all joy! I'm living at the doorway of heaven at ninety-three, aware that any day could be my last. Joy is all around me. My heart overflows with gratitude for this joy. It has not diminished over time. It grows more radiant each and every day, with the promise of heaven set before me. The hymn writer said it best:

> Oh, I want to see Him, look upon His face,
> There to sing forever of His saving grace;
> On the streets of Glory let me lift my voice,
> Cares all past, home at last, ever to rejoice.[2]

Oh, I want to see him! I am almost there. I can almost see his face. And *he is Joy!*

A PRAYER TO REVERE THE ENJOYABLE GOD

Father, all true joys in life find their most profound origin in you. You don't suggest, you command us to enjoy you. But our hearts are often too distracted, too mangled, too stony to delight in you as we should. We often find sin sweet and you bland, not because you are not ultimately satisfying, but because our affections are out of touch with reality. Change our hearts. Intensify our disgust at sin and our delight in you. Break our addictions to self-destructive pleasures. May we find ourselves so filled to the brim with your life-giving presence that there is simply no room left in our hearts for sin. Be glorified in us as we are increasingly satisfied in you. Amen.

REFLECT

Having completed chapters 6–10, ponder these questions for personal study or group discussion:

1. What do you see as the most prominent substitutes for God in which people seek their ultimate joy in our culture? Now the hard question: What are some of the most prominent substitutes for God in your own pursuit of joy?

2. We have explored several reasons why God hides. Try to put at least three of those reasons in your own words. Then try to explain why God's commitment to our lasting happiness and his hiddenness do not contradict one another.

3. Try to state at least four blessings that come from having God as your Father. What habits could you form on a daily basis to live more aware of your privileged status as an adopted child of the Creator of the universe?

REPENT

In the left column, write down ways that you revere God in his supreme enjoyability. In the right column, list ways that your life does *not* revere him. We often wear rose-colored glasses when we introspect, so pray with the psalmist, "Search me, O God, and know my heart! Try me and know my thoughts! And see if there be any grievous way in me, and lead me in the way everlasting!" (Ps. 139:23–24). Ask yourself honestly: *Do I enjoy God? In what ways do I live like he is the ultimate source of human satisfaction? Do I look to some other thing as my primary source of joy?*

HOW I AM REVERING	HOW I AM *NOT* REVERING

Pray your way down the left column. Thank God for any ways that you are living out his supreme enjoyability. Recognize that any ways in which you actually revere him are not from your own willpower but from his grace so he gets the praise and thanks. Then pray down the right column, confessing any ways in which you are not enjoying him as you should. Ask him to recalibrate your emotions so that he is sweet and irresistible and sin is rotten and gross to you.

RESOURCES

Here are great theological resources to take your capacity to enjoy God to the next level:

Uche Anizor, *Overcoming Apathy: Gospel Hope for Those Who Struggle* (Crossway, 2022).

Augustine, *Confessions* (Word on Fire Classics, 2017).

Boethius, *Consolation of Philosophy* (Penguin Classics, 1999).

Jonathan Edwards, *The End for which God Created the World* (CreateSpace, 2014).

C. S. Lewis, *Surprised by Joy: The Shape of My Early Life* (HarperOne, 2017).

C. S. Lewis, *The Weight of Glory* (HarperOne, 2001).

John Piper, *Desiring God: Meditations of a Christian Hedonist* (Multnomah, 1996).

R. C. Sproul, *Enjoying God: Finding Hope in God's Attributes* (Baker, 2017).

Joni Eareckson Tada, *When God Weeps: Why Our Suffering Matters to the Almighty* (Zondervan, 1997).

Philip Yancey, *Disappointment with God: Three Questions No One Asks Aloud* (Zondervan, 1997).

PART 3

VICTORIOUS

GOD RULES

OVER THE COMING CHAPTERS, WE WILL EXPLORE THE VICTORIOUS POWER AND sovereignty of God and its impact on our actions together. We will be asking and seeking answers to questions like these:

What in the universe, if anything, lies beyond the scope of God's sovereignty?

Is God sovereign over the little things, the minutiae of life, or over the big picture, the grand story of human history?

Is God the author of evil and suffering?

How does embracing the truth of God's sovereignty set us free from anxiety, exhaustion, and despair?

How can we affirm God's sovereign rule and victory when the sky seems to be falling and it feels like all is lost?

READINGS

To prepare your soul for the coming chapters, set aside a few minutes to read, really read—slowly, prayerfully, thoughtfully—through the following texts on the victorious power and sovereignty of God. Ask God to open your heart and mind to what he is saying to you about himself and how you can best respond to that truth about him with reverence.

JOB 42:1-2

Then Job answered the LORD and said:

> "I know that you can do all things,
> and that no purpose of yours can be thwarted."

ISAIAH 14:27

> For the LORD of hosts has purposed,
> and who will annul it?
> His hand is stretched out,
> and who will turn it back?

ISAIAH 46:8-10

> "Remember this and stand firm,
> recall it to mind, you transgressors,
> remember the former things of old;
> for I am God, and there is no other;
> I am God, and there is none like me,
> declaring the end from the beginning
> and from ancient times things not yet done,
> saying, 'My counsel shall stand,
> and I will accomplish all my purpose.'"

PSALM 135:6

> Whatever the LORD pleases, he does,
> in heaven and on earth,
> in the seas and all deeps.

ACTS 4:24-28 (NIV)

"Sovereign Lord," they said, "you made the heavens and the earth and the sea, and everything in them. You spoke by the Holy Spirit through the mouth of your servant, our father David:

> "'Why do the nations rage
> and the peoples plot in vain?
> The kings of the earth rise up
> and the rulers band together

against the Lord
    and against his anointed one.'

Indeed Herod and Pontius Pilate met together with the Gentiles and the people of Israel in this city to conspire against your holy servant Jesus, whom you anointed. They did what your power and will had decided beforehand should happen."

EPHESIANS 1:11-12 (NIV)

In him we were also chosen, having been predestined according to the plan of him who works out everything in conformity with the purpose of his will, in order that we, who were the first to put our hope in Christ, might be for the praise of his glory.

RHYTHMS

Revering God isn't just a matter of filling our heads with new information. It includes forming habits. Choose two or more of the following suggestions this week to help you better live in sync with the sovereign victory of God:

1. An ancient Middle Eastern king named Nebuchadnezzar labored under the delusion of his own sovereignty. It drove him past the brink of his sanity. Read how he came to recognize God's sovereignty in Daniel 4:28–37. Pray along with his realization of God's everlasting dominion in verses 34–35.

2. Make a list of the three biggest pains in your life. Lift them one by one into God's sovereign hands.

3. Ask the Holy Spirit to search your heart, revealing any anxieties that may be lurking there. Spend fifteen minutes in silence, surrendered to the Spirit.

THE SOVEREIGNTY
CIRCLE

WE HAVE SEEN SOMETHING, HOWEVER SMALL, OF THE RELIABILITY AND ENJOYABILITY of God. But God is not only thinking and feeling. He is also a God of doing, a God of action, and a God of power. If I have not offended you yet, then brace yourself. We turn now to one of the most offensive truths in the entire Bible. It scandalized some of the greatest minds in the history of theology. Jonathan Edwards, who has been branded "America's first and best homegrown philosopher"[1] called it "a horrible doctrine."[2] His protégé David Brainerd approached it with "a heart full of raging opposition."[3] R. C. Sproul called it "an ugly thought" and "fought against it tooth and nail."[4] For my first seven years as a believer, I bristled at the very idea. I made a pact with myself in college that if the Bible really taught it, I would bid farewell to the Bible forever.

Then Edwards had what he called "a wonderful transformation." What had seemed horrible became "a delightful conviction" for him, "exceedingly pleasant, bright, and sweet."[5] What Brainerd once opposed he found to be a source of "infinite wisdom, suitableness, and excellency."[6] Sproul said that the doctrine that "haunted" him eventually "burst upon my soul" and "revealed the depth and the riches of the mercy of God."[7]

I broke my silly college pact. Shortly after graduation, having lost much sleep and sanity over the doctrine, I boarded a flight to the Netherlands. A friend gave me a tattered teal copy of Edwards' *Freedom of the Will* to help pass the long hours over the Atlantic. When I took off from LAX, I shook my fist at the doctrine. By the time the plane touched down in Schiphol, I had bowed my knee. A joy, security, and awe that I never thought possible came rushing into my spiritual life.

That difficult and delightful doctrine is the sovereignty of God. As you read what follows, you may feel like shaking your fists, plugging your nose, or tossing this book in a blender. If so, then you are in good company. You just may be on the brink of discovering something more "pleasant, bright, and sweet" than anything you've ever experienced.

In the opening weeks of my Theology 1 class at Biola University, I draw a big circle on the board. I write "The Sovereignty Circle" in big letters. Then I ask my students, "What belongs inside and what belongs outside this circle of divine power?" This is not a question for people with elbow patches on their blazers to ponder in ivory towers. It is a question that touches every one of our lives in more ways than we know. As Martin Luther said, "If I am ignorant of God's works and power, I am ignorant of God Himself; and if I do not know God, I cannot worship, praise, give thanks or serve Him, for I do not know how much I should attribute to myself and how much to Him."[8]

What, then, belongs in the sovereignty circle? Do supernovas, black holes, the aurora borealis, and great white sharks? Psalm 135:6: "Whatever the LORD pleases, he does, in heaven and on earth, in the seas and all deeps" (cf. Job 38–39). Draw an exploding star and a shark inside the sovereignty circle.

What about all so-called chance phenomenon? Proverbs 16:33: "The lot is cast into the lap, but its every decision is from the LORD" (cf. Acts 1:24). Draw rolling dice or a flipping coin in the sovereignty circle.

What about the rise and fall of nations? Job 12:23: "He makes nations great, and he destroys them" (cf. Ezra 1:1; 6:22; Prov. 21:1; Acts 14:16; 17:26). Draw a burning flag in the circle.

What about suffering that seems totally senseless? Matthew 10:29: "Not one [sparrow] will fall to the ground apart from your Father" (cf. Isa. 45:7). Jesus was executed "according to the definite plan and foreknowledge of God" (Acts 2:23). Draw a dead bird inside the circle, then a cross.

What about the human heart? "I will give you a new heart, and a new spirit I will put within you" (Ezek. 36:26). Human talent? "What do you have that you did not receive?" (1 Cor. 4:7)? Human plans? "The heart of man plans his way, but the LORD establishes his steps" (Prov. 16:9). Draw yourself in the circle.

Human politics? "The king's heart is a stream of water in the hand of the LORD; he turns it wherever he will" (Prov. 21:1). Human salvation? Romans 9:16: "It depends not on human will or exertion, but on God, who has mercy" (cf. John 6:37–44; Rom. 8:30; Eph. 1:3–10). Our next heartbeat? Our every breath? The next move we make? Acts 17:28: "In him we live and move and have our being." Fill the circle.

What exists outside of the sovereignty circle? The answer is the same as what unicorns dream of—nothing. From exploding stars to subatomic particles, from the death of sparrows to the death of his beloved Son, from sorrow to salvation, *God is the enthroned King of his entire universe.* He always does whatever he pleases however he pleases whenever he pleases to whomever or whatever he pleases in accordance with his holy nature. He is never surprised, and his sovereign will is never sabotaged. His will cannot be stopped any more than a pinwheel could stop a tornado or a sandcastle could stop a tsunami. God prevails. He succeeds. He reigns. He rules. Nothing—from the pits of suffering to the peaks of salvation—lies beyond the scope of his sovereign rule. God is victorious.

God is the enthroned King of his entire universe.

That's part of what it means for God to be God. He "works all things according to the counsel of his will" (Eph. 1:11). He declared, "My counsel shall stand, and I will accomplish all my purpose" (Isa. 46:10). Job said, "I know that you can do all things, and that no purpose of yours can be thwarted" (Job 42:2). Isaiah acknowledged, "For the LORD of hosts has purposed, and who will annul it? His hand is stretched out, and who will turn it back?" (Isa. 14:27). The psalmist sang, "Our God is in the heavens; he does all that he pleases" (Ps. 115:3).

I warned you that this is not an easy doctrine, but it is essential if we are to have a God worthy of reverence. As A. W. Pink said, "A 'god' whose will is resisted, whose designs are frustrated, and whose purpose is checkmated, possesses no title to Deity, and so far from being an object of worship, merits nothing but contempt."[9]

WHERE IS GOD WHEN THE SKY IS FALLING?

IS IT A STRETCH TO LOCATE THE SUFFERING AND EVIL ACTIONS OF CREATURES INSIDE the circle of divine sovereignty? Let's time travel back to the first century to see how the earliest Christians answered that question. In a Jerusalem home, surrounded by worried Christians, we hear the following prayer as recorded for us in Acts 4:24–28:

> Sovereign Lord, who made the heaven and the earth and the sea and everything in them . . . truly in this city there were gathered together against your holy servant Jesus, whom you anointed, both Herod and Pontius Pilate, along with the Gentiles and the peoples of Israel, to do whatever your hand and your plan had predestined to take place.

What prompted this prayer? The apostles Peter and John had recently encountered a man with disabilities, a regular among the broken bodies assembled daily at the Beautiful Gate of the temple. After Peter told the man, in the name of Jesus Christ of Nazareth, to rise up and walk, the man ran and jumped for joy for the first time in his life. Peter and John shunned the credit and publicly declared the power of the resurrected Lord Jesus. Five thousand men responded by giving their allegiance to Christ. Such wondrous and subversive preaching left the religious and political power brokers in Jerusalem "greatly annoyed" (Acts 4:2). They took Peter and

John into custody and handed down a harsh sentence, saying essentially, "Shut up about Jesus or we will shut you up!" Luke's historical narrative makes it clear that those issuing the death threat were the same cast of characters who conspired in the execution of Jesus.[1] In other words, this was no empty threat.

Upon their release, Peter and John broke the bad news to the gathered saints. Fear and anxiety would have been predictable emotional reactions to such a credible death threat. So what did the early church do? They prayed. Who did they pray to? The opening word of their prayer sheds light on their theology of power. They prayed to the *Despota*, a Greek word from which we get the English *despot*,[2] which conveys absolute power.[3] Good English translations render it "Sovereign Lord." Luke surrounded the term with impressive power titles—priests, the temple captain, Sadducees (4:1), rulers, elders, scribes (4:5, 8, 23), the high priest and all who were of high-priestly descent (4:6), the council (4:15), kings and rulers (4:26), Herod and Pontius Pilate (4:27). But God and God alone merits the title *Despota*. He "who made the heaven and the earth and the sea and everything in them" (4:24) was in charge, not those conspiring religious and political power brokers. Our fate is in God's hands, not the hands of power brokers.

From there, the early church's prayer turned to the execution of Jesus. When it seemed like evil had triumphed over good, like creatures had bested their Creator, the praying Christians made a staggering theological claim. In conspiring to crucify Jesus, these malevolent human agents succeeded only in doing "whatever [God's] hand and . . . plan had predestined to take place" (4:28). The *cheir*, or hand of God, is "an image of his power . . . to denote sovereign control."[4] It is the same hand of God that liberated the Jews from Egyptian slavery,[5] and that Nebuchadnezzar acknowledged could never be hindered.[6]

As if that weren't powerful enough, the prayer adds the *boulē* of God—his will, his purpose, his plan. It is God's *boulē* that no human hand can overthrow in Acts 5:38–39.[7] Jesus's execution was not happenstance. It was not improvised. It was not a setback or a surprise. It was God's plan, promised centuries and millennia before the day of Jesus's crucifixion.[8]

What do the hand and plan of God do? Here we meet a fourth power term in the early church's short prayer. The Sovereign Lord's (*Despota*) hand (*cheir*) and plan (*boulē*) predetermine. This verb—*proorisen*—is only ever used of the Creator, never the creature's action in Scripture.[9] What did God predetermine according to the early Christians? Nothing less than the execution of Jesus, a theological fact that the early church cited to draw courage as they faced a new potentially deadly religious and political threat. The sky seemed to be falling on the Christians in Jerusalem. *Should we run for the hills? Hide in caves? Panic? Silence ourselves? Where are you, God?*

They recalled that, amid terrifying news, God is right where he has always been—*on his throne.*[10] The Sovereign Lord's hand and will can predetermine suffering and evil without in any way compromising his absolute goodness, a truth they would have learned well from reading their Old Testaments.[11] With this deep theology of divine providence, the early Christians "continued to speak the word of God with boldness" (4:31).

Amid terrifying news, God is right where he has always been—on his throne.

As the Acts narrative unfolded from that prayerful house, God's enemies—both human and demonic—attempted to rain down on the sparks of the early church, turning it to ash and smoke. Each time it was as if God snapped his sovereign fingers and turned the water to gasoline midair and the good news spread like wildfire from Jerusalem to Samaria and to the ends of the earth. What might happen if we took our enthroned God as seriously as the early church did?

THE COUNTERCULTURE
IN THE AGE OF ANXIETY

IF WE TOOK GOD'S SOVEREIGNTY OVER SUFFERING AND EVIL AS SERIOUSLY AS OUR
first-century brothers and sisters, then we would look far more countercultural than we do.

Western culture has been through an age of faith, an age of enlighten-
ment, an age of science, and so on. What label best describes our present age?
Princeton's Robert George dubs it the "age of feeling."[1] If George is right,
then there is one feeling in particular that most defines our age—anxiety.

We find ourselves in what indie rock band Arcade Fire brands the
"Age of Anxiety." Anxiety disorders now affect a whopping one-third of
adolescents between the ages of thirteen and eighteen.[2] Before 2009, 37
percent of students who visited university counseling centers cited anxiety
as their problem. By 2016 the percentage jumped to 51 percent and continues to climb.[3] In 2020 the American Psychological Association declared
"a national mental health crisis."[4] Chapman University released its 2022
Survey on American Fear, with fear of corrupt government officials topping
the list for four out of five Americans. Over half of Americans live in chronic
fear of nuclear attacks, pollution, chemical warfare, economic collapse, and
World War III.[5]

Sure, there are many contributing factors—the world-shrinking effects
of social media that bombard us with gruesome global headlines faster than
anytime in human history, political upheaval, coddling parenting styles built

on the false premise of human fragility (as Jonathan Haidt has argued[6]), and more. But I believe there is a profound theological factor behind our age of anxiety. To help you grasp this factor, I'd like you to meet a friend named Tilly.

Tilly was full of objections against God.[7] We sat across from one another at a local brewery as she rapid-fired objections like a tommy gun. "What about evolution?" "What about crusades and inquisitions?" "What about all the evil and suffering in the world?" Five or so minutes passed until I spoke up.

"You have a lot of great questions, Tilly. I take them seriously. I'd be happy to try to answer them if that's what you want. But can I ask you something first?"

Tilly nodded.

"What if I spent the next few hours answering every question to your intellectual satisfaction? What if God's existence was beyond all reasonable doubt for you, what then? Would you bow the knee? Would you let God be God of your life?"

Her reply was instant and emphatic. "No!"

"Okay, then. Thanks for being honest. It would be a waste of our time if I offered what I think are compelling reasons to believe in God. Even if God's existence was beyond doubt for you, you're telling me that you still would never entrust your life to him. Why is that?" I asked.

"To be honest," Tilly replied after a thoughtful pause, "the thought of God's existence makes me feel"—she searched for exactly the right word—"it makes me feel *panic*." That was exactly the right word. For anyone who has ever had the unpleasant (though extremely common) experience of a panic attack, you know what it feels like. Panic feels like losing all control. It is the head-spinning sensation of utter powerlessness and doom. That was how the very idea of God made Tilly feel.

"It sounds like you feel better when you feel in control. Is that right?" I asked.

"Yes," Tilly replied.

"It sounds like you prefer to white-knuckle the steering wheel of your own life, to turn left when you want, right when you want, speed up and slow down when you want. Is that fair to say?"

"Yes."

My next question was not intended as a gotcha moment. "So, how's that working out for you?" I asked.

From the resulting streaks of mascara down her cheeks, the answer was obvious—"Not great."

Now Tilly and I were ready to have the right conversation.

All of us have a Tilly inside. We want to be in control but feel threatened by the topsy-turvy universe. We are anxiously aware of how easily our white-knuckle attempts to steer toward brighter futures may send us careening into trees, lampposts, rockslides, or brick walls. There's just too much beyond our control. We hatch grand plans; God laughs (Ps. 2:4). No amount of protecting, planning, or thinking can give us the unflinching security we seek.

No amount of overprotecting, overplanning, or overthinking can give us the unflinching security we seek.

Returning to our age of anxiety, allow me to float a theory. One defining mark of our age is what Charles Taylor calls "the immanent frame." "This frame," says Taylor, "constitutes a 'natural' order, to be contrasted to a 'supernatural' one, an 'immanent' world, over against a possible 'transcendent' one." It is not so much a belief but the "sensed context in which we develop our beliefs," "an unchallenged framework."[8] Like water to a fish, we inhabit and don't question the immanent frame, and like those fish, we swim through life oblivious to the reality of everything that transcends our bowl. It is living life as if electric bills, heartburn, hamburgers, social media feeds, insomnia, traffic, and chemical reactions make up "real life," while God, angels, demons, miracles, and a grand story of cosmic redemption are somehow less than real or largely irrelevant to day-to-day existence.

Life in the immanent frame is a kind of practical atheism, and it is hardly just for atheists. We may have the *Westminster Shorter Catechism* memorized. We may happily affirm God's "most holy, wise, and powerful preserving and governing [of] all his creatures," yet still live as if we are at the mercy of impersonal forces or our own willpower. Nodding our heads at the doctrine of God's sovereignty and internalizing it so it forms the existential and emotional premise of how we process life are two very different things.

When we live detached from the transcendent, we still need, deep down, what only a transcendent God can give us. We try to fill his infinite shoes. When we try to be sovereign ourselves, we don't trust in the only one who is actually sovereign. As creatures, we buckle under a weight that can be sustained only on Creator-sized shoulders. The predictable psychological result of life trapped in the immanent frame is often catastrophic fear and anxiety.

I am not arguing that a failure to live in light of God's sovereignty is the *only* source of anxiety; overactive amygdalas, past traumas, and even that espresso shot or habanero-drenched hot wing can play a part.[9] We are, after all, not ghosts but embodied souls, and our bodies can have a massive impact, for better or for worse, on our mental and spiritual states. (If you don't believe me, try making a habit of praying on your knees and/or with your arms outstretched and notice the effects a physical posture of reverence can have on your soul.)

Nevertheless, all the physical disciplines, aromatherapies, massages, and selective serotonin reuptake inhibitors in the world cannot get at the root of anxiety if we maintain the illusion of our own sovereignty. Like Tilly (and like me far more often than I care to admit), the extent to which we do not trust in God as sovereign is the extent to which we try to be sovereign ourselves. That is a recipe for mental exhaustion and chronic anxiety.

For all our attempts at divine authority, just ponder for a moment how small we are in an immanent frame. Bleak medical diagnoses happen every day, cars collide, fault lines quake, active shooters rampage, politicians plot, governments collapse, nuclear arsenals exist, economies tank, planets warm, meteorites stray through space, and George Lucas keeps making sequels. If there is no *Despota*—no sovereign Lord—then something like existential dread is indeed the proper logical and psychological response to existing. Poets like Arthur Rimbaud, philosophers like Arthur Schopenhauer, novelists like Albert Camus, painters like Francis Bacon, composers like John Cage, and filmmakers like Stanley Kubrick understood this well. To forget what they understood so well, we may distract ourselves by filling our handheld screens with oily smudges, bombarding our brains with happy stimulants, or otherwise "amusing ourselves to death," as Neil Postman famously observed.[10]

Fear him or you can find a way to fear virtually everything else.

There is a far better solution. Open the immanent frame. Take the lid off the box of your closed cosmos and let the Transcendent cast everything in a new light. Join the early Christians of Acts 4 who refused to believe that the bleak facts of legal death threats and crucifixes are all there is to "the real world." Tap into the reality that a transcendent God exists and sits enthroned. Fear him or you can find a way to fear virtually everything else.[11]

"THIS, PLEASE, CANNOT BE THAT"

SOME THEOLOGIANS CONTEND THAT GOD IS SOVEREIGN IN A GENERAL SENSE, THAT is, he will accomplish his overarching goals in human history and may, at crucial moments in the plotline, step in with a more hands-on approach. But they reject a comprehensive sovereignty.[1] Perhaps Hollywood director Paul Thomas Anderson is closer to the mark than such theologians.

Anderson wrote most of his underappreciated cinematic masterpiece *Magnolia* over a period of two weeks, holed up in a Vermont cabin, scared to leave on account of a snake he had spotted outside. (Keep that snake in mind.) The film opens with a narrator pontificating about three stories with a shared theme, what theologians would call "providence." First, the 1911 hanging of three men for the murder of Sir Edmund William Godfrey, resident of Greenberry Hill, London. His murderers were Joseph Green, Stanley Berry, and Daniel Hill—Green, Berry, Hill.

The narrator jumps to a 1983 story of a diver named Delmer Darion found in full scuba gear dead atop a tree. He had been accidentally slurped from Lake Tahoe into a scooper plane to fight a nearby forest fire, piloted by one Craig Hansen. Two nights prior, a down-on-his-luck Hansen attacked Darion at a nearby Reno casino where the unfortunate scuba enthusiast worked as a blackjack dealer. "The weight of the guilt and the measure of coincidence [was] so large Hansen took his life."[2]

Then comes the third story, the astounding death of seventeen-year-old

Sydney Barringer in 1959, an unsuccessful suicide turned successful homicide. Barringer decided to step off the roof of his nine-story apartment building, unaware of the safety net installed by window washers below that would have saved his life. Three stories into his fall, Sydney Barringer suffered a fatal shotgun blast to the stomach, fired during a domestic dispute on the sixth floor. The shooter turned out to be Faye Barringer, attempting to frighten Arthur Barringer—Sydney's parents. The typically unloaded weapon had been loaded six days prior by none other than their son—Sydney Barringer, who had grown tired of their acrimonious disputes. Thus, Sydney became an accomplice to his own murder.

Anderson concludes, "It is in the humble opinion of this narrator that this is not just 'something that happened.' This cannot be 'one of those things.' This, please, cannot be that. . . . This was not just a matter of chance."[3]

In 2021 John Piper released a brilliant theological tome called *Providence*. The audiobook runs over an entire day, clocking in at twenty-six hours. P. T. Anderson, not a Christian, much less a theologian, captures in a mere six minutes on the big screen a deep truth that Piper elucidates on paper. Indeed, *each and every* moment in the Bible (all seventy-five hours in audiobook form as read by Max McClean) can be accurately described by Anderson's words: "This is not just 'something that happened.'"

Acts retells the conversion of the first African, an Ethiopian, to faith in Jesus. In fact, this African is the first case of a nonethnically Jewish person finding salvation in Jesus in all of Acts. During the earliest eras of the church, Africa proved to be rich soil from which much beautiful Christianity sprouted, including such theological luminaries as Athanasius, Augustine, Clement, Cyprian, and Tertullian. Consider the historical account Luke offered.[4]

An angel beckoned Philip to stroll the road from Jerusalem to old Gaza. It was a strange request as Gaza had become a no-man's-land and the road to this ancient ghost town was all but deserted. With more than 250,000 miles of roads zigzagging the Roman Empire, Philip ended up on this particular desolate fifty-mile stretch at just the right time for his path to intersect with an Ethiopian. This is not just "something that happened."

The Ethiopian was a man of tremendous power and influence, an official to the African queen Candace, who was in charge of her entire treasury (Acts 8:27). The Ethiopian, therefore, was one of the .0000001 percent with the means to (1) afford the journey to and from Jerusalem, (2) foot the bill to travel by chariot, and (3) acquire a hard-to-come-by Isaiah scroll (as printing presses wouldn't exist for another millennium and a half). This wealthy Ethiopian happened to read the scroll (1) out loud, (2) within earshot of Philip, and (3) not in Ethiopian or any other language but in the common Greek that Philip could understand.

The precise book and chapter the Ethiopian read aloud in Greek was what we know as Isaiah 53, a passage so clearly about the good news of Jesus that Charles Spurgeon described it as "a Bible in miniature, the gospel in its essence."[5] Old Testament scholar Franz Delitzsch famously said that Isaiah 53 "looks as if it had been written beneath the cross upon Golgotha,"[6] though it was, in fact, written (read: prophesied) centuries earlier.

The Ethiopian could have read any scroll, Plato's *Republic* or *The Egyptian Book of the Dead*. But he was reading the Old Testament. Within the Bible, he could have been reading the census lists in Numbers—"from Simeon, Shelumiel the son of Zurishaddai," and so on—or rules for dealing with household mold in Leviticus.[7] But the Ethiopian was reading the single-most christological chapter out of the 929 chapters of the Old Testament. "This cannot be 'one of those things.'"

The Ethiopian invited Philip into his chariot to explain Isaiah 53. Philip happened to be among the few who could articulate clearly how the Suffering Servant of Isaiah 53 is, in fact, Jesus. At the moment when the good news of Jesus—the "lamb that is led to the slaughter" (v. 7)—made sense to the Ethiopian, the chariot passed a body of water, a rarity in this stretch of parched Middle Eastern desert. There Philip baptized the Ethiopian who continued on his journey "rejoicing," bringing the best news in the universe to the African continent, where millions more would come to rejoice in Jesus, the Suffering Servant of Isaiah 53.

It is in the humble opinion of this narrator that this is not just "something that happened." This cannot be "one of those things." This, please, cannot be that. . . . This was not just a matter of chance. Nothing is.

Think again of the snake outside the Vermont cabin where Anderson wrote *Magnolia*. Without that slithering reptile, Anderson would likely not have barricaded himself inside a cabin to crank out the *Magnolia* script. There is another snake who had something to do with the writing not just of *a* great story, but *the* Story for all time. Please don't misinterpret my point. I am not saying we should

Nothing in the plotline of reality, composed as it is by history's Great Scriptwriter, is a matter of chance.

thank the deceptive serpent, bent as he is on vandalizing everything true, good, and beautiful. I am not weighing in on old infra- versus supralapsarian disputes or how precisely Satan and our first parents fell. Nothing in the plotline of reality, composed as it is by history's Great Scriptwriter, is a matter of chance. Desolate roads, pricey scrolls, bodies of water in the desert, even snakes—indeed all the suffering you will ever endure and joy you will ever savor—are hardly matters of chance. "These, please, cannot be that."

LETTERS TO A FATHER
FROM THE BLACK HOLE

IF GOD WERE *MERELY* SOVEREIGN, THEN THERE IS A POSSIBILITY THAT COULD demolish all peace of mind. What if God were all-powerful but not all-good, someone like the *Deus deceptor* Descartes worried about, a God who flexes his omnipotence to deceive and destroy us? Our brief study of divine sovereignty would be incomplete without acknowledging that there is not a tyrant, sociopath, or cosmic killjoy on the throne. Rather, a loving *Father* reigns, and his rule produces joy, not panic.

Why does the fatherhood of God make all the difference? Whenever I throw my seven-year-old son Hendrik into the air and catch him, he does not scream in horror. He has no control whatsoever, and yet he laughs hysterically. "Again, Daddy, again!" When we wrestle, Hendrik has no idea what is coming next. A piledriver? A turnbuckle fly? A flying wedgie of doom? He howls with joy precisely because he has no idea what's coming next.

My son can experience the total loss of control as freedom and euphoria rather than panic. Why? If a total stranger nabbed Hendrik and started hurling him into the air or attacking him with flying wedgies of doom, you had better believe he would be terrified (at least until I pummeled the stranger). The difference is obvious. Hendrik knows me. He trusts me. He knows that I am more powerful than him, but, crucially, he also knows that I channel that superior power for his good because I love him.

We don't have to experience our lack of control as panic, because the sovereign God of the Bible is not a creepy stranger. He is a loving Father. In the Old Testament, God reveals himself as a lawmaker, judge, groom, healer, warrior, potter, shield, avenger, architect, doctor, light, fire, lover, rock, tower, king, shepherd, lion, eagle, star, shadow, fountain, mother,[1] and even as Father from time to time, fifteen times to be precise.[2] Yet in the New Testament, a homeless Jewish rabbi speaks freely and frequently of God as Father, no fewer than 168 times in the four gospels. He invites us to pray, "Our Father . . ." (Matt. 6:9). Jesus's hyperfocus on the fatherhood of God nearly gets him killed (John 5:18–20).

"What is a Christian?" asked J. I. Packer. "The richest answer I know is that a Christian is one who has God as Father,"[3] he answers. "You sum up the whole of New Testament religion if you describe it as the knowledge of God as one's holy Father. If you want to judge how well a person understands Christianity, find out how much he makes of the thought of being God's child and having God as his Father."[4]

This theological truth scratches a deep existential itch—the universal human need for good, strong fathers. Problems abound when that need is not met. "We know the statistics," said Barack Obama, "that children who grow up without a father are five times more likely to live in poverty and commit crime; nine times more likely to drop out of schools and twenty times more likely to end up in prison. They are more likely to have behavioral problems, or run away from home, or become teenage parents themselves."[5] In his fascinating book *Faith of the Fatherless: The Psychology of Atheism*, Paul Vitz documents how history's most influential atheists either had dead fathers (e.g., Nietzsche, Hume, Russell, Sartre, Camus, and Schopenhauer) or abusive and weak fathers (e.g., Hobbes, Voltaire, Feuerbach, Freud, Stalin, Hitler, and Mao).[6]

The fatherhood of a sovereign God is grounds for trading panic for joy when life doesn't go our way.

Consider the timeless playground taunt, "My dad could beat up your dad" (a taunt I always welcomed as my own father happens to be a ninth-degree Kung Fu San Soo black belt master). Maybe you had a good strong father; maybe you didn't. The fact is that if you trust in Jesus, then you have the strongest Father in existence, and he is good. As we can call him "Abba," so he calls us sons and daughters, beloved, fed, clothed, heard, understood, forgiven, cherished, wanted, held, supported, celebrated. The fatherhood of a sovereign God frees us to trade panic for joy when life doesn't go our way.[7]

Guido De Bres penned the *Belgic Confession of Faith* in 1561 in hopes of convincing the Roman Catholic King Philip II that Protestants were not violent revolutionaries to round up and send to the gallows. In 1567 he was arrested and imprisoned at the hands of the Inquisitors. He found himself in a notorious dungeon called the "Brunain," or "Black Hole." It was "very bleak, obscure, and dark," De Bres wrote. "The air is poor and it stinks. On my feet and hands I have irons, big and heavy."[8]

From the Black Hole, De Bres composed what one scholar described as "one of the most touching, faith-filled, heart-wrenching, God-glorifying pieces of writing that no one knows about."[9] To his beloved wife, Catherine, De Bres wrote about God's sovereignty. "It is very true that human reason rebels against this doctrine and resists it as much as possible and I have very strongly experienced this myself." Most of us can relate. He continued, "When I was arrested, I would say to myself . . . 'We ought not to have been arrested.' With such thoughts I became overwhelmed." Then came De Bres's breakthrough. He told Catherine,

> Then my heart began to feel a great repose. I began then to say, "My God . . . may your will be done. I cannot escape from your hands. And if I could, I would not, since it is happiness for me to conform to your will." These thoughts made my heart cheerful again. . . . I pray you, my dear and faithful companion, to join me in thanking God for what he has done.[10]

Twelve days later, May 31, 1567, in the town of Valenciennes in northern France, Guido De Bres died by hanging. His words to Catherine: "Remember that I did not fall into the hands of my enemies by mere chance, but through the providence of my God who controls and governs all things, the least as well as the greatest. . . . How then can harm come to me without the command and providence of God? It cannot happen unless one should say that God is no longer God."[11] How did De Bres go from wallowing in self-pity to facing the gallows without flinching? He trusted in the sovereignty of the God he described as "the father to poor orphans."[12] Do you feel panicked, lost, alone, overwhelmed, unwanted, useless, ashamed? Run to your sovereign Father. Like the father in Jesus's parable of the prodigal son, he's already running toward you.[13]

MICHAEL HORTON ON THE VICTORIOUS SOVEREIGNTY OF GOD

Michael Horton is an author, speaker, and celebrated systematic theologian. He serves as the J. Gresham Machen Professor of Theology and Apologetics at Westminster Seminary California, editor-in-chief of *Modern Reformation* magazine, and president and host of the nationally syndicated radio broadcast *The White Horse Inn*. He is also a man who reveres God. This is his story of how the victoriousness of the sovereign God has impacted his life.

Receiving emails from vendors asking, "How did we do?" is irritating. It's not enough that I bought something from them; now I have to take a test. Frankly, I all too often follow the same obnoxious protocol in my daily life—"How did I do?" In a performance culture like ours, I want to feel like my performance counts, that it's noticed. My fallen heart can even twist something like giving to others and make it less about them and more about me. Like Martin Luther five hundred years ago, we can drive ourselves to the brink of our own sanity by trying to prove ourselves. "How am I doing?" can become an obsession, leaving us constantly preoccupied and worrying about ourselves instead of revering and enjoying God.

It is in that state of self-obsession and the utter loss of security in ourselves that the victories of our sovereign God become so precious. Like many others, the doctrine of God's sovereignty scared me at first. I thought it was about extinguishing my freedom and obliterating my identity. Gradually, I came to see in Scripture that God's sovereignty is the only reason I really have both freedom and identity. It's not like a seesaw where God's sovereignty rises at the expense of our human responsibility, or vice versa. Rather, it is

God's initiating, effectual, and perfecting grace that moves us from the bondage of the will to freedom in Christ.

This directly contradicts my/our performance mentality. God isn't waiting around for us to get our act together, use our free will properly, and perform for him. Rather, our sovereign Father redeemed us by his Son "at the right time." "While we were still *weak* . . . Christ died for the *ungodly*. . . . While we were still *sinners*, Christ died for us. . . . While we were *enemies* we were reconciled to God by the death of his Son" (Rom. 5:6–10, emphasis added). He redeemed us not when we proved ourselves worthy in any way whatsoever, but when all that we proved was our utter ungodliness, sinfulness, and enmity against him. Scripture offers a clear answer to "How did I do?" "There is no one righteous, not even one" (Rom. 3:10 NIV). My own performance is worthy of death, and so is yours (Rom. 6:23).

How did I—Michael Horton—do? Trust me, you don't want to know. God knows me and my sin-ridden track record, but he adopted me as his cherished son anyway. The important question in every sermon, prayer, evangelistic conversation, and family and personal devotional time is, "How did *God* do?" Because of what *he* did, does, and will do, I am assured of everlasting life. "So then it depends not on human will or exertion, but on God, who has mercy" (Rom. 9:16). "How did I do?" is the wrong question, a question that will lead us down a path of chronic self-doubt and despair. The right question, the more reverent question is "What did the sovereign God do for me in Christ? What victory has he won on my behalf?"

Paul's answer was that *while we* were dead in trespasses and sins, unable to make the slightest move toward God,

> *God*, being rich in mercy, because of the great love with which he loved us, *even when we were dead* in our trespasses, *made us alive* together with Christ—by grace you have been saved—and raised us up with him and seated us with him in the heavenly places in Christ Jesus, so that in the coming ages he might show the immeasurable riches of his grace in kindness toward us in Christ Jesus. For by grace you have been saved through faith. And this

is not your own doing; it is the gift of God, not a result of works, so that no one may boast. (Eph. 2:4–9, emphasis added)

Does this good news of God's sovereign grace imply that we toss good works out the window? Not at all. Paul continued, "For we are *his workmanship*, created in Christ Jesus for good works, which *God prepared beforehand*, that we should walk in them" (Eph. 2:10, emphasis added). We do not offer good works to God to put him in our debt or prove our worthiness. Because of the omnipotent God's victory over sin and condemnation through Christ, we can live lives of gratitude instead of guilt, freedom instead of fear. We don't do that by worrying about ourselves all the time. "We do this by keeping our eyes on Jesus, the champion who initiates and perfects our faith" (Heb. 12:2 NLT).

Over four decades of looking to Jesus, I have found that the doctrine of God's sovereignty—a doctrine that once led me to throw the Bible across the room after reading Romans 9—has become a profound and precious relief from bondage to the law of self-creating, self-sustaining, and self-saving performance. I can step off the hopeless treadmill of asking, "How am I doing," and rest in what God has done, the sovereign victory he accomplished on my behalf through Christ's incarnation, obedient life, vicarious death, bodily resurrection, and glorious ascension. By his grace, you can too.

A PRAYER TO REVERE THE VICTORIOUS GOD

Father, you are all-powerful. And you direct that omnipotence to work all things—even life's heartaches and horrors—to our good. All the undefinable terrors, all the bad news, all the pulse-escalating panic in the universe cannot separate us from your fatherly love. In your sovereignty, there is no such thing as wasted pain or superfluous suffering. Even when it seems like evil and suffering are winning, you will prevail. You are victorious in your sovereignty, and we are therefore "more than conquerors." In our age of anxiety, make us counterculturally fearless. Amen.

REFLECT

Ponder these questions for personal study or group discussion:

1. We can all relate to Thom Yorke, lead singer of experimental British rock band Radiohead. Describing his state of mind on their first three albums—*Pablo Honey*, *The Bends*, and *OK Computer*, Yorke recalls, "The problem for me if I'm honest is that I wasn't enjoying it 'til later on because I had my hands so stuck on that steering wheel, white knucklin'. I didn't want to make a mistake. I was terrified of making a mistake." In that state of what he calls "control freakery," Yorke became "unbearable." In which areas of your life are you most prone to being an unbearable control freak? How's that working out for you?

2. Does that fact that God is sovereign over suffering mean that, this side of heaven, we will always see and understand what he is up to in our suffering? If not (which is the right answer), what do you think are some of the reasons God may withhold giving us crystal-clear explanations behind all our pain?

3. What theological truth can you apply to your life and how you pray from the way that Guido de Bres faced his arrest and execution?

REPENT

In the left column, write down ways that you revere God in his supreme victoriousness. In the right column, list ways that your life does *not* revere him. We often wear rose-colored glasses when we introspect, so pray with the psalmist, "Search me, O God, and know my heart! Try me and know my thoughts! And see if there be any grievous way in me, and lead me in the way everlasting!" (Ps. 139:23–24). Ask yourself honestly: *Do I rest in God's sovereignty? Are there any ways I pretend to be sovereign myself, subjecting myself to far more stress and anxiety than I need to?*

Pray your way down the left column. Thank God for any ways that you are living out his sovereignty. Recognize that any ways in which you actually revere him are not from your own willpower but from his grace so he gets the praise and thanks. Then pray down the right column, confessing any ways in which you are not living out God's sovereignty. Ask him for a supernatural dose of faith.

HOW I AM REVERING	HOW I AM *NOT* REVERING

RESOURCES

Here are great theological resources to take your reverence for the sovereignty of God to the next level:

John Calvin, *The Secret Providence of God* (Crossway, 2010).

D. A. Carson, *Divine Sovereignty and Human Responsibility* (Wipf and Stock, 2002).

Anthony Carter, *Black and Reformed: Seeing God's Sovereignty in the African-American Christian Experience* (P&R, 2006).

Stephen Charnock, *The Existence and Attributes of God* (Crossway, 2022).

Jonathan Edwards, *Freedom of the Will* (CreateSpace, 2012).

John Frame, *The Doctrine of God: A Theology of Lordship* (P&R, 2002).

J. I. Packer, *Evangelism and the Sovereignty of God* (IVP, 2012).

John Piper, *Providence* (Crossway, 2021).

Thaddeus Williams, *God Reforms Hearts: Rethinking Free Will and the Problem of Evil* (Lexham Academic, 2022).

R. K. McGregor Wright, *No Place for Sovereignty: What's Wrong with Freewill Theism* (IVP Academic, 1996).

PART 4

ETERNALLY LOVING

GOD IS FATHER, SON, AND HOLY SPIRIT

OVER THE COMING CHAPTERS, WE WILL EXPLORE THE ETERNAL LOVE OF THE TRIUNE God and its impact on our relational lives together. We will be asking and seeking answers to questions like these:

Why can the God of the Bible, as opposed to, say, the god of Mormonism or Islam, be *eternally* loving?

Does God's passionate pursuit of his own glory make him self-centered and egomaniacal?

What is the doctrine of the Trinity, and why is it so precious, biblical, and love inspiring?

Is it possible to argue from the wrongness of reckless driving or the rightness of allowing traffic to merge to the existence of the triune God?

What is the "anti-Trinity" and how can we resist its evil agenda?

READINGS

To prepare your soul for the coming chapters, set aside a few minutes to read, really read—slowly, prayerfully, thoughtfully—through the following texts on the eternal love of the triune God. Ask God to open your heart and mind to what he is saying to you about himself and how you can best respond to the love of the Father, the Son, and the Holy Spirit with reverence.

MATTHEW 28:18-20

And Jesus came and said to them, "All authority in heaven and on earth has been given to me. Go therefore and make disciples of all nations, baptizing them in the name of the Father and of the Son and of the Holy Spirit, teaching them to observe all that I have commanded you. And behold, I am with you always, to the end of the age."

LUKE 3:21-22

Now when all the people were baptized, and when Jesus also had been baptized and was praying, the heavens were opened, and the Holy Spirit descended on him in bodily form, like a dove; and a voice came from heaven, "You are my beloved Son; with you I am well pleased."

JOHN 6:37-40

"All that the Father gives me will come to me, and whoever comes to me I will never cast out. For I have come down from heaven, not to do my own will but the will of him who sent me. And this is the will of him who sent me, that I should lose nothing of all that he has given me, but raise it up on the last day. For this is the will of my Father, that everyone who looks on the Son and believes in him should have eternal life, and I will raise him up on the last day."

JOHN 17:20-26

"I do not ask for these only, but also for those who will believe in me through their word, that they may all be one, just as you, Father, are in me, and I in you, that they also may be in us, so that the world may believe that you have sent me. The glory that you have given me I have given to them, that they may be one even as we are one, I in them and you in me, that they may become perfectly one, so that the world may know that you sent me and loved them even as you loved me. Father, I desire that they also, whom you have given me, may be with me where I am, to see my glory that you have given me because you loved me before the foundation of the world. O righteous Father, even though the world does not know you, I know you, and these know that you have sent me. I made known to them your name, and I will continue to make it known, that the love with which you have loved me may be in them, and I in them."

1 JOHN 4:7-11

Beloved, let us love one another, for love is from God, and whoever loves has been born of God and knows God. Anyone who does not love does not know God, because God is love. In this the love of God was made manifest among us, that God sent his only Son into the world, so that we might live through him. In this is love, not that we have loved God but that he loved us and sent his Son to be the propitiation for our sins. Beloved, if God so loved us, we also ought to love one another.

RHYTHMS

Revering God isn't just a matter of filling our heads with new information. It includes forming habits. Choose two or more of the following suggestions this week to help you better live out the eternal love of the triune God:

1. Early in the day, make a list of three loving things you can do for a family member, friend, or neighbor. Then follow through and do those things, praying that through them the triune God would make his love better known.

2. Make a list of aspects of your identity, including personality traits you are known for, your nationality, political persuasion, talents, and so on. Then, at the very top, write, "Love gift of the triune God of infinite and eternal love," since that is the highest identity that defines you. Pray to the Father, Son, and Holy Spirit, thanking them for making you who you are.

3. One of the most common ways love is expressed in the New Testament is by giving financially to help those in need. Find a need you can help with. Deprive yourself of a few weekly luxuries and cheerfully give the surplus money as a tangible manifestation of God's love.

THE INFINITELY
WORST GOD

AS WE TURN TO THE ETERNAL LOVE OF GOD, LET US BEGIN BY PONDERING ETERNALITY, the theological fact that God is not bound by time because God made time.

It was a sunny day at the San Clemente Pier. Waves were crashing. Surfers were surfing. Bikini bodies were slowly baking. The blue and chrome Amtrak Pacific Surfliner was keeping schedule, gliding parallel to the shoreline, triggering railroad crossing bells along the way. At a concrete picnic bench, I struck up a conversation with two Mormon elders, each in their late teens, attired in their standard-issue dark slacks and pressed white shirts. As an ex-Mormon myself, I have always loved exchanging ideas with Joseph Smith's Latter-day Saints, many of whom I count as dear friends. These two missionaries, with an enviable assignment to the California beach town of San Clemente, shared with me about the Mormon doctrine of eternal progression. I was fascinated.

They cited Mormon "prophet" Lorenzo Snow, "As man is, God once was; as God is, man may become."[1] They paraphrased Joseph Smith, who said,

> God himself was once as we are now, and is an exalted man, and sits enthroned in yonder heavens. That is the great secret. . . . For I am going to tell you how God became God. We have imagined and supposed that God was God from all eternity. I will refute that idea. . . . You have got to

learn to be gods yourselves, and to be kings and priests to God, the same as all gods have done before you, namely, by going from one degree of glory to another, and a small capacity to a great one, from grace to grace, from exaltation to exaltation.[2]

I asked a simple question. "Does that mean that God, your heavenly father, also has a heavenly father, a man who progressed to godhood before him?"

"Yes," was their reply.

"Did the heavenly father's heavenly father, your heavenly grandfather, I suppose, also have a heavenly father?"

"Yes," came the reply. Here they were faithfully in step with their founding prophet Joseph Smith when he said, "If Jesus Christ was the Son of God, and John discovered that God the Father of Jesus Christ has a Father, you may suppose that he had a father also. When was there ever any son without a father? And where was there ever a father without also first being a son? . . . Hence if Jesus had a father, can we not believe that *he* had a father also?"[3]

You might see where this is going. "Does the heavenly father's heavenly father's heavenly father have a heavenly father?"

"Yes."

"So how far back does that go?"

They responded, like Joseph Smith who compared time to a beginning-less and endless ring, that it has been going on forever. The process of men becoming gods had no starting point.

"Okay," came my next question, "once a man becomes God, does he max out his goodness, or does he continue progressing, getting better and better?"

"Well," they replied, "the doctrine is called *eternal* progression for a reason. We are always getting better, always progressing." In Smith's words, "going from one degree of glory to another . . . from grace to grace, from exaltation to exaltation."

"Fair enough," I said. "Does that mean your heavenly father's heavenly father is slightly more progressed than he is?" I was met with confused looks. "Your doctrine of eternal progression means that your heavenly father's heavenly father's heavenly father is even more progressed than the God you worship. And if this process of men becoming gods and continuing to progress has been going on for an infinite past, as you say, then you know what that means?"

"What?"

"It means that there are literally an infinite number of men who became gods who are more progressed, more advanced as gods than your heavenly father. Logically, this means (and I did not mean this with cruelty or as a gotcha moment) that your heavenly father is literally the infinitely worst god in existence." The nearby sets of crashing waves seemed to take on a symbolic meaning.

Contrast the heavenly father of my dear Mormon friends with the King of kings and Lord of lords we meet in Scripture:

"Therefore you are great, O Lord God. For there is none like you, and there is no God besides you." (2 Sam. 7:22)

From everlasting to everlasting you are God. (Ps. 90:2)

"Before me no god was formed,
	nor shall there be any after me." (Isa. 43:10)

"For I the Lord do not change." (Mal. 3:6)

Jesus Christ is the same yesterday and today and forever. (Heb. 13:8)

Every good gift and every perfect gift is from above, coming down from the Father of lights, with whom there is no variation or shadow due to change. (James 1:17)

"I am the Alpha and the Omega," says the Lord God, "who is and who was and who is to come, the Almighty." (Rev. 1:8) [What comes before alpha in the Greek alphabet? Nothing. What comes before God? Nothing.]

We, like Joseph Smith's heavenly father and grandfathers, are time-bound. We are in process. We are not pure being, we are becoming. Outside circumstances shape and reshape us. Our plans change, our identities change, our desires change. For creatures like us, the past is mostly unknown and often forgotten, the present is full of ambiguity, and the future is a con-stellation of ten billion question marks. We are creatures, not the Creator. As creatures we are contingent. "About every four seconds," said Charles Octavius Boothe, man "must drink in the air, in order to keep his little spark of life aglow. His life is not in himself. Not so with God. The sources of life are all in him."[4]

The self-existing God is not bound by space because he made space. So he is not bound by time because he made time. God surely acts within the timeline, but since he made that line and exists beyond it, he sees our past, present, and future with absolute clarity.

There was never a time when God was not fully who he is, and there will never be a time when he will not be fully who he is.

There was never a time when God was not fully who he is.

No force, no pressure, no catastrophe can alter who God is. As A. W. Pink put it, "He cannot change for the better, for he is already perfect; and being perfect, he cannot change for the worse."[5] Herman Bavinck echoed, "The doctrine of God's immutability is of the highest significance for religion. The contrast between being and becoming marks the difference between the Creator and the creature. Every creature is continually becoming. It is changeable, constantly striving, seeks rest and satisfaction, and finds this rest in God, in him alone, for only he is pure being and not becoming."[6]

Thus, we have a solid foundation to affirm not only that God is loving; he is *eternally* loving. In a world where emotions vacillate, friends betray, lovers leave, families split, and heart monitors go flat, an eternal love is what we all crave.

IS GOD OR TOD AN EGOMANIAC?

WE TURN NOW FROM ETERNALITY TO THE LOVE SIDE OF GOD'S ETERNAL LOVE. WE ARE immediately struck with an objection. How can God be loving if he seems so egotistical?

Why did God create the universe and populate our small corner of the cosmos with over a hundred billion images of himself over the millennia, including you and me, and about 385,000 new images of himself per day (Gen. 1:26–31; Num. 14:21; Isa. 43:7)? Why was Israel created and chosen as God's people (Gen. 2:1–2; Isa. 43:6–7; 49:1–3; Jer. 13:11)? Why were they rescued from Egyptian slavery (Ex. 14:4, 18; Ps. 106:6–8; Ezek. 20:5–9)? Why were they given the Law (Ex. 20:3–5), left to wander in the wilderness (Ezek. 20:13–14, 21–22), granted victory over the Canaanites (Josh. 24:12–14; 2 Sam. 7:23), given a king (1 Sam. 12:19–23) and a temple (1 Kings 8:41–45), restored from captivity (2 Kings 19:34; 20:6; Isa. 48:9–11; Ezek. 36:22–23, 32), and given prophets (Zech. 2:5; Hag. 1:8; Mal. 2:2)? Turning to the New Testament, why did God send his Son (John 4:34; 7:8; 17:4; Rom. 15:9)? Why did Jesus die and rise bodily from the grave (John 12:27–28; Rom. 3:25; 1 Pet. 1:3)? Why will the Son return (John 17:24; 2 Thess. 1:9–10; Rev. 21:23)? Why does God bless, choose, predestine, adopt, redeem, forgive, and seal us (Eph. 1:3–14)? What is the ultimate aim of the Christian life (Matt. 5:16; 1 Cor. 10:31; 1 Peter 4:11)? The answer remains the same through the Old and New Testaments—God's glory.

God's glory—the manifestation of the gravitas and glow of his manifold perfections—is the chorus to which the song of Scripture returns again and again, down to its last page, with the command, "Worship God" (Rev. 22:9).

To better grasp why some find this biblical truth so objectionable, imagine we change a single letter and turn *God* to *Tod*. What would you think of a mere mortal named Tod who was supremely passionate about his own glory? You would likely not think of Tod as noble for being the center of his own universe and pursuing his glorification above all else. He would be an egomaniac who needed to be taken down a few pegs, like a prima donna, a cult leader, a fascist dictator, or a "like"-obsessed social media influencer. Why is it praiseworthy that God seeks his own glory, but obnoxious and evil for Tod to do the same?

This is precisely the problem that drove Brad Pitt away from his Southern Baptist upbringing in America's Bible Belt. In the A-list actor's own words from an interview with *Parade* magazine, "I didn't understand this idea of a God who says, 'You have to acknowledge me. You have to say that I'm the best, and then I'll give you eternal happiness. If you won't, then you don't get it!'" It seemed to be about ego. I can't see God operating from ego, so it made no sense to me."[1]

How might we answer all the Brad Pitts out there who question the alleged egomania of God?

Tod's problem, unlike God, is that, as a finite creature, he thinks too highly of himself. Imagine we could put a number value to capture the value of any created thing. Let's say a pile of dirt is a plus five, a brick of gold is a plus one hundred, a bowl of kale is a minus ten, and so on. If Tod is a plus five thousand but thinks and acts like a plus five million, then we would spot the discrepancy and properly consider Tod a delusional egoist. We would not join in on his self-praise. We would likely seek ways to broadcast his faults and move him down in the social pecking order.

Finite creatures are capable of overestimating themselves precisely because they are finite. This is one of those strange places where what is possible for us— like lying or learning—is impossible for God precisely because he is God. It is impossible to overestimate the value of an infinite being.

It is logically and metaphysically impossible to give God too much glory.

We could no more ascribe more glory than is due to an infinite Creator than we could count past infinity or draw a square circle. It is logically and metaphysically impossible to give God too much glory.

The reason some mistake the God who seeks his glory as an egomaniac is because they blur the all-important distinction between God as Creator and ourselves as creatures. It's wrong for us to pursue ultimate glory for ourselves because we, by nature, are not ultimate. It would be wrong for God or for us to pursue anything less than God's supreme glory because he is, by nature, supreme. African American theologian Lemuel Haynes echoed, "There is no conceivable object that bears any proportion with the glory of God, and for him to ever aim at anything else would be incompatible with his perfections."[2]

Moreover, as John Piper loves to remind us, "God is most glorified in us when we are most satisfied in him."[3] God's passion for his own glory is not at odds with our joy. It is not like Stalin, Sauron, or Emperor Palpatine's passions for their own glory. They exerted power as a zero-sum game, spreading their tyranny and everyone else's misery around the earth, Middle-earth, or a galaxy far, far away. No. God is as committed to our joy as he is committed to his glory because God's glory consists in part of our enjoyment of him. As Jonathan Edwards concludes his classic *The End for Which God Created the World*, "God's respect to the creatures good, and his respect to himself, is not a divided respect. . . . [God's] supreme regard to *himself*, as it arises from . . . the creatures exercising a supreme regard to God . . . in beholding God's glory, in esteeming and loving it, and rejoicing in it.[4] C. S. Lewis concurs: "The Westminster Catechism says that man's chief end is 'to glorify God and enjoy him forever.' But we shall then know that these are the same thing. Fully to enjoy is to glorify. In commanding us to glorify him, God is inviting us to enjoy him."[5]

In God's kindness and creativity, he makes misty waterfalls, juicy mangoes, flickering fireflies, sizzling whitewash, harmonizing songbirds, babbling brooks, and earth-shaking thunder for us to enjoy. If God made the chief end of our existence the enjoyment of waterfalls, mangoes, and all other created delights, then he would be short-changing us. Each of these finite enjoyments and all finite enjoyments combined could not satiate our thirst for the infinite. If God made anything other than his infinite self the highest joy we could attain, then our souls would be forever restless, starved, and disillusioned. "In your presence there is fullness of joy; at your right hand are pleasures forevermore" (Ps. 16:11).

There is something still more profound we can say about why Tod, but not God, would be egotistical to seek his own glory, and it has everything to do with the Trinity. To this precious doctrine we turn next.

"GOD IN THREE PERSONS..."

THERE IS ANOTHER REASON IT IS IMPOSSIBLE FOR GOD TO BE AN EGOMANIAC, A reason that pulls us down to the bedrock of reality, a foundation so metaphysically deep that the word *downward* loses all meaning. It's as deep as we can go. I speak of the Trinity.

If our view of bedrock reality begins with oneness—whether it be the Hindu's Brahman, Plato's "Good," or Stephen Hawking's infinitely dense singularity—it will end with a unity that devours all beautiful diversity. If it begins with many-ness—whether it be the earth, wind, fire, and water of Empedocles, the infinite physical particulars of Anaxagoras, or the warring group-identities of Robin DiAngelo—it will end by obliterating all precious unity. This is the age-old problem of the one and the many, a problem that haunted such ancient philosophers as Thales, Anaxagoras, Heraclitus, and Democritus. How can we have unity that doesn't devour diversity and diversity that doesn't destroy unity? Apart from the God of the Bible, it becomes an unsolvable and ultimately bloody problem.

But in Christianity everything starts with a God who is one and many, the one God who exists as three inter-loving persons—the Father, the Son, and the Holy Spirit. Here neither unity devours diversity nor vice versa. We avoid both individual-crushing totalitarianism and lonesome individualism. We discover a way of being human in our romances, our families, our communities, and our nations that is truly humanizing because it mirrors something of the triune God who made us in his image.

Notice the difference between Tod and the triune God. Tod can be an egomaniac because he is one person with one nature. Any glory Tod seeks would be directed toward his singular person and would, therefore, be self-centered. God, however, is not one person with one nature. He is tripersonal. The one God exists, has always existed, and will always exist as Father, Son, and Holy Spirit—three eternally inter-loving divine persons.

Occasionally the friendly neighborhood cultist likes to point out that the word *Trinity* appears nowhere in the sixty-six books of Scripture. That much is true. But it doesn't tell us much. The word *omnibenevolence* cannot be found in the text, but even die-hard cultists affirm that God is all-good. What matters is not the presence or absence of a specific word, but whether the meaning that a given word conveys is true to the text.

The word *Trinity*—or *Trinitas* in Latin, as coined by Tertullian (AD 165–220)—is simply a label to describe the sum of three clear biblical teachings. The doctrine stands on three solid pillars:

1. **Pillar 1:** There is one and only one God (Deut. 6:4; Isa. 43:10).
2. **Pillar 2:** The Father is God (John 20:17), the Son is God (Isa. 9:6; John 5:18–20; 8:58; 20:27–29; Rom. 9:5; Col. 1:15), and the Holy Spirit is God (Acts 5:3–5; 2 Cor. 3:17–18).
3. **Pillar 3:** The Father is not the Son, the Son is not the Father, and neither is the Holy Spirit; rather, they are three distinct, inter-loving persons (Luke 3:21–22; John 17:20–26).

By rejecting the first pillar that there is one and only one God, you end up with *tritheism*, the view of Joseph Smith and the Mormon church. In Smith's words, "I have always declared God to be a distinct personage, Jesus Christ a separate and distinct personage from God the Father, and that the Holy Ghost was a distinct personage and a Spirit: and these three constitute three distinct personages and three Gods. If this is in accordance with the New Testament, lo and behold! we have three Gods anyhow, and they are plural: and who can contradict it?"[1]

To answer Smith's question, Moses can contradict it (Deut. 4:35; 6:4; 32:39), Nehemiah can (Neh. 9:6), David can (Ps. 86:10), Isaiah can (Isa. 43:10), Jesus can (Mark 12:29), Paul can (1 Cor. 8:4; 10:19–20), and, perhaps most surprisingly, *The Book of Mormon* and *Doctrine and Covenants* can

(Almah 11:26–29; Moses 1:6; 2:3–7; DC 20:17, 19, 28). They all affirm that there is one and only one God.

By rejecting the second pillar, you end up with a view held by modern-day Jehovah's Witnesses called *Unitarianism* (also known as Arianism, after a fourth-century heretic in Alexandria, Egypt, named Arius). For the Unitarian, the Father is God, the Son a created being below God, and the Spirit an impersonal force. The problem here is that Scripture does not shy away from calling Jesus "Mighty God" (Isa. 9:6), "equal with God" (John 5:18), the "I am" (John 8:58), "my Lord and my God" (John 20:28), "God over all" (Rom. 9:5), "in the form of God" (Phil. 2:6), "the image of the invisible God" (Col. 1:15), and "the radiance of the glory of God and the exact imprint of his nature" (Heb. 1:3). For those still doubtful of the full divinity of Jesus, perhaps a straightforward three-step argument may help:

1. Jesus is the Creator (John 1:3; Col. 1:16; Heb. 1:8–10).
2. The one true God—LORD in caps—is the Creator (Isa. 44:24).
3. Therefore, Jesus is the one true God.

By rejecting the third pillar, you end up with a view called *modalism* (the view of modern-day Oneness Pentecostals and Jesus Only groups, also called Sabellianism after the third-century Libyan heretic named Sabellius). For the modalist, the Father, Son, and Spirit are one God who exists as one person, who takes on three consecutive modes of existence, first as Father, *then* as Son, *then* as Holy Spirit. Just as I can be a professor at 3:00 p.m., a human jungle gym at 5:00 p.m., and a bad cook at 7:00 p.m., so God is one person playing distinct roles when creating the universe, redeeming the world, and powering the church.

At Jesus's baptism, we don't see three consecutive modes; we encounter three simultaneous divine persons—the Son being immersed in the Jordan River, the Spirit descending as a dove, and the Father declaring from heaven, "You are my beloved Son; with you I am well pleased" (Luke 3:21–22). That word "beloved" exposes the fatal flaw with modalism. Modes cannot love one another; persons can.

Here we circle back to the difference between an egomaniac like Tod and the triune God. The Father does not hoard glory for himself. "The Father loves the Son and has given all things into his hand" (John 3:35; cf. 13:3). "All that the Father has is mine" (John 16:15), said Jesus. "If I glorify myself," Jesus declared, "my glory is nothing. It is my Father who glorifies me" (John 8:54). The night before his execution, Jesus prayed, "Father, the hour has come; glorify your Son that the Son may glorify you" (John 17:1).

Like his Father, Jesus is not a narcissist. "I honor my Father" (John 8:49), and "I love the Father" (John 14:31), he professed. Jesus accomplishes whatever we ask in his name not for himself but "that the Father may be glorified in the Son" (John 14:13). That is not self-centeredness; it is love—Father glorifying Son, Son glorifying Father. The triune God is not only not narcissistic; he is anti-narcissistic and always has been. "Father," Jesus prayed, "glorify me in your own presence with the glory that I had with you before the world existed" (John 17:5).

The triune God is not only not narcissistic; he is anti-narcissistic and always has been.

And Jesus said of the third person of the Trinity, the Holy Spirit, "But when the Helper comes, whom I will send to you from the Father, the Spirit of truth, who proceeds from the Father, he will bear witness about me" (John 15:26). The Spirit, like Father and Son, is revealed to us not as elbowing others offstage, hogging the spotlight to bask in applause. His mission is to obey and glorify Father and Son.

So when we mortals glorify God—which is our "chief end"—we are not glorifying an egomaniac. We are glorifying a God whose very essence is self-giving community—Father glorifying Son, Son glorifying Father, Spirit glorifying Father and Son.[2] The triune God is the living and loving antithesis of egomania.

Even here we do not meet a snobby clique of three persons stockpiling all glory for themselves. No. The loving dance among the divine persons—known to theologians as the "perichoresis"—is not a centripetal or inward spinning dance like a toilet flushing or a black hole in space. Perichoresis is centrifugal or outward spinning. It reaches *out* to us that we, too, might be swept off our feet and drawn into the loving choreography of the self-giving God. Jesus wants us to be with him "to see my glory that you have given me because you loved me before the foundation of the world" (John 17:24). Oh, to be swept up in that eternal love of God in three persons!

"...BLESSED TRINITY"

WE HAVE SEEN THAT THE TRINITY IS BIBLICAL AND THE OPPOSITE OF EGOMANIA, but is the doctrine reasonable?

Twenty years ago, I sat at my desk where I worked as a researcher at a countercult apologetics organization in Southern California. For months, much of my brain space had been filled with a kind of obsession over a single question. There are arguments for God as beginner, God as designer, God as moral lawgiver, and so on. Aquinas's famous five arguments could get a logical thinker to an unmoved mover, a first cause, a necessary being, an ultimate good, and a supreme intelligence. But is there a good argument that could take us all the way to the "God in three persons, blessed Trinity," in the words of the old hymn?

One day the light bulb turned on. My fingers on the keyboard of the bulky old PC could barely keep up. First, let me state the argument in a seemingly outrageous way.

> *If you believe that reckless driver on the road who cut you off was wrong to do so, then you should believe in the Trinity.*

We could fill in reckless driving with basically any moral action—right or wrong, small- or large-scale—and reach the same conclusion. It was wrong for the online stranger to troll, the telemarketer to harass, the identity thief to hack, the politician to lie, the spouse to cheat, the father to whip, the racist to hate, the terrorist to detonate the vest, the slave trader to steal humans, the Gestapo to round up Jews, and so on. It was right for the driver to allow the merge, the sibling to share the last bite, the whistleblower to expose the corruption, the hero to jump on the grenade, the church to serve the poor, the abolitionists to free the slaves, and so on. Pick any right or wrong action.

Next consider what we actually mean when we say "right" or "wrong." We mean something more than "I personally don't like infidelity, child abuse, terrorism, racism, human trafficking, or genocide," the way a man might not like foam in his coffee or mustard on his hot dog. We also mean something more than "I'm with the masses who have decided by majority opinion to call slavery, racism, and genocide wrong." We all know if Wilberforce, Douglass, Tubman, and Lincoln's abolitionist efforts failed, the Ku Klux Klan overtook America, and the Third Reich defeated the Allies—slavery, racism, and genocide would remain evil as ever, despite popular opinion. Questions of ultimate morality cannot be decided at a ballot box.

By "right" and "wrong," we also mean something more than firing or misfiring synapses. To say the serial killer's spree was a matter of an overabundance of, say, C fibers firing in his amygdala, is not to explain evil, but to explain it out of existence. It turns blameworthy perpetrators into blameless victims of their own brain chemistry. Reducing morality to molecules gives every misanthrope in history the ultimate copout. It is not the religious copout "The devil made me do it," but the secular version: "My neurons made me do it."

The thing about objective morality is that the harder we try to refute it, the faster it refutes us. Even the most die-hard moral relativist abandons his anything-goes attitude the moment the burglar makes off with his property, the slanderer sullies his reputation, or the dog walker allows his animal to do his business on the relativist's lawn. Jean-Paul Sartre, the existentialist littérateur who vehemently rejected all transcendent categories of right and wrong and argued that "all things are permissible,"[1] committed much of his time and energy to counter the evils of French colonialism and the "race murder" it unleashed in Algeria. Friedrich Nietzsche, who saw himself as a courageous superman flying above and "beyond good and evil," spoke with the moralistic passion of a Baptist preacher against the evils of nationalism and anti-Semitism. Atheist Michael Ruse, who from one side of his mouth argues that ethics is "an illusion fobbed on us by our genes,"[2] cannot help but confess out of the other side of his mouth that "the man who says that it is morally acceptable to rape little children is just as mistaken as the man who says, 2 + 2 = 5."[3]

After demonstrating in painstaking detail why every godless attempt to account for morality falls flat, atheist Arthur Leff concluded,

> Nevertheless:
> Napalming babies is bad
> Starving the poor is wicked
> Buying and selling each other is depraved
> Those who stood up and died resisting Hitler, Stalin, Amin, and Pol Pot—and General Custer, too—have earned salvation.
> Those who acquiesced deserve to be damned.
> There is in the world such a thing as evil
> [All together now:] Sez who?
> God help us.[4]

The existence of real right and wrong points us to the existence not just of an impersonal moral code but of a personal moral encoder. In Leff's words, "If it is to fulfill its role, the evaluator must be the unjudged judge, the unruled legislator, the premise maker who rest on no premises, the uncreated creator of values. Now what would you call such a thing if it existed? You would call it Him."[5]

The point becomes clear if we ponder for a moment the fact that any morality worth its salt must feature love. Strip love from our vision of right and wrong and you would no more have morality than you would have a Tarantino movie with no blood. Love, by its very nature, cannot just be an "it," or an impersonal force. This was the problem with Plato's ultimate being, "The Good." Plato's "Good" was not a person, but a force, and therefore no more capable of love than electricity, magnetism, or gravity. Morality then points us to a supreme standard of good—a personal, loving *who* rather than a loveless *what*.

Morality then points us to a supreme standard of good—a personal, loving who rather than a loveless what.

Augustine took us farther. "What, then, is love," asked the African bishop, "except a certain life which couples or seeks to couple together some two things, namely, him that loves, and that which is loved?"[6] True love requires not just a single *who* but, at a minimum, a plural *whos*, at least a lover and a beloved. But how do we get as far as the Trinity?[7]

Anselm offered us a key: "What good, therefore, does the supreme Good lack, through which every good is? Therefore, thou art just, truthful, blessed, and whatever it is better to be than not to be. For it is better to be just than not just; better to be blessed than not blessed."[8]

From here the tumblers fall into place one by one. If we're speaking of the "supreme Good," then it is better [read: more loving] to reveal yourself to humanity than to keep that love unrevealed, unshared, and unenjoyed by others. A being who reveals himself in time-space history to manifest his love is better than some being hiding away from the world, hoarding the love for himself, like a dragon in some heavenly lair.

So we must look to the so-called revealed religions to see if any candidates measure up to the standard of perfect love. Buddhism is atheistic while Hinduism centers on an impersonal Brahman. It is better to exist and be personal than not exist or be impersonal, so we must search on. According to Islam, Allah both exists and is personal. But he is a lover without a beloved unless he makes other beings to receive his divine affection. Since the highest love is interpersonal, requiring both a lover and a beloved, Allah's love is contingent and he cannot be eternally loving. Returning to Anselm's insight—"Thou art . . . whatever it is better to be than not to be"—it is better to be eternally loving than requiring the creation of other beings to become loving. Put differently, interpersonal love cannot be an essential attribute of Allah's divine nature. The same problem afflicts the Jehovah of the Jehovah's Witnesses, who was all alone until he created Jesus. Alas, we must continue our search.

Perhaps polytheism could get us to a perfect love. The polytheist believes that multiple divine beings exist and are personal. But they, too, fail as candidates for Supreme Love. Let's say Zeus loves Hera, Osiris loves Isis, or the Mormon heavenly father loves Jesus. Here love is something like redness in an apple. Redness is some property that exists above and beyond apples that they may or may not express. There are, after all, green, yellow, and even white apples. If Zeus, Osiris, or Smith's heavenly father chooses to express love, then he himself is not the ultimate source or standard of love but is choosing to express something that exists above and beyond himself. But again, love, unlike redness, is not a *something*. It is personal. It is *Someone*. As John said, "God is love" (1 John 4:16). All that can be said of Zeus, Osiris, or Smith's heavenly father is that he *expresses* love. But it would require an altogether different kind of a being, a being who is not one among many in a pantheon of deities, in order to say that he *is* love. With Anselm's help, we can say it is better to *be* love than to express a love that exists above oneself.

Our search narrows. I taught comparative religion for nearly ten years. I was raised Mormon, spent countless hours studying sacred texts and conversing with Muslims, Hindus, Jehovah's Witnesses, and more. There is something utterly unique about the God we meet in the Bible.[9] We can say with John that he "is love" in a way we can't say of any other god. The God of the Bible is a God of perfect love and, therefore, the source and standard of all goodness because he not only exists, he not only reveals himself, he is not only personal—he is *tripersonal*. As Father, Son, and Holy Spirit, God need not look above himself to instantiate some love that exists above and beyond him. He need not create a universe and populate it with other beings in order to give and receive interpersonal love. As Jesus himself said, "Father . . . you loved me before the foundation of the world" (John 17:24). Our search for perfect love reaches its destination on our knees before the Father, the Son, and the Holy Spirit. If you believe people are truly wrong to drive recklessly, abuse children, and enslave, hate, and massacre one another; if you believe people are truly right to share with, sacrifice for, protect, liberate, and save one another, then you should also believe in the Trinity; and not merely believe, but bow in worship before he who "is love," "God in three persons, blessed Trinity."

> **Bow in worship before he who "is love," "God in three persons, blessed Trinity."**

20

THE ANTI-TRINITY

IMMANUEL KANT THOUGHT THAT "TAKEN LITERALLY, ABSOLUTELY NOTHING worthwhile for the practical life can be made out of the doctrine of the Trinity."[1] I am convinced by Scripture and experience that the great German philosopher could not have been more wrong on this point. The one God who exists as three inter-loving persons has everything to do with "the practical life." The Trinity shapes how we break anti-loving cycles in our hearts, how we pray, how we worship, how we do church, how we build relationships, and more.

Perhaps Kant's assessment was informed by a failure of eighteenth-century European churches to intentionally live out Trinitarian realities. As J. Scott Horrell laments, "We have done little to consciously express Trinitarian belief in our daily lives and in the community and mission of the church."[2] In other words, we need not only Trinitarian *orthodoxy*—correct doctrine of the Trinity—but also Trinitarian *orthopraxy*—correct practice that accurately reflects the reality of one God who exists as three inter-loving persons. Jesus prayed for his church to form a kind of angled mirror.[3] We are to be so united together in love that we direct the world's gaze upward to behold the triune God of love (John 17:11–24). In John's gospel, Jesus expressed his desire for the world to see the reality of love within the Trinity no less than eight times (3:35; 5:20; 10:17; 14:31; 15:10; 17:23, 24, 26). Are our churches cracked mirrors refracting little light from above, or are we reflecting the triune God clearly?

We could list many reasons why churches fail to clearly reflect Trinitarian reality to the world. I'd like to focus on one reason that is rarely considered.

We often fail to reflect the Trinity because *we do not have a robust enough doctrine of the anti-Trinity.* Before sewing a scarlet *H* (for "heretic") onto my corduroy jacket, allow me to define "the anti-Trinity."

THE ANTI-TRINITY		THE TRINITY	
"The Father of Lies"		"The Father of Lights"	
John 8:44 1 Peter 5:8 John 17:15 Eph. 6:12 John 10:10 James 4:7	The devil is evil, on a destructive mission for his glory's sake. Narrow focus on this truth leads to blaming our evils on the devil and an unhealthy obsession with demons.	The Father is God, on a redemptive mission for his glory's sake. Narrow focus on this truth leads to Arianism and a failure to worship the Son and the Holy Spirit.	James 1:17 Eph. 4:6 1 Peter 1:3 Matt. 5:45 John 4:23 John 10:29
"The Flesh"		God Who "Became Flesh"	
Rom. 8:13 Gal. 5:19–20 Ps. 51:1–12 1 Peter 2: 11 Col. 3:5–10 Matt. 15:8–20	The sin nature is evil, an internal driving force away from God toward death. Narrow focus on this truth leads to morbid introspection and ignoring spiritual warfare.	The Son is God, who lived flawlessly, died as our substitute, and rose bodily. Narrow focus on this truth leads to Jesus Only theology and a failure to worship the Father and the Spirit.	John 1:1, 14 Isa. 9:6–7 Heb. 1:3–13 Col. 1:15–17 Rom. 9:5 John 20:28
"The Spirit of the Age"		"The Spirit of Truth"	
1 Cor. 2:12 Rom. 12:2 James 4:4 Titus 2:12 1 John 2:16 Eph. 2:1–5	The world is evil, moving people deeper into the illusion of their own godhood. Narrow focus on this truth leads to us-them xenophobia and culture war.	The Holy Spirit is God who indwells and empowers the Christian life. Narrow focus on this truth leads to "charismania" and a failure to worship the Father and Son.	John 14:16 Ezek. 36:26 Acts 5:3–9 2 Peter 1:21 Gal. 5:22–23 John 16:8–14

Trinitarian heresies tend to focus on one divine person or another while devaluing the other two. Arius, in the fourth century, upheld the Father's divinity while devaluing the Son and Spirit. Many within today's Jesus Only movement have done the same with the Son at the expense of the Father and Spirit, and so on. A biblical view of the Trinity demands that our theology is not *FATHER*, Son, and Holy Spirit. Or Father, *SON*, and Holy Spirit. Or Father, Son, and *HOLY SPIRIT*. A biblical view exalts the one God who exists as *FATHER*, *SON*, and *HOLY SPIRIT*—all equally divine persons, each worthy of worship, love, and awe.

Yet the Bible also reveals an unholy anti-Trinity—three destructive forces at work against the triune Creator's mission. Protestant Reformers like Martin Luther saw these three forces accurately as the world, the flesh, and the devil. I call these three "the anti-Trinity," not because they afford us with some kind of analogy of how one God could exist as three persons (they offer no such analogy), but because the world, the flesh, and the devil are set directly at odds against the redemptive mission of the triune God. We must not downplay the reality of any of these three malevolent forces as we join the triune God's mission. Biblically, who are the members of the anti-Trinity?

The Devil

The devil cannot be allegorized away as some fictional villain like Darth Vader or the Joker. In the Bible, Satan and his legions are really there and launch moment-by-moment warfare against God. The Father, the first member of the holy Trinity, is our great "justifier," declaring us not guilty (Rom. 3:26), a God who "never lies" (Titus 1:2), and who "gives . . . life" (Acts 17:25). Satan, the first member of the anti-Trinity, is the great "accuser" (Luke 22:21; Rev. 12:10), "the father of lies" who "was a murderer from the beginning" (John 8:44). We must prayerfully suit up with the armor of faith, truth, and the gospel, and fight back against Satan's power with Scripture's power (Eph. 6:10–18). If we ignore the first member of the anti-Trinity then we live out a kind of oxymoronical "Christian naturalism," oblivious to invisible warfare, naked on the battlefield, duped by the devil's great trick of convincing the world that he doesn't exist.

If we stop with the Father of Lies, then we become a kind of inverted mirror image of the Arian who limits his concept of God to the Father. Arianism keeps people from engaging in worship of the Son and the Spirit as they should. Likewise, limiting our concept of evil to the devil keeps us from engaging the flesh and the world as we should. With such an inadequate view of the anti-Trinity, we end up with an unhealthy, superstitious fixation on the invisible world. We find Satan in every sniffle, fear demons in every dark corner, and blame

We end up obsessed with the "father of lies" rather than awestruck at the "Father of lights."

Beelzebub for our own self-induced blunders. "The devil made me do it," we may say, when in reality, "My own stupidity and addiction to the rush of sin made me do it." We end up obsessed with the "father of lies" (John 8:44) rather than awestruck at the "Father of lights" from whom all good things come (James 1:17).

The Flesh

The second unholy member of the Bible's anti-Trinity was often referred to by Paul as "the flesh." By "flesh" Paul did not mean our hundred or so pounds of carbon and H_2O but was referring to the sin nature, that drive within all of us to do things our own way, in our own power, for our own glory. It's that force inside you pulling you like a giant invisible magnet back into those same self-destructive sins.

Pop band INXS was not far from Scripture when they sang, "Every single one of us has a devil inside"[4] (see Gen. 6:5; Jer. 17:9; Eccl. 9:3; Matt. 15:19; Eph. 2:1–3). Narrowing our view of evil to devils out there causes us to ignore the "devil" *in here*, the evil propensities within our own hearts. We are all "possessed" by that evil force Paul called our "flesh" (Gal. 5:19–20; Col. 3:5–10; Rom. 8:13). What are we to do with the second member of the anti-Trinity? Paul, again using warfare terminology, commanded us to kill it prayerfully by the power of the Holy Spirit (Rom. 8:13). The Puritans used to call this sacred duty "mortification." If we are not orthodox enough in our view of the anti-Trinity, if we limit our concept of evil only to the flesh, then we may grow preoccupied with ourselves, morbidly introspective, and stray naked into spiritual warfare against the devil *out there*.

The World

The 6.6-sextillion-ton sphere spinning around the sun is not some evil force according to the Bible. God called the world "good" when he made it. "World" in the anti-Trinity refers not to earth but the "spirit of the age," the system that hails greedy consumption, boundless sexual exploration, and other soul-crushing vices as virtues (Eph. 4:17–20; 2 Peter 2:12–14; 1 John 2:16). It measures people's status in terms of the name brands on their shoes, the notches on their bedpost, or the followers on their Instagram account. It is the axis of cultural forces that conspire for the worship of the finite over and against the infinite God. Friendship with this world makes us the "enemy" (James 4:4, there's that warfare language again) of the God who wants so much more for his creatures.

We are not commanded to build compounds, stockpiled with guns, barbed-wired off from this world. We are called to live *in* this world in a radically countercultural and redemptive way. We are to think of ourselves as Paul did—"crucified . . . to the world" (Gal. 6:14), our desires to indulge in its self-destructive pleasures hanging dead and powerless. We are to be nonconformists against the pattern on this world (Rom. 12:2), refuting a system of self-exaltation with lives of irrefutable, self-sacrificial love.

Limiting our concept of evil to this member of the anti-Trinity leaves us detrimentally imbalanced. We find ourselves on a self-righteous crusade against all the evil forces in culture—those snowflake lefties *out there*, those Christmas-canceling secularists *out there*, those monkey-brained evolutionists *out there*. We disregard the evils *in here*, the corruption in our own hearts. It is, after all, far easier to blame the unbelieving world than face ourselves squarely in the mirror. Is it any wonder with such an inadequate view of the anti-Trinity that the loudest spokespeople against culture's evils are often the same names making scandalous headlines with their own personal evils? When we only battle external evils, we leave our internal evils unexamined and unopposed.

The anti-Trinity is no match for a triune God of eternal love.

We also become so obsessed with political culture wars that we become prayerless and oblivious to the reality of spiritual warfare. Without a biblical awareness of the anti-Trinity, we become the very evils we are fighting.

To echo our original thesis: *we fail to reflect the Trinity well when we do not have a robust enough doctrine of the anti-Trinity.* We reduce evil to the world, the flesh, *or* the devil, when all three are daily at war against our joy in God and the joy of the nations. Which member(s) of the anti-Trinity do *you* most often ignore? Where does your soul stand unguarded? Do not be intimidated, overwhelmed, or discouraged. The anti-Trinity is no match for a triune God of eternal love.

FRED SANDERS ON THE
ETERNAL LOVE OF GOD

Fred Sanders is one of the world's leading systematic theologians who specializes in the doctrine of the Trinity. He serves as a professor in Biola University's Torrey Honors College. He is also a man who reveres God. This is his story of how the eternal love of the triune God has impacted his life.

In the year that I became a Christian, I was a teenager with what I suppose must be a pretty predictable set of problems. I was fearful about an uncertain future, deeply lonely and unconvinced I was lovable, embarrassed about my obvious shortcomings, and so on. I guess a lot of young people have some version of these feelings: a little bored, a little scared, a little ashamed. As I started going to church and reading the Bible, I gradually began to understand things better. Underneath my felt needs, I began to recognize my real needs: reconciliation with God, forgiveness of sin, and power to live for Christ. God met me where I was and took me somewhere better than I knew. The things I didn't even know were problems (my refusal to give glory to God) were solved in a way that also happened to solve many of the things I did know were problems (insomnia, defensiveness, risky behavior).

Something similar happened in my understanding of who God is, and this is where the theology really starts to kick in. Because God had moved into my life and solved my spiritual problems at their root, I recognized just how much I benefited from his grace. In a lot of ways, I began to relate to God as my problem solver, my provider, my teacher. In one sense, this was fine: we finite and fallen creatures are always needy, never self-sufficient. So of course God gets our attention and attracts our gratitude as the one who meets our needs. But after a few months of rejoicing in God's wonderful availability to me, and of growing in prayer and Bible study, I noticed that something was wrong. Somehow it was still just me at the center of the whole project, and God was orbiting my needs like some gracious satellite. That couldn't be right. I actually wanted to be called out of myself, to something greater than myself. As I read and reread the Bible, it became clear to me that I needed to be decentralized from my own life story and situation. God had to be the center.

I kept some notes back then, and one heading under which I started writing down relevant Bible passages was "Notes for a Gospel Outside of Me." What I meant by that, though I was groping in the dark and barely had words for it at the time, was that I knew I needed God to be central. My relation to God needed to become theocentric rather than me-centric. And if that was going to happen, I would have to recognize that God's own divine life had a lot going on in it, up above my head, without reference to me in the first place. Of course I wanted God to have something to do with me eventually, but what I was dying to find was a way of grasping how God's own eternal life and liveliness was independent of me.

Every time I found a passage (whether in the Bible or in a devotional book, including things by C. S. Lewis and J. I. Packer) that suggested the depth and independence of the life of God, I would write it down in a notebook under that heading "Gospel Outside Me." Gradually I accumulated several pages of these passages. Slowly I noticed that the richest expressions of them had a few things in common. They tended to name the Father and the Son: "Father, glorify me in your presence with the glory I had with you before the world began" (John 17:5 NIV). Sometimes they also named the Holy Spirit: "[Jesus] rejoiced in the Holy Spirit and said, 'I thank you, Father" (Luke 10:21). "This is my beloved Son, with whom I am well pleased" (Matt. 3:17). The bigness of this conception of God began to dawn on me. The greatness of what existed between the Father, Son, and Holy Spirit began to outflank my own intellectual horizon.

And then something happened. I read a really bad Christian book that a friend recommended. I forget the name of it now, and its author, but I remember that it was relentless in its message that God's love for me was at the center of the universe. It was very straightforward in saying it: there was nothing deeper than God's love for me, for me, for me. This forgettable book was a catalyst for me; it was the lie that made me perceive the truth. God's love for me was not the central thing. God's love in itself was the one great thing, and it had its own secure foundation, without which there would be no love for me to be invited into or rescued by. Furthermore, those notes I was taking about how the Father loved the Son in the Holy Spirit—they were the concrete details I had been needing in order to understand God's absolute, sovereign self-sufficiency. The Trinity met my need for a God whose life was about more than just meeting my needs. This was the foundation for a gospel that certainly reached down and saved me, but that was securely anchored in something about as far outside of me as it was possible to get.

In the decades since then, I've learned a lot more about the triune God. I've written several books and articles about the doctrine, and I never get tired of teaching about it in churches and even in academic settings. The love of the Father and the Son in the unity of the Holy Spirit continues to be my lifeline and my anchor, and the more I study it the more certain I am that this gospel that made all the difference for me has its source in a vast, profound reality that is way outside of me but draws me in closer and closer.

A PRAYER TO REVERE THE
ETERNAL LOVE OF GOD

God, you are the one true God, and you reveal yourself to us as three coequal, coeternal persons—Father, Son, and Holy Spirit. We can say most truly that you are love. Draw us into the divine dance of infinite affection. May we see our true origin, our identities, and our destinies as wrapped up and secure in your intra-Trinitarian affection. As John 6, 10, and 17 reveal, we are living, breathing love-gifts bestowed by the Father to the Son as the expression of your infinite affection. What an incredible identity! May we be worthy of it by living lives marked by extraordinary love. May we love you, our brothers and sisters in Christ, and our unbelieving neighbors with such a depth and authenticity that more people are drawn to you, the God in three persons, blessed Trinity. Amen.

REFLECT

Ponder these questions for personal study or group discussion:

1. State the three solid biblical pillars of the doctrine of the Trinity in your own words.

2. Do your best to explain in your own words why it is essential for God to be triune in order to say truly with John that "God is love."

3. These chapters argued that we must match our Trinitarian orthodoxy (good doctrine) with Trinitarian orthopraxy (good practice or living). Brainstorm four or five ways, as a church, that we can better live out the eternal love of the triune God.

REPENT

In the left column, write down ways that you revere the triune God in his eternal love. In the right column, list ways that your life does *not* revere him. We often wear rose-colored glasses when we introspect, so pray with the psalmist, "Search me, O God, and know my heart! Try me and know my thoughts! And see if there be any grievous way in me, and lead me in the way everlasting!" (Ps. 139:23–24). Ask yourself honestly: *Do I take God's eternal love for me seriously, or do I allow myself to stew in thoughts and feelings that I am unlovable?*

Pray your way down the left column. Thank God for any ways that you are living out his eternal love. Recognize that any ways in which you actually revere him are not from your own willpower but from his grace so he gets the praise and thanks. Then pray down the right column, confessing any ways in which you are not living out his eternal love. Ask him for a supernatural dose of faith.

HOW I AM REVERING	HOW I AM *NOT* REVERING

RESOURCES

Here are great theological resources to take your reverence for the eternal love of the triune God to the next level:

Augustine, *On the Trinity* (New City, 2012).

Matthew Barrett, *Simply Trinity: The Unmanipulated Father, Son, and Holy Spirit* (Baker, 2021).

John Owen, *Communion with the Triune God* (Crossway, 2007).

Vern Poythress, *The Mystery of the Trinity: A Trinitarian Approach to the Attributes of God* (P&R, 2020).

Michael Reeves, *Delighting in the Trinity: An Introduction to the Christian Faith* (IVP, 2022).

Fred Sanders, *The Deep Things of God: How the Trinity Changes Everything* (Crossway, 2010).

Fred Sanders, *The Triune God* (Zondervan Academic, 2016).

Scott Swain, *The Trinity: An Introduction* (Crossway, 2020).

Carl Trueman and Brandon Crowe (editors), *The Essential Trinity: New Testament Foundations and Practical Relevance* (P&R, 2017).

James White, *The Forgotten Trinity: Recovering the Heart of Christian Belief* (Bethany House, 1998).

PART 5

REDEMPTIVE

GOD SAVES SINNERS

OVER THE COMING CHAPTERS, WE WILL EXPLORE THE REDEMPTIVE GRACE OF GOD and its impact on our moral lives together. We will be asking and seeking answers to questions like these:

> Isn't it a bit outdated and gauche to speak of sin and God's wrath?
> Why does the gospel sound like nonsense to nonbelievers when we talk about the gory crucifixion of Christ as the supreme expression of God's love?
> What drove Isaiah, Paul, and Martin Luther to despair, and what truth that is utterly unique to a Christian worldview set them free?
> How much does our free will factor into our salvation?
> Whose understanding of God's grace comes closest to the Bible— Pelagius the Brit's, Cassian the Roman's, Arminius the Dutchman's, or Augustine the African's?

READINGS

To prepare your soul for the coming chapters, set aside a few minutes to read, really read—slowly, prayerfully, thoughtfully—through the following texts on the redemptive grace of God. Ask God to open your heart and mind to what he is saying to you about himself and how you can best respond to that truth about him with reverence.

JOEL 2:13

"And rend your hearts and not your garments.
Return to the LORD your God,
for he is gracious and merciful,
slow to anger, and abounding in steadfast love;
and he relents over disaster."

EPHESIANS 2:1-5, 8-10

And you were dead in the trespasses and sins in which you once walked, following the course of this world, following the prince of the power of the air, the spirit that is now at work in the sons of disobedience—among whom we all once lived in the passions of our flesh, carrying out the desires of the body and the mind, and were by nature children of wrath, like the rest of mankind. But God, being rich in mercy, because of the great love with which he loved us, even when we were dead in our trespasses, made us alive together with Christ. . . . For by grace you have been saved through faith. And this is not your own doing; it is the gift of God, not a result of works, so that no one may boast. For we are his workmanship, created in Christ Jesus for good works, which God prepared beforehand, that we should walk in them.

2 CORINTHIANS 12:9-10

But he said to me, "My grace is sufficient for you, for my power is made perfect in weakness." Therefore I will boast all the more gladly of my weaknesses, so that the power of Christ may rest upon me. For the sake of Christ, then, I am content with weaknesses, insults, hardships, persecutions, and calamities. For when I am weak, then I am strong.

1 CORINTHIANS 15:10

But by the grace of God I am what I am, and his grace toward me was not in vain. On the contrary, I worked harder than any of them, though it was not I, but the grace of God that is with me.

TITUS 2:11-14

For the grace of God has appeared, bringing salvation for all people, training us to renounce ungodliness and worldly passions, and to live self-controlled, upright, and godly lives in the present age, waiting for our blessed hope, the appearing of the glory of our great God and Savior

Jesus Christ, who gave himself for us to redeem us from all lawlessness and to purify for himself a people for his own possession who are zealous for good works.

RHYTHMS

Revering God isn't just a matter of filling our heads with new information. It includes forming habits. Choose two or more of the following suggestions this week to help you better live out the redemptive grace of God:

1. God's saving grace was meant to be shared. Ask God to set divine appointments for you this week with nonbelievers, opportunities to share the gospel. When God brings people across your path, don't shy away. Boldly share the best news in the universe.

2. God has the power to reform hearts. Make a list of five people you would love to see receive new, believing hearts, and pray for each of them by name.

3. Ask the Holy Spirit to help you identify three anti-loving patterns in your daily life. Pray as Paul did for the Thessalonians that God would cause you to "increase and abound in love" (1 Thess. 3:12).

FIRST, THE BAD NEWS

WITH AN INFECTIOUS SMILE AND SOOTHING SOUTHERN DRAWL, THE PREACHER takes the stage of the old Houston Rockets stadium, renovated to accommodate the forty-three thousand congregants of Lakewood Church. The weekly television broadcast will reach seven million more in approximately a hundred countries. He says inspirational things like, "Have confidence in yourself." "You can choose to change." "I don't do wrong on purpose. . . . I know my heart is right."[1] In an interview with CBN news, he declared, "When I see thousands of people before me, it just doesn't come out of me to say, 'You guys are terrible, and you're going to hell.' I'd rather say that God is a God of mercy."[2]

I sincerely wonder what the prophet Jeremiah would say to Joel Osteen. Jeremiah described the human heart as "deceitful above all things, and desperately sick" (Jer. 17:9). Or Solomon, who said, "The hearts of the children of man are full of evil, and madness is in their hearts while they live" (Eccl. 9:3). Or Jesus, who said, "Out of the heart come evil thoughts, murder, adultery, sexual immorality, theft, false witness, slander" (Matt. 15:19), and who warned of hell more often than he spoke of heaven.[3] Jesus and the Jewish prophets didn't refuse to speak of God's wrath because they would "rather say that God is a God of mercy." They spoke brazenly about human depravity and divine wrath precisely because without them, the mercy of God cannot shine forth in all its extraordinary, ill-deserved, and pride-crushing mercifulness. The extent to which we downplay or ignore the bad news is the extent to which we reduce God's good news to sentimental fluff.

If we're basically good, then we don't need Jesus as a Savior to move us from depraved to saved. We only need him (if at all) as a life coach to move us from good to great. But a life-coach Jesus is not the Jesus we meet in the text of Scripture.

The problem is not with Joel Osteen's pulpit alone. (For the record, it is not the *man* Joel Osteen I target but the man's ideas; I make a standing offer to treat the man to a meal, with an open Bible between us.) Centuries before the Texan megachurch pastor, Pelagius taught that "human nature is uncorrupted,"[4] Erasmus argued that "it is in the power of every man to keep what is commanded,"[5] and Charles Finney preached that "men have power or ability to do all their duty."[6] The problem is far bigger than any single pastor today. Osteen finds himself in good company with 71 percent of Americans and 65 percent of self-identifying evangelicals believing that we are born innocent.[7] We also have the psychological phenomenon of the self-serving bias, our well-documented tendency to exaggerate our strengths and downplay our shortcomings. As Solomon said long before the psychologists caught up, "every way of a man is right in his own eyes" (Prov. 21:2). One-hundred percent of 829,000 high school students rated themselves above average in their ability to get along with others, with 25 percent ranking themselves in the top 1 percent.[8] Ninety-four percent of college professors believe themselves to be superior to their average colleagues, with 25 percent considering themselves "truly exceptional."[9] Ninety-one percent of Americans believe that "the best way to find yourself is by looking within yourself."[10] The mainstream says the answers are within our hearts. The Bible tells us what we know in our most honest moments—our hearts are the problem.

Seeing ourselves as basically good people[11] turns the meaning of the cross to nonsense. Ask Christians today to articulate the reason Jesus died on the cross. A hefty share who have never heard of the twelfth-century Frenchman Peter Abelard or his moral exemplar theory of atonement would likely echo his perspective. The cross of Jesus is about God showing how much he loves us by willingly sending Jesus to die for us, modeling how we too should love sacrificially. There's truth there, but not nearly enough.

Many of us have heard the cliché that goes like this: "I asked Jesus how much he loved me, and Jesus said, 'This much!' Then he stretched out his arms and died." Surely something profound is missing here. Imagine a lover professing his love for his beloved. "I love you," he declares, then picks up a nearby ceramic coffee mug and shatters it on his forehead. As blood streaks down his temples, he exclaims, "I really love you," and presses his palm on the glowing red circle of a nearby electric stovetop. As smoke and stench fill the room, he shouts, "I really, really love you," and bolts for the fifth-story window and launches himself through the glass to the pavement below.

If the cross is merely God's expression of love, then why all the prolonged agony of crucifixion? Lashing, public humiliation, a criminal's death, spikes through the wrists and ankles, a Roman spear under the rib cage and through the pericardium seem totally, gruesomely unnecessary. God could simply profess his love and spend eternity showering us with blessings to demonstrate his infinite affection. The death of Jesus sounds just as nonsensical to nonbelievers when we explain it as an expression of God's love for us while editing out—perhaps for fear of appearing judgmental—the sobering reality of God's just wrath against human rebellion. The wrath of God is the shape his goodness takes when he confronts anything that seeks to defy, corrupt, or vandalize what is true, good, and beautiful. If our cross is not the intersection of divine love *and* divine wrath, then it is not the cross of Christ.

We must avoid a common caricature. There stands a raging father, face red, ears smoking, forehead veins pulsing, fists cocked, ready to rain down blows of fury until his son stands in the way to take the beating, thereby changing the father's mind toward us from hate to love. The Bible says the opposite. "For God so *loved* the world, that he gave his only Son" (John 3:16, emphasis added).

If our cross is not the intersection of divine love and divine wrath, then it is not the cross of Christ.

"God shows his *love* for us in that while we were still sinners, Christ died for us (Rom. 5:8, emphasis added). "In this is love, not that we have loved God but that he loved us and sent his Son to be the propitiation for our sins" (1 John 4:10).[12]

Consider six images of what God, the love-motivated Father, accomplished by sending his Son to die for us. God sent Christ as an atoner (2 Cor. 5:18–21; Rom. 5:8–10; Col. 1:19–21), a battlefield hero (Gen. 3:15; Col. 2:15; Heb. 2:14–15; 1 John 3:8), a chain breaker (Mark 20:28; John 8:36; Gal. 5:1; 1 Peter 1:18–19), a defense attorney (Isa. 53; Rom. 3:23–28; Gal. 3:1; 1 John 2:1–2), an eternal priest (Lev. 4–6, 12; Eph. 5:2; Heb. 2:14–17; 9:12–14), and a forsaken son (Ezek. 16; Isa. 53; Matt. 27:46; Eph. 1; Heb. 13:11–13). What good is the Atoner to those who don't realize they are in a state of rebellion against their Creator? What good is the Battlefield Hero to those who don't realize they are the devil's prisoners of war? What good is the Chain Breaker to those who don't realize their slavery to sin? What good is the Defense Attorney to those who justify their criminality, a priest to those who don't reckon seriously with entering the holy of holies, or a forsaken son to those who don't see themselves as outcasts? Unless we reckon honestly with the reality of sin and the divine justice it warrants, we will never see God's grace to us in Christ for all that it is.

There is a reason jewelry shops display their diamonds against a backdrop of black velvet. There is a reason a full moon is more breathtaking after sunset. There is a reason Romans 1–3 precedes Romans 4–16. Take the familiar sitcom setup line, "I have some good news and I have some bad news. Which do you want to hear first?" If we prefer the good news first, then the bad news is that there is no good news. It is only if we take the bad news first—the reality of sin and the divine wrath it deserves—that the good news is actually good news.

WRATH

WHY DO WE DOWNPLAY OR DENY THE WRATH OF GOD,[1] AND THUS DIMINISH THE amazing grace of God? When was the last time you heard a sermon on divine wrath or sang a song exalting God for his righteous fury against evil? Why do we often hold an unreasonable bias against this hopeful—yes, hopeful—doctrine?

1. The Middle Schooler Problem

It is easy to care way too much about what people think. We censor ourselves to avoid being cast out of culture's cool crowd. We live in an age where anything goes and the only sin is calling anything sin. The very idea of a transcendent God who passes judgment on human action seems offensive, even appalling, to many. The just judgment of God means that our subjective feelings are not the final authority. That is, damnable heresy by today's standards. We shortchange God's wrath rather than face the possible wrath of our neighbors.

Yet, both Old and New Testaments speak again and again about God's righteous fury against evil (Num. 11:33; 2 Kings 22:13; John 3:36; Rom. 1:18; Eph. 5:6; Col. 3:6; Heb. 3:11; 4:3; Rev. 6:16; 14:10, 19; 15:1, 7; 16:1; 19:15). A. W. Pink noted that "there are more references in Scripture to the anger, fury, and wrath of God, than there are to his love and tenderness."[2] Test your heart. Which are you more concerned about: human rejection or divine revelation?

2. The Problem of Subway Theology

At the international hoagie chain Subway, every customer has the freedom to tailor a sub to his or her precise specs. Subway theology says, "Yes, go heavy on the love of God. Slather on divine compassion. Add an extra helping of grace and mercy. But hold the wrath. A God who punishes sin to the utmost, no thank you. A holy God who judges unholiness, hard pass."

We find ourselves immersed in consumer culture, conditioned to believe that reality can be easily adjusted to align with our preferences. The Cheesecake Factory menu boasts "more than 250 dishes made fresh from scratch every day." The original McDonald's menu offered 9 options in 1940. It has ballooned to 145 items today. Psychologist Barry Schwartz conducted research at a midsize local supermarket where he counted 85 brands of crackers, 150 lipsticks, 230 soup options, 275 cereal options, 285 varieties of cookies, and a whopping 360 types of shampoo, conditioner, hair gel, and mousse.[3]

With a superabundance of options, why not include theology among the products over which personal preference rules supreme? The problem with lumping theology in with crackers, shampoo, and lipstick is that we end up reversing the metaphysical order of reality. We bow to a god chiseled in our own image rather than to the actual God who made us in his image. Theology becomes a thinly veiled form of self-worship. That is not theology at all; it is idolatry.

3. The "Little Wing" Problem

A third reason we underappreciate God's wrath is that many of us are rightfully jaded by human wrath. The Bible has much to say about how human expressions of wrath go wrong. Hence, God's command, "Refrain from anger, and forsake wrath! Fret not yourself; it tends only to evil" (Ps. 37:8). We are commanded to be "slow to anger" because "the anger of man does not produce the righteousness of God" (James 1:19–20 cf. Col. 3:8).

Imagine a world in which the only guitars that exist have cracked bodies, bent necks, and rusty strings. Every guitar has either been smashed into a Marshall full stack or doused with lighter fluid and set ablaze. Playing a guitar masterpiece like Jimi Hendrix's "Little Wing" in such a world would be cringeworthy at best. The sublime chord changes and lead lines would sound like dying cats. That would not mean that the beauty of "Little Wing" does not exist, only that humanity is terrible at instantiating it.

Humanity is busted. Human nature is out of tune with reality. We are cracked, smashed, bent, and as charred as Hendrix's Stratocaster after the 1967 Monterey International Pop Festival. The dissonant, terrible ways we express wrath do not mean that there is no such thing as good wrath. As C. S. Lewis recounted, "A man does not call a line crooked unless he has some idea of a straight line."[4] As Jon Foreman sings, "The shadow proves the sunshine."[5] The dissonance points toward the resonance.

As busted humans, our wrath, unlike God's, is easily *unhinged*. Emotion overwhelms all reason. It is not about justice; it is a tantrum. "Wrath is fierce and anger is a flood" (Prov. 27:4 NASB). Our wrath, unlike God's, is easily *misdirected*. It is a poor judge who punishes the innocent and cowers before the guilty. "Acquitting the guilty and condemning the innocent—the LORD detests them both" (Prov. 17:15 NIV). Our wrath, unlike God's, is easily *disproportionate*. The punishment does not fit the crime. "Unequal weights and unequal measures are both alike an abomination to the LORD" (Prov. 20:10). Our wrath, unlike God's, is easily *hypocritical*. We punish others as if we ourselves are righteous when we are anything but. "You hypocrite, first take the log out of your own eye, and then you will see clearly to take the speck out of your brother's eye" (Matt. 7:5).

Because God is altogether holy, his wrath is never hypocritical.

In a profound sense, God is not wrathful. He is not wrathful in the fallen ways that we are wrathful. God's wrath is never unhinged because he is never overcome by emotion. God's wrath is never misdirected because he is all-knowing. God's wrath is never disproportionate because he is just. God's wrath is never hypocritical because he is altogether holy.

The truth is that we have a soul-deep longing for true wrath.[6] Derek Rishmawy observes, "We honestly don't want a God who looks at sin, idolatry, murder, oppression, racism, sexism, rape, genocide, theft, infidelity, child abuse, and the thousand dirty 'little' sins we'd like to sweep under the rug, and just shrugs his shoulders and *lets it go*."[7]

What is infinitely worse than a God of wrath? A God without wrath. Deep down we know this. Hitler took a self-inflicted bullet to the head in Berlin's *Führerbunker*. Does that somehow balance the scales with the millions of divine image bearers he exterminated? No. This is how ancient Jews of the Old Testament often viewed God's wrath, not with embarrassment but with exultation. For all the unrighted wrongs of this world, ultimate justice will prevail. Hallelujah! The evasive murderer, the sexual predator, the human trafficker, the political con artist, the corruptor of children, the greedy televangelist, the well-paid terminator of nascent human life, the self-righteous Pharisee, the drug lord, the racist, the swindler, the pornographer, the active shooter—as Johnny Cash sang, "Sooner or later God'll cut you down."[8] J. I. Packer concludes, "The character of God is the guarantee that all wrongs will be righted someday; when the 'day of God's wrath, when his righteous judgment will be revealed' (Rom. 2:5 NIV) arrives, retribution will be exact, and no problems of cosmic unfairness will remain to haunt us. God is the Judge, so justice will be done."[9]

It's easy to point to the Hitlers of history, the killers, con artists, child predators, and other misanthropes and pray along with the self-satisfied Pharisee, "I am not like other men" (Luke 18:11). The sobering truth is that we, too, deserve infinite wrath for our offenses against an infinite being. So let us, instead, join the tax collector beating his breast and crying, "God, be merciful to me, a sinner!" (Luke 18:13). When we throw ourselves at the mercy of God the Father, he offers us Jesus our *hilasmos*, our propitiation (1 John 2:1–2), our wrath taker. In Jesus there is no divine wrath that we could possibly experience on account of our lawbreaking. Every last bullet of divine justice was fired into his flesh on the cross; we stand behind him without a scratch as the just executioners' magazines click empty. The demands of divine justice have been satisfied by Christ on our behalf. If we edit divine wrath from our understanding of God, then we reduce the cross of Christ to a nonsensical display of divine love alone, rather than the glorious intersection of God's just wrath and radical love for sinners like us.

HOLY ROLLERS

GOD'S GRACE FOILS ANY WELL-MEANING ATTEMPT AT POLITICAL CORRECTNESS TO blur all faiths together and say they all hold the same basic truth. To grasp this point, meet Guinness record holder Mohan Das. Das, better known as "Lotan Baba" or the "rolling saint," expresses his faith by rolling in the dirt, literally. Come monsoon rain or desert shine, he rolled over four thousand kilometers in India alone and was attempting to roll all the way to England. A shopkeeper quoted by Reuters News Service said, "I just looked outside and there was this idiot rolling along the ground."[1] Before his holy rolling career, Das spent twelve years standing in place and eating only grass as an act of penance.

It would be easy to look at Baba and concur with the shopkeeper. Going to such ridiculous measures seems idiotic. If Lotan Baba is an idiot, then so am I. So are most of us. For some, "rolling" takes the form of rigid adherence to the five pillars of Islam. Others follow the Four Noble Truths and Eightfold Path of Buddhism, the teachings of the Watchtower, Professor Peterson's twelve rules for life, or the latest fitness guru's shredded ab regimen. Others "roll" by broadcasting their virtue—metaphorically shouting, *See, I'm a good person too!*—through their social media posts and hashtags. We roll our way into the confessional booth, the temple, the cathedral, the protest, or the gym. Most of us feel like we have something to prove. *See, I'm worthwhile. I'm enlightened. I merit love because I [fill in the blank].* But it's a losing game, and deep down we know that already.

The holiness of God renders all of our holy rolling futile. To be holy—*qadosh* in Hebrew—means to be set apart, sacred, unique, transcendent, existing above and beyond all evil and corruption. Ancient Hebrew had no such thing as bold or italic font, exclamation points, or underlining to add emphasis to a word or phrase. Instead, they used repetition, and triple repetition was the most emphatic statement you could possibly make.[2] In Isaiah 6 the prophet beholds God in his temple on his throne. The thresholds quake, smoke billows, seraphim circle and declare that the LORD is *qadosh, qadosh, qadosh*. This phrase, known as the *trisagion*, is still repeated by Jews all over the world in daily prayers and Sabbath services. The LORD isn't just "holy," or even "holy, holy"; he is "holy, holy, holy" (Isa. 6:3)—*__HOLY!!!__* in all caps, bold font, italicized, underlined, with exclamation points.

Notice Isaiah's reaction. He declared, "Woe is me! For I am lost" (Isa. 6:5). Isaiah was born into nobility. He saw royals enthroned and even pronounced woe on them. With King Uzziah recently deceased after a fifty-two-year reign, Isaiah beheld *the* King, with a capital *K*. This time the woe he pronounced was on himself. Isaiah in verse 5 was a man doomed, cursed, ruined, unraveled, and utterly despairing over himself. The holiness of the *__HOLY!__* God incinerated any sense of his own goodness.

> **The LORD is holy, holy, holy—**
> *__HOLY!!!__* **in all caps, bold font,**
> *italicized, underlined, with*
> *exclamation points.*

Centuries later, another renowned Jewish theologian, Paul, met God incarnate and concluded, "Wretched man that I am!" (Rom. 7:24). Then Paul rebranded himself as the chief of sinners (1 Tim. 1:15). All of his own impressive *torah*-keeping and religious accomplishments amount to a steaming pile of *skybala*, Greek for refuse, festering sewage, rotting waste, and even feces.[3]

Fast-forward a millennium and a half. In his public debut as a Catholic cleric, Martin Luther had to pray the prayer of consecration over the Communion elements at Mass. When the big moment came, Luther's pulse skyrocketed. He had to say eleven words: "We offer unto Thee, the living, the true, the eternal God." Panic froze his lips. Luther's first Mass, his moment in the spotlight, ended in horror. Luther recalled, "I was utterly stupefied and terror-stricken. . . . Who am I, that I should lift up mine eyes or raise my hands to the divine Majesty? The angels surround him. At his nod the earth trembles. And shall I, a miserable little pygmy, say 'I want this, I ask for that'? For I am dust and ashes and full of sin and I am speaking to the living, eternal and the true God."[4]

To stave off his sense of terror before a holy God, Luther took to living an extreme monastic life for nineteen years. He fasted for days at a time. He slept blanketless in his stone monastery cell, nearly freezing to death in the subzero German winters.[5] He would spend up to six hours a day in the confessional booth cataloging his every blunder to his eye-rolling father confessor.[6] None of it worked.

Isaiah, Paul, and Luther each realized that no amount of holy rolling could dazzle a holy, holy, holy God or save his soul. Thankfully, their stories do not end in despair.

After pronouncing woe on himself, Isaiah narrated, "Then one of the seraphim flew to me, having in his hand a burning coal that he had taken with tongs from the altar. And he touched my mouth and said: 'Behold, this has touched your lips; your guilt is taken away, and your sin atoned for'" (Isa. 6:6–7).

These three men each realized in his own way that no amount of holy rolling could dazzle a holy, holy, holy God.

After confessing his wretchedness, Paul asked, "Who will deliver me from this body of death?" and answered, "Thanks be to God through Jesus Christ our Lord!" (Rom. 7:24–25). Paul expounded, "I am not ashamed of the gospel, because it is the power of God that brings salvation to everyone who believes. . . . For in the gospel the righteousness of God is revealed—a righteousness that is by faith from first to last, just as it is written: 'The righteous will live by faith'" (Rom. 1:16–17 NIV).

Pondering those very words in the fall of 1515, likely while perched on the latrine (the toilet was discovered by German archaeologists in 2004), woe-stricken Luther found his "gate to heaven." Luther said,

> Although an impeccable monk, I stood before God as a sinner troubled in conscience, and I had no confidence that my merit would assuage him. Therefore I did not love a just and angry God, but rather hated and murmured against him. Yet I clung to the dear Paul and a great yearning to know what he meant. . . . Then I grasped that the justice of God is that righteousness by which through grace and sheer mercy God justified us through faith. Thereupon I felt myself to be reborn and to have gone through open doors into paradise.[7]

These three theologians were united by despair—not a nihilistic despair but a realistic despair, the kind that reckons honestly with the utter futility of our own holy rolling. Isaiah compared his "righteous deeds" to *idim bagad*—Hebrew for used menstruation rags (Isa. 64:6). Paul described the righteousness of his own as *skybala*—Greek for trash, waste, and feces (Phil. 3:8). Luther described himself as *reiffe dreck*—German for ripe manure.[8] Yet Isaiah looked forward to God's promise of the Suffering Servant, "pierced for our transgressions" and "crushed for our iniquities" who would bring us peace (Isa. 53:5). Paul looked to God who by sending Jesus became both "just and the justifier" (Rom. 3:26). Luther came to "behold God in faith . . . [and] look upon his fatherly, friendly heart in which there is no anger nor ungraciousness."[9]

We should swap hopeless despair for the kind of despair—Luther's *anfechtung*—that drives us, exhausted and self-disenchanted, into the Father's arms through the crucified Christ. We do not sing, "My hope is built on my spiritual performance, my capacity to parse Greek verbs, or dance exegetical circles around the cultists on my doorstep." With the old hymn we sing, "My hope is built on nothing less than Jesus' blood and righteousness."

24

HEALTHY, BATTERED, DEAD, OR ROBOTS?

HAVING ESTABLISHED THAT WE ARE SAVED BY GOD'S REDEMPTIVE GRACE ALONE, we face a question with enormous implications for how we worship, pray, doubt, suffer, evangelize, and more. How far must God's grace go to save sinners like us? The history of reflection on the Scriptures has yielded five ways to answer that question.

In the lecture hall, I clarify these theological options by choosing an unsuspecting student. Let us say that I seek to establish a friendship with a student named Colton. My first option would be to simply make the offer, "Hey Colton, let's get a cup of coffee. I'll buy." He has the freedom to accept or shun my offer. This is, more or less, how a view known as Pelagianism presents God's grace toward us. In the early fifth century AD, a British monk named Pelagius (along with Coelestius, Julian of Eclanum, later Charles Finney, and now Joel Osteen) taught that God need only extend commandments, invitations, and warnings. We have power in our natural, God-given state to freely say yes or no to God's offer. God would never command the impossible. *Ought* implies "can"[1] because every divine command corresponds to a human power to keep it. We are highly morally competent creatures.

Pelagius's idea that we have God-affirming power within ourselves holds tremendous sway in today's church. Such optimism is right at home within a self-glorifying culture that tells us that the answers (rather than the problems) lie within ourselves. A whopping 91 percent of Americans believe that "to find the answers we must look within."[2] This view of human power (and the minimal view of divine power it entails) has captivated millions through the media platforms of Joel Osteen and other self-help superstars. Church historian Philip Schaff draws out some implications of this popular Pelagian perspective: "If human nature is uncorrupted, and the natural will competent to all good, we need no Redeemer to create in us a new will and a new life, but merely an improver and ennobler; and salvation is essentially a work of man."[3]

This moves us to a second way we might understand the grace God extends to establish a relationship with us. In this scenario, I make the offer, "Colton, let's get a cup of coffee," but to my shock and horror, Colton has been mugged. He lies sprawled and twitching on the ground, bruised and bleeding. In his battered state, Colton cannot simply say, "Sure!" and join me in a kindly stroll to the Eagle's Nest, Biola University's best coffee shop. But he can at least wiggle a pinky to signal that, yes, he would like to join me. At that point, I would go to work bandaging wounds, administering medicine, getting Colton back on his feet so he can make the full free effort to join me for a cup.

Here we meet the semi-Pelagian understanding of divine grace, which also happens to be the official view of the Roman Catholic Church. A fourth-century abbot named John Cassian taught that saying yes to God is far more difficult than Pelagius thought. We are not healthy and capable. Our free will has been severely maimed ever since the fall of Adam and Eve. Our willpower is not obliterated, but it is battered and bruised. God sees whatever frail, quivering movements we make toward him and supplies us with enough medicating grace to fully and freely embrace him.[4]

Next comes the theology of Arminianism. For the sixteenth-century Dutchman James Arminius (and his seventeenth-century followers called the Remonstrance), our power is not unscathed by the fall of Genesis 3, as Pelagius believed. Nor is it wounded yet capable of slight Godward motion, as Cassian taught. In this view, when I say, "Let's get a cup of coffee," poor Colton is dead. I offer coffee to a corpse. Said Arminius, "The mind of man, in this state, is dark, destitute of the saving knowledge of God, and, according to the Apostle, incapable of those things which belong to the Spirit of God."[5] John Wesley echoed, "Since the fall, no child of man has a natural power to choose anything that is truly good."[6]

Since Colton can't respond, Arminianism demands drastic action. I must charge the defibrillator paddles, yell, "Clear!" and jolt life into Colton's corpse. In Arminian theology, God extends such life-giving action to everyone, thereby bestowing new powers of free will—the *possibilitas boni et mali*—to accept or reject him.[7] Thanks to this life-giving divine action (which Arminians dub "prevenient grace"), all of us freshly resuscitated "Coltons" can say yes or (and here's the key to understanding Arminian theology) say no to God. The Remonstrants said, "Man does not have saving faith of himself nor by the power of his own free will. . . . It is necessary that he be regenerated by God, in Christ, through his Holy Spirit, and renewed in understanding, affections or will, and all powers, in order that he may rightly understand, meditate upon, will, and perform that which is truly good."[8] Note well, man *may*, not man *will* choose God. It follows that "with respect to the mode of this grace . . . it is not irresistible. . . . Man is able of himself to despise that grace and not to believe, and therefore to perish through his own fault."[9]

Augustine went further. The fourth-century African bishop thought that, yes, we are dead in sin.[10] God's offer of salvation would be akin to me offering Colton's corpse a cup of coffee. But for Augustine, when God charges the defibrillator and jolts life into our spiritual corpses, his life-saving action is so drastic, gracious, and transformative that we *will* say yes to him, not *may* say yes to him. For Augustine, we come to God as "the Delightful Conqueror"[11] who applies "efficacious powers to our will,"[12] to "rejoice to thee, in thee, and for thee."[13] God does not merely *resuscitate*, he *reforms* our hearts such that we find a relationship with our unfailing heavenly medic irresistible.[14] In the words of Francis Turretin, "[God infuses] his vivifying Spirit, who, gliding into the inmost recesses of the soul, reforms the mind itself, healing its depraved inclinations and prejudices. . . . [God] so sweetly and at the same time powerfully affects the man that he cannot (thus called) help following God."[15]

God charges the defibrillator and jolts life into our spiritual corpses.

Augustine's theology stands in contrast to our final option, the creepiest scenario by far. I cannot bear the thought of Colton shunning my offer. I team up with some colleagues in the computer science department to design a sophisticated artificial affection chip. I scout out Colton's apartment, sneak in under cover of nightfall, and install the hardware into his sleeping brain. He wakes up with an irrepressible urge—"Must get coffee with Thaddeus. *Beep-boop-bop.* Must get coffee with Thaddeus." And there I sit sipping a flat white with a human I have effectively turned into a living Chatty Cathy doll—pull the string and out comes the preprogrammed "I love you."

Fortunately, no theologian to my knowledge has advocated such a view in church history,[16] and for good reason.[17] While atheists like Denis Diderot, B. F. Skinner, Jacques Monod, Daniel Dennett, Alex Rosenberg, and Sam Harris have argued for such determinism (as their brain chemistry presumably determined them to do), nowhere does the Bible present humans as soulless automatons.[18] We are believing, disbelieving, and choosing moral agents. Why, then, would I bother including this robotic view among our options? Because the Augustinian view is often confused with Chatty Cathy determinism, turning otherwise helpful dialogues into a series of straw men.

What, then, sets Augustine's theology apart from a world of preprogrammed dolls? In Augustine's view, there are significant, willing, and believing human agents loving God because they *want* to. In the Chatty Cathy view, by contrast, there are only heartless automatons expressing the mere syntax of love because they *have* to. Turretin further distinguished the Augustinian view:

> With respect to the actual [conversion], the principal cause is indeed God, but the proximate and immediate cause is man, who (excited by the Holy Spirit and imbued with the habits of faith and love) believes and loves. . . . Hence it appears that man is not like a log and a trunk in his regeneration as our opponents falsely charge upon us. . . . The Spirit does not force the will and carry it on unwillingly to conversion, but glides most sweetly into the soul . . . and operates by an infusion of supernatural habits by which it is freed little by little from its innate depravity, so as to become willing from unwilling. . . . The will so renewed and acted upon immediately acts, converting itself to God and believing.[19]

We have now clarified five ways to understand God's grace. We have a grace that requests (Pelagianism), a grace that repairs (semi-Pelagianism), a grace that resuscitates (Arminianism), a grace that reforms (Augustinianism), and a grace that robs us of our humanity. The real question is not which view we personally like, but rather which view does the Bible teach?

A BRIT, A ROMAN, A DUTCHMAN, AND AN AFRICAN WALK INTO A BAR

WHEN IT COMES TO ACCEPTING GOD'S OFFER OF SALVATION, OUR THEOLOGICAL PICTURE now looks like this:

> **Pelagianism:** All can, some will. God's grace merely *requests* of our competent hearts.
>
> **Semi-Pelagianism (Cassianism):** All barely can, some will. God's grace *repairs* our battered hearts.
>
> **Arminianism:** None can until God works; then all can and some will. God's grace *resuscitates* every dead heart so they may love him.
>
> **Augustinianism:** None can until God works; then all who can will. God's grace *reforms* dead hearts so they will love him.
>
> **Chatty Cathy Determinism:** None can, none will, because there are none, only robots. God *robs* our hearts of humanity.[1]

Who got it right? Whose theology, if any, can be found in the text of Scripture?

In the early fifth century, the pope of Rome, Zosimus, gave his stamp of approval to Pelagianism, deeming it within the bounds of Christian orthodoxy. Thankfully, a team of African theologians, led by Augustine, exposed Pelagianism for the heresy that it is. We are not morally able in our natural state to obey God's commands by flexing our undamaged free will. The Bible teaches that we are dead in sin, enemies of God, hostile to him, totally incapable of submitting to his law, unable to please him, and unable to understand or receive the things of his Spirit (Eph. 2:1; Col. 1:21; Rom. 8:7–8; 1 Cor. 2:14). For making too much of human goodness and therefore too little of God's grace, Pelagianism was condemned as heresy at no less than three church councils—in Carthage in 418, Ephesus in 431, and Orange in 529.

But the ghost of Pelagius lives on. Three-quarters of Americans today agree that the Bible teaches, "God helps those who help themselves,"[2] with many believing it to be one of the Ten Commandments. The phrase actually comes not from the Bible but from a British politician named Algernon Sidney in the late seventeenth century. The Bible is clear: God does not help those who help themselves, but those who are utterly broken and beyond self-help (see Ezek. 16). Where are the Augustines of the twenty-first century who will exorcise the spirit of Pelagius from our churches and boldly herald again the good news of salvation by God's grace alone? I pray you are reading this now.

That leaves us with the Roman, the Dutchman, and the African. Unlike Cassian the Roman, the Bible does not teach that we are mangled but still able to freely, albeit feebly, reach toward God. Rather, in our fallen state we are no more capable of upward movement toward God than a cadaver on the mortician's slab. When the Bible says we were dead in trespasses and sins (Eph. 2:1), dead means dead.

This leaves us with two options and the question between "may" and "will." For Arminius, God jolts us to life to resuscitate our free wills so that we *may* (or may not) freely accept him. For Augustine, when God jolts us to life, he reforms our hearts so radically that we *will* accept him, without reducing us to robots in the process. God's saving grace for Arminius is resistible, for Augustine irresistible. What does the Bible say?

The Great Cardiac Surgeon replaces the stones in human chests with hearts of flesh.

The Old Testament gives three metaphors of God's gracious action in human hearts. All three occur in the context of God introducing the new covenant.[3] God circumcises hearts (Deut. 30:6), writes his law in hearts (Jer. 31:33), and performs a stone-to-flesh heart transplant (Ezek. 36:26). God circumcises a heart "so that you will love the LORD your God with all your heart and with all your soul" (Deut. 30:6). When he writes his law in hearts, he declares, "I will be their God, and they shall be my people" (Jer. 31:33). When the Great Cardiac Surgeon replaces the stones in human chests with hearts of flesh, he promises that he will "cause you to walk in my statutes and be careful to obey my rules" (Ezek. 36:27).

If these passages are about Arminian heart resuscitation,[4] then we face a strange possibility. It becomes possible to have a divinely circumcised, etched, transplanted heart and still say no to God, step outside his covenant, and curse yourself. Nowhere in the text do we find such bizarre contradictory creatures—humans who are *in the new covenant* by virtue of their new hearts who are simultaneously *outside the new covenant* by using those new hearts to reject God to their own damnation.

The New Testament offers still deeper insight into whether God resuscitates hearts that can say no to him or reforms hearts that will say yes to him. John 6:37 speaks of the Father giving the Son people. In John's view, every believer is a living, breathing "I love you" spoken by a triune God, from Father to Son (John 17:20–26).

Jesus declared, "All that the Father gives me will come to me" (John 6:37).[5] Who "will come to" Jesus? "All that the Father gives" to him. The Father "gives" in the present tense. People "will come" in the future tense. Grammatically, this is like saying, "All the governor pardons (present) will enjoy (future) freedom from death row." The prisoners' enjoying freedom rests on the prior actions of the governor. Similarly, if you believe in Jesus, then you were not the prime mover behind that belief. Rather, you believe in the Son because the Father first gave you to the Son as an expression of his intense affection for the Son. You cannot credit your salvation to your superior smarts or spiritual chops. The convict has the governor to thank for his enjoying freedom. You have God the Father to thank for your coming to / believing in the Son.

Arminianism requires us to reverse John's verbs. All who come (present) to the Son [with their autonomous free power], will be given (future) by the Father. For John, however, we do not believe to *become* intra-Trinitarian love-gifts; we believe *because* we are intra-Trinitarian love-gifts. "All" the Father gives will come to the Son. For John it lies beyond the scope of possibility that anyone the Father wants to give his Son as a living, conscious, worshiping "I love you" would not, in fact, come to the Son.[6]

This raises an important question. Do humans like us have enough power to mar the full, radiant expression of God's love within the Trinity? John helps us answer that question. The Father's "will" (*thelema*) is that the Son would lose none of all that the Father has given him and that the Son would raise up the complete gift on the last day (6:38–40). If we could resist Jesus with self-destructive finality, then we could prevent the Son from doing his Father's will. Do we possess such intra-Trinitarian love-blocking power? Jesus counters, "No one can come to me unless the Father who sent me draws him. And I *will* raise him up on the last day" (6:44, emphasis added).[7]

Arminius leads us away from this blessed assurance. Merely resuscitated hearts (as opposed to reformed hearts) can be drawn by the Father but reject the Son, and therefore *not* be raised up into glory. If God's will to the Son is that he lose not a single love gift (6:38–40) and we have the autonomous power to lose ourselves, then we can keep the Son from perfectly fulfilling his Father's will. If the Son could fail to perfectly fulfill the Father's will, then the cross is emptied of its saving power.[8]

John 6 is hardly an isolated text. For Arminius, all receive resuscitated hearts, and the difference between those who are saved and those who are not depends precisely on how different people use the same gift of free will. But Paul did not mince words when he said that salvation "depends not on human will and exertion, but on God, who has mercy" (Rom. 9:16). Everyone the Father calls will be justified, and everyone he justifies will be glorified (Rom. 8:30). "He chose us in him

> **God gets 100 percent of the credit and glory for my salvation, for making it both a possibility and a reality.**

before the foundation of the world, that we should be holy and blameless before him. In love he predestined us for adoption to himself as sons through Jesus Christ, according to the purpose of his will" (Eph. 1:4–5). The African had it right.

Four more arguments support Augustine.

1. You Are Not Smarter or More Spiritual

If Arminianism is true and I have accepted Jesus, then what conclusion must I draw when I look at those who reject him? We were all graced with the same free will to accept or reject. Why did I accept and others reject? Arminianism logically requires that I made better use of my God-given willpower than those who reject. The only thing that moves my salvation from being a mere possibility to an actuality is my free choice to say yes to Jesus.[9] In the words of Arminius, "'What then' you ask, 'does Free Will do?' I reply with brevity, 'It saves.'"[10] If the Dutchman is right, then I could pat myself on the back for somehow being smarter or more spiritual than unbelievers, and I leave the door open for pride. I know myself well enough—shlub that I am—to know that is absurd. God gets 100 percent of the credit and glory for my salvation, for making it both a possibility and a reality.[11]

2. God's Success Does Not Rest On Human Validation

If Arminianism is true and God's saving grace is resistible, then we face an unnerving prospect. If everyone has the free will to say no, then it is at least possible, metaphysically speaking, for everyone to, in fact, say no. It follows that there is a possible world for Arminians in which God's desire to save his creatures utterly failed, and Jesus's death did not save a single soul. Heaven would be a ghost town. Arminianism makes it possible that televangelist Kenneth Copeland was right when he heretically declared, "I was shocked when I found out who the biggest failure in the Bible actually is. . . . The biggest one in the whole Bible is God."[12] The only reason God's plans were not utterly sabotaged in our world is that at least some humans chose to freely accept Jesus. A God whose redemptive success rests on whether humans autonomously accept him is not the God we meet in Scripture. The God of Scripture "does all that he pleases" (Ps. 115:3), "does according to his will among the host of heaven and among the inhabitants of the earth" (Dan. 4:35), says, "My counsel shall stand, and I will accomplish all my purpose" (Isa. 46:10), "can do all things, and that no purpose of [his] can be thwarted" (Job 42:2), and "works all things according to the counsel of his will" (Eph. 1:11).

3. God's Grace Never Damns

Arminianism turns saving grace into damning grace. How so? Arminianism requires a particular notion of free will called libertarian free will. Libertarian free will says that we must have the free agency to choose otherwise if we are to be held morally responsible for our actions. To be praiseworthy or blameworthy for our actions, we must be able to resist all physical forces, the coercion of others, our own strongest desires, and all divine influence.[13] Imagine a universe in which God resuscitates no one. All remain dead in sin. In such a universe, no one could choose God. Therefore, on a libertarian account of freedom, no one could be blamed for *not* choosing God. Thus, hell would be vacant. However, the moment God bestows the Arminians' prevenient grace, resuscitating hearts so that they now have the freedom to accept or reject him, something horrific occurs. Now, since humans have the ability to say yes to God, they suddenly become blameworthy for saying no to him. In the Bible, grace saves otherwise blameworthy sinners. Arminian grace damns otherwise blameless sinners.

4. I Am a Shlub (and So Are You)

A final reason the African got it right and the Dutchman had it wrong is more of a personal than a theological reason. I know that if my salvation was 99.999 percent God's grace and .001 percent up to me and my proper use of my God-given willpower, I would find a way to muck up my .001 percent and damn myself. My salvation must be 100 percent God's doing. In Spurgeon's words salvation must be *"all* of grace,"[14] I believe that is the most honest and consistent way to sing with Paul, "To him be glory" (Eph. 3:21), with Peter, "To him belong glory and dominion forever and ever" (1 Peter 4:11), and with every creature in the universe, "To him who sits on the throne and to the Lamb be blessing and honor and glory and might forever and ever" (Rev. 5:13).

Have I solved every mystery about how God's grace works in human hearts? Obviously not. I have likely raised more questions than I have answered. If Augustine was right, does this strip humanity of meaningful free will? Does it make God the author of evil? Does it clash with the Bible's teaching that God desires all people to be saved? Does it render our sharing of the gospel pointless? The short answer to all four questions is no. To better understand how God's sovereign, heart-reforming grace does not reduce us to robots, compromise his goodness or love, or hamper evangelism, I pray you will dive into the sea of helpful resources that go deeper than I have in this chapter.[15] (I also include the best cases against the Augustinian view of reforming grace for you to ponder.[16])

I leave you with some questions to consider. What do you believe when you are on your knees? Do you pray that God would make unbelieving loved ones' salvation actual or possible? Do you ask him to resuscitate them to a point where they can continue to reject him, or that he would so radically reform them that they will accept him? When you find anti-loving patterns in your own heart, can you pray as Paul prayed for the Thessalonians, "May the Lord make [me] increase and abound in love" (1 Thess. 3:12)? When you see church people backbiting and churches splitting, do you pray like Jesus that God would make them one (John 17:21), as if God actually has the power to answer such a prayer? Can you pray with St. Francis, "O Divine Master, grant that I may not so much seek . . . to be loved as to love,"[17] or with Thomas à Kempis, "Let me be possessed by thy love, and ravished from myself! Let me love thee more than myself"?[18] Can you echo John Donne, "Batter my heart, three person'd God. . . . Take me to you, imprison me, for except you enthrall me, shall never be free, nor chaste, except thou ravish me."[19] In the words of poet Janette . . . Ikz:

> Take hold of my chest
> Firmly place your word
> Begin compressions
> Keep blood
> Circulating within me
> Defibrillate this heart
> May it only be synced
> To the rhythm of your word.[20]

Do you believe God has enough grace and power to answer such prayers without reducing us to Chatty Cathy dolls? Of course you do. So says J. I. Packer, "what you do is pray in categorical terms that God will, quite simply and decisively save them. . . . You would not dream of making it a point in your prayer that you are not asking God actually to bring them to faith, because you recognize that that is something he cannot do. . . . Your confidence in asking rests upon the certainty that he is able to do what you ask. . . . On our feet we may have arguments about it, but on our knees we are all agreed."[21] Augustine the African was right, "He to whom is given by God the love of God, and the love of our neighbor for God's sake; he indeed, ought to pray insistently that this gift may be . . . increased in him."[22]

ERIK THOENNES ON THE REDEMPTIVE GRACE OF GOD

Erik Thoennes is a former professional athlete, pastor, speaker, and author who serves as a professor of theology at Biola University's Talbot School of Theology. He is also a man who reveres God. This is his story of how the redemptive grace of God has impacted his life.

I hate grace. I realize that's a horrible thing for a Christian, never mind a Christian theology professor, to say, but it's true. On my best days, when I'm thinking rightly, I understand that my whole life depends on God's grace and that without it I have nothing I need or really want. But I realized a long time ago that there is something deep in my heart that hates grace. It comes from the influence of the old me, even though that version of myself died with Christ when I repented and trusted Jesus and started my new life in him when I was a little kid. Grace is what frees me from the filthy rags of my self-righteousness and the impossible burden of proving myself worthy of God's kindness. But on some days, my pride and the Father of Lies tell me that I need to earn, prove, demonstrate, deserve, and somehow make myself worthy of God's love and forgiveness. Such self-centeredness completely defies the heart of the gospel. Even though I've been walking with Jesus for over half a century, it's a battle for me to rest in the sufficient grace of God through the finished work of Christ. It's not hard for me to admit this because I know I'm not alone in my bent toward self-sufficiency. You may see yourself in these lyrics of hip-hop artist Hank Murphy as I do:

> I'm having a hard time with Grace today.
> Every time she comes close, I hide my face. . . .

It's true I don't deserve her
She's a princess, I'm a beggar. . . .
What's wrong with me? . . .

This love-hate relationship with grace that Murphy describes is fundamentally the conflict between finding my identity in my sinful self or in Christ. At the same time, I'm both drawn by the Spirit and repelled by my sin, which rejects God's liberating kindness. This pride is at the heart of our shared depravity, which is an exchange of God dependence for self-dependence. This leads to the ultimate defamation of God's character when we exchange the glory of God for our own glory (Rom 1:21–23). The truth is, it's idiotic for me to attempt to resist grace and try to prove myself.

In my experience, being a man adds to the problem. Men often have a particularly hard time giving up the need to prove themselves, especially me, having been a three-sport competitive athlete during my most formative years. I grew up and played football in a town where football was like a religion and then in college and professionally until I was twenty-eight. Athletes learn that talent, effort, and extreme discipline are the foundations of success over the long haul. "You only get out of it what you put into it" is one of the cardinal doctrines of being a serious athlete. This doctrine applies to athletics and many other endeavors in life. But if you bring that mentality into your relationship with God, you will work *for* your salvation instead of working *out* your salvation, which is a fatal mistake.

I've also spent most of my life in an academic environment, which can easily reinforce the competitive, accomplishment-based mindset. It has been crucial for me to recognize that while my experience of intimacy with God can be affected by what I do, the most important truth about me—my standing before God—is by nothing but sheer divine grace *alone*. When the gospel wins the battle of my mind and heart, I flee to the God of grace to receive what I need. Yes, it is a hit to my ego, but a much-needed and life-giving hit. Only Jesus provides the perfect obedience and atoning work by which I can stand before my Maker with joy and confidence.

But as a theology professor who lectures on grace often, and as the pastor of a church with *Grace* in its name, you might think this comes easy. It doesn't. But it helps to preach the gospel to myself often. As the great Scottish evangelist Robert Murray M'Cheyne said, I need to take ten looks at Christ for every one look at myself. You and I live in a culture that constantly encourages us to be self-absorbed rather than Christ-dependent. I know how desperately I need the Bible and the Spirit of God to saturate my mind and heart if I am going to break out of the prison of self.

Being part of my local church, filled with wonderful, gospel-grounded people, has also been a great help to my growing reliance on Jesus's sufficiency rather than on my accomplishments. And God has used my wife in profound ways to deepen my understanding and experience of God's grace. Her example of walking in grace and showing me, our children, and many others gracious kindness has been a beautiful encouragement and exhortation to rest in Jesus. Adopting and raising our four children has been a major source of growth for me as I've sought to show my children the grace that their heavenly Father has for them. This has been a real challenge as I battle my sin, but by God's grace I'm making progress and trust that there is enough grace for me, even when I fail to be the man I should be. Ministry partners and mentors along the way have also played a vital role in being able not only to believe but to live out God's redemptive grace.

Amid the joys and trials of life, the cry of my heart is to be able to truly say and believe with the apostle Paul that "I have been crucified with Christ. It is no longer I who live, but Christ who lives in me. And the life I now live in the flesh I live by faith in the Son of God, who loved me and gave himself for me" (Gal 2:20). I want to live at the end of myself and at the feet of Jesus. Resting in God's sufficient grace can be hard, but God has promised never to quit on his children until we all get home looking just like Jesus and hearing, "Well done." Jesus paid it all, and when I'm able to rest in his perfect righteousness and payment for my sin, I learn to love his amazing grace more each day and walk in the freedom and joy that he alone provides.

A PRAYER TO REVERE THE REDEMPTIVE GOD

Father, without you we are radically depraved and utterly incapable of saving ourselves. We deserve your infinite just wrath. Save us sinners by your grace and by amazing grace alone through the finished work of Jesus. Remove from us our hearts of stone and give us hearts of flesh. Circumcise our hearts and write your law on them. Cause us to increase and abound in love. May your heart-reforming grace have its way with us that all the glory, honor, praise, and thanks may be yours for all eternity. Extend that same reforming grace to [name five people who do not yet know God]. Amen.

REFLECT

Ponder these questions for personal study or group discussion:

1. Why do you think it is so easy to downplay the fact of sin and stay silent about the wrath of God? In what ways is it unloving to neglect these theological realities?

2. It is easy to slide from grace back into self-powered performance mode. What are three or four daily habits we might form to stay better attuned to the good news of God's redemptive grace?

3. Why do you think so many Christians in the twenty-first century, according to studies, seem stuck in Pelagianism and oblivious to how radical God's grace really is? What can we do to spur today's church back to the gospel?

REPENT

In the left column, write down ways that you revere God in his redemptive grace. In the right column, list ways that your life does *not* revere him. We often wear rose-colored glasses when we introspect, so pray with the psalmist, "Search me, O God, and know my heart! Try me and know my thoughts! And see if there be any grievous way in me, and lead me in the way everlasting!" (Ps. 139:23–24). Ask yourself honestly: *Do I recognize my moment-by-moment utter dependence on God's grace? Do I in any way depend on my own self-righteousness? Can I truly say that my identity and destiny are by his grace?*

HOW I AM REVERING	HOW I AM *NOT* REVERING

Pray your way down the left column. Thank God for any ways that you are living out his redemptive grace. Recognize that any ways in which you actually revere him are not from your own willpower but from his grace so he gets the praise and thanks. Then pray down the right column, confessing any ways in which you are not living out his grace. Ask him for a supernatural dose of faith.

RESOURCES

Here are great theological resources to take your reverence for the redeeming grace of God to the next level:

Augustine, *On Grace and Free Will* (GLH Publishing, 2016).

John Bunyon, *Grace Abounding to the Chief of Sinners* (Banner of Truth, 2018).

Robert Farrar Capon, *The Parables of Grace* (Eerdmans, 1990).

Michael Horton, *Justification (Vols. 1-2)*, New Studies in Dogmatics (Zondervan Academic, 2018).

Michael Horton, *Putting Amazing Back into Grace: Embracing the Heart of the Gospel* (Baker, 2002).

Tim Keller, *The Prodigal God: Recovering the Heart of the Christian Faith* (Penguin, 2011).

Martin Luther, *Bondage of the Will* (Revell, 2005).

R. C. Sproul, *The Holiness of God* (Tyndale, 1998).

Charles Spurgeon, *All of Grace* (CreateSpace, 2017).

Carl Trueman, *Grace Alone: Salvation as a Gift from God: What the Reformers Taught and Why It Still Matters* (Zondervan Academic, 2017).

James White, *The God Who Justifies: The Doctrine of Justification* (Bethany House, 2001).

PART 6

EXPRESSIVE

GOD MAKES BEAUTY

OVER THE COMING CHAPTERS, WE WILL EXPLORE THE EXPRESSIVE ARTISTRY OF GOD and its impact on our creative lives together. We will be asking and seeking answers to questions like these:

How does the creative power of God make sense of the big bang, the periodic table, the earth, the emergence of life, the diversity of species, and human agency?

Can we look to the stars to find human meaning?

How many arguments are there for the existence of a creative God—five, a dozen, 150, or billions?

What is God's crowning creative achievement (and no, it is not the coffee bean)?

If we are all designed to be just like Jesus, don't we become identical carbon copies in a way that obliterates our individual identities?

READINGS

To prepare your soul for the coming chapters, set aside a few minutes to read, really read—slowly, prayerfully, thoughtfully—through the following texts on the expressive artistry of God. Ask God to open your heart and mind to what he is saying to you about himself and how you can best respond to that truth about him with reverence.

GENESIS 1:1

In the beginning, God created the heavens and the earth.

PSALM 19:1 (NASB)

The heavens tell of the glory of God;
and their expanse declares the work of His hands.

PSALM 139:13–16

For you formed my inward parts;
you knitted me together in my mother's womb.
I praise you, for I am fearfully and wonderfully made.
Wonderful are your works;
my soul knows it very well.
My frame was not hidden from you,
when I was being made in secret,
intricately woven in the depths of the earth.
Your eyes saw my unformed substance;
in your book were written, every one of them,
the days that were formed for me,
when as yet there was none of them.

ISAIAH 64:8

We are the clay, and you are our potter;
we are all the work of your hand.

EPHESIANS 2:10

We are his workmanship, created in Christ Jesus for good works, which God prepared beforehand, that we should walk in them.

RHYTHMS

Revering God isn't just a matter of filling our heads with new information. It includes forming habits. Choose two or more of the following suggestions this week to help you better live out the expressive artistry of God:

1. Look up at night. Just stand there, neck cricked upward for a minute or two, and thank God for what you see.

2. Go for a walk or hike in whatever bit of nature you can find around you. Breathe in deeply, thanking God for oxygen. Step reflectively, thanking God that the conditions on earth are just right for you to walk around and not float away or collapse dead.

3. Go treat someone like the beautiful image bearer of God they are.

4. Now let's up the ante. Think of three people you have a really hard time with, maybe a public figure you disagree with about virtually everything, maybe a boss or coworker, maybe a neighbor or family member. Think this true thought toward them—*image bearer of God*. Then pray for all three and ask God to recalibrate your emotions toward them. Remember, Jesus calls us beyond neighbor-love to love our enemies (Matt. 5:44).

BLIND LEAPS OF ATHEISM

THE FIRST VERB IN THE FIRST SENTENCE ON THE FIRST PAGE OF THE BIBLE IS THE
Hebrew word *bara'* (pronounced baw-rah). "In the beginning, God *created*
the heavens and the earth" (Gen. 1:1, emphasis added). The first time God
introduced us to himself in all of Scripture, his creativity took center stage.
He built the canvases of space, sky, ocean, and land the first three creation
days, then spent the next three filling those canvases with beauty—stars,
sun, moon, flying animals, sea creatures, land critters, and beasts. Then, as
his creative finale, he designed human beings in his image to carry forward
his work of multiplying beauty in the world.

God used a one-word description after each creation day—*tov*—as
in, "It was *good*." The emphasis of Genesis 1 falls less on *moral* goodness
and more on *aesthetic* goodness, that is, beauty. It is beautiful that there
are stars, clouds, hummingbirds, scarlet macaws, blue whales, clown fish,
barracudas, cocoa trees, magnolias, purple sage, chipmunks, German
shepherds, and Clydesdales. The fall of Genesis 3 left creation marred and
groaning (Rom. 8:20–22). Yet God has graciously preserved plenty of *tov*
in the world worth enjoying. In a rare moment of theological reflection, Sir
Arthur Conan Doyle's Sherlock Holmes pontificates, "What a lovely thing
a rose is. . . . Our highest assurance of the goodness of providence seems
to me to rest in the flowers. . . . Other things . . . are all really necessary
for our existence in the first instance. But this rose is an extra. Its smell
and its color are an embellishment of life, not a condition of it. It is only
goodness which gives extras."[1]

The Creator, because he is good, evidently cares about beauty for beauty's sake. He adds scents, colors, tastes, sounds, and textures to his creation that do not necessarily add to the universe's functionality from an engineer's perspective, but add to its aesthetic power.

Look around. Put a flower in your face and breathe it in. Pet a dog. Savor a strawberry. Count the black spots on a ladybug's back. Listen to the birds' staccato melodies, the sibilant sizzle of waves, or the bass rumble and crackling treble of thunder. God is wonderfully expressive. It follows from Genesis 1 that we do not *fabricate* beauty in the universe, we *find* beauty that was already there before we encountered it, beauty that would remain beautiful even if we all went belly-up tomorrow. There is such a thing as objective beauty because God—the final authority on the nature of reality—declares it to be so. Beauty exists in the eye of the ultimate beholder, and is therefore more than an arbitrary human projection into the void.

> **There is such a thing as objective beauty because God—the final authority on the nature of reality—declares it to be so.**

Some may reply, "Believing God made everything—what a leap of faith!" One way to test the validity of a belief is to assume its falsehood to see if the alternative make more or less sense of the world. So, let's assume for the moment that there is no creator God. Pretend that Genesis 1 is pure fiction. Will we find our worldview more factual and defensible, or will we face longer and longer leaps of blind faith?

Let's begin, well, at the beginning. If there is no Creator, we may ask, then how do we get *anything at all from nothing at all*? It was Jean-Paul Sartre who said that all philosophy begins with the question "Why is there something rather than nothing?" It was that very question that my high school teacher Dr. Chris posed to my senior class. We were on a field trip down a hiking trail in Whiting Ranch, California, where a gigantic fallen oak tree had become known as the "Philosophy Tree." You are supposed to choose a branch, sit, and ponder the mysteries of existence. It must have been a slow day in Orange County news because the *OC Register* sent a journalist to report on the musings of a couple dozen seventeen-year-olds sitting on a fallen oak pondering why there is something rather than nothing. "Well," I replied with a totally unjustified confidence, "God must have gotten bored, so he decided to make something." That's the answer that the *OC Register* quoted and credited to yours truly. (Yes, my first official published philosophical and theological statement was, well, heresy.) God did not create out of boredom or neediness but out of a superabundance of triune joy and expressive glory.

Logically, there are only four possible answers to Sartre's query. First, we could deny that there is something. The universe is just a massive illusion, like the Hindu concept of *maya* or Hollywood's *The Matrix*. The quickest way to debunk this option is to ask whoever defends it to give you all their illusionary money or the illusionary keys to their illusionary car or stand in front of illusionary oncoming traffic. You will learn quickly that option one is unlivable, making it impossible to practice what we preach.

A second possibility is that the something—the universe—is indeed real but has always existed. It had no beginning and therefore requires no Beginner. There are good scientific reasons for rejecting an eternal cosmos. Big bang cosmology demonstrates that time itself began.[2] The fact that the universe is winding down, slowly running out of energy toward a state of equilibrium, or heat death, also suggests that the universe hasn't always been here. If the universe is running out of energy and has been around forever, then certainly an infinite past would have been enough time for it to have already expired. The fact that there's enough energy left to power a light bulb or your smartphone, therefore, counts against the eternal universe hypothesis.

Then comes the philosophical argument. Now is happening, well, now, and again now, and now. If the universe had no beginning, then there would be an infinite number of hours, years, and millennia that would have to transpire before now, as you read this sentence. If there were an infinite number of moments that had to transpire before now, then we could never get to now. Therefore, the universe began.[3]

So there is something—the universe—and it has not always been. Option three is that the universe came from nothing at all. The something came from nothing. This is metaphysically impossible. As David Hume put it, *ex nihilo nihil fit*—from nothing, nothing comes. This leaves us with a final logical possibility—the universe is real, the universe began, and it began not from nothing but from Someone. We could call it the Genesis 1:1 option—"In the beginning, God created the heavens and the earth."

We encounter a second faith leap required to deny God's existence. How do we get a *tailored bang from chance*? Cosmologists in recent years have discovered that for the big bang to be successful and not just collapse back in on itself, there had to be very fine-tuned conditions.[4] How did a successful bang come by sheer chance, with no one dialing in the precise conditions for an expanding universe?

Third comes the leap of how we got a *heavy universe from a light universe*. Twenty years ago my university classmates and I shuffled into the lecture hall and found our seats. Our professor, Dr. Stangl, tall, tweed-coated, with thick Coke-bottle glasses, had his back to the class, scribbling away at a massive equation that took up around thirty feet of chalkboard. He eventually turned to face the class, revealing tears streaming down his cheeks from behind his thick spectacles. "Isn't God's math beautiful?" he exclaimed. No one had a clue. He was literally crying at math. (I, too, have cried at math, but for entirely different reasons.) Dr. Stangl explained that he had just written out the equations for nuclear fusion as it occurs in the core of collapsing stars, how every variable had to be precisely balanced or the whole process would break down. The universe would remain lifelessly stuck at the top of the periodic table. Dr. Stangl marveled at the sheer mathematical genius required for such equations to work and form heavy, life-sustaining elements.[5] By denying the Great Mathematician, atheism requires extraordinary faith that mindless molecules are somehow capable of manifesting marvelous math.

Two and a half millennia ago David sang, "The heavens tell of the glory of God; and their expanse declares the work of His hands" (Ps. 19:1 NASB). That verse is actually truer today than when it was first written. David could look up and be wonderstruck at the creative genius of God. Dr. Stangl had—and indeed we have—the tremendous advantage, thanks to scientific progress, of appreciating intricacies and wonders of the heavens in far more detail than an ancient Jewish king could. Psalm 19:1 becomes even more evident with each deep space photograph the James Webb Space Telescope relays back to earth. We don't invent; we discover that even more wonder has been swirling over our heads than our ancestors realized.[6]

> **We don't invent; we discover that even more wonder has been swirling over our heads than our ancestors realized.**

So far we have seen three leaps of faith required to reject God's existence, how we got anything from nothing, a tailored-bang from chance, and a heavy universe from a light universe. But the first verse of the Bible says not only that God created the "heavens" but also the "earth." So let's return home to our little blue marble to identify four more leaps.

MORE LEAPS
OF ATHEISM

ONCE WE MOVE DOWN THE PERIODIC TABLE, HOW DO WE GET THE HEAVY ELEMENTS together to form a planet finely tuned for the emergence of biological life? Can blind luck explain how we got a planet with the precise axial tilt, ozone layer, oxygen-to-nitrogen ratios, number of star companions, distance from the sun, surface gravity, thickness of crust, rotation period, and other life-essential features?[1] How do we get an *earth fit for life from space dust*?

Even if we somehow have an earth fit for life without an intelligence involved, the next leap is a massive one. Could a mindless material process ever grant us *intricate life from nonlife*? Scientists call this the problem of "abiogenesis." Getting the heavy elements aligned in just the precise configuration to form amino acids, proteins, and a single living cell, then having that cell survive and reproduce seems like too astronomical a leap of improbability to many minds. In Darwin's day, cells were thought of more or less as tiny bags of goo. With the breakthroughs of microbiology and biochemistry, we have been able to peer into the cellular world. It is hardly gelatinous goo. It is an elegant microcosm of order, information, coding, efficiency, functionality, and design.

These advances in understanding the building blocks of life are so compelling that they convinced one of the most influential atheists of the twentieth century to change his mind on the God question. Antony Flew, philosophical heavyweight and former Oxford don, shocked the world in 2004 when he went public with his newfound belief in a transcendent intelligence. In 2008 came the book no one in their wildest dreams thought would have Tony Flew's name on the cover. It was called *There Is a God: How the World's Most Notorious Atheist Changed His Mind*. In Flew's words,

> My whole life has been guided by the principle of Plato's Socrates: Follow the evidence, wherever it leads. . . . DNA has shown, by the almost unbelievable complexity of the arrangements which are needed to produce (life), that intelligence must have been involved. . . .[2] It has become inordinately difficult even to begin to think about constructing a naturalistic theory of the evolution of that first reproducing organism.[3]

Even if we could somehow get a reproducing single-cell organism without a higher intelligence involved, how do we get *species from a single cell?* Earth features a vast, complex, sometimes comical array of species. (Consider the emu, the cassowary, or the Chinese crested dog and tell me God doesn't have a sense of humor.) Where did all the new genetic information come from to generate the millions of diverse plant and animal species above, underneath, and around us?[4]

Let us be generous and assume that our atheist friends could somehow turn each of the faith leaps above into rational steps. Good for them, but their problems have only just begun. The next leap is a doozy, not a single leap but multiple leaps under one heading. How do we get *man-the-agent from man-the-animal?* Once the atheist climbs Darwin's evolutionary tree and reaches man-the-animal, something astounding happens—consciousness emerges. If our story of human origins starts with dumb, mindless matter—an unconscious "It"— then how can we explain what's going on in our minds this very moment? Consider nine dimensions of being conscious:

> Atheism requires multiple leaps of blind faith, including how to get . . .
>
> **A**nything from nothing
> **T**ailored bang from chance
> **H**eavy universe from a light universe
> **E**arth fit for life from space dust
> **I**ntricate life from nonlife
> **S**pecies from a single cell
> **M**an-the-agent from man-the-animal

1. Choice Making

We make thousands of choices a day. If you were created in the image of a choice-making Mind, this comes as no surprise. But can meaningful choices be reduced to a natural world that operates by either physical determinism or random quantum indeterminism?[5] If we could so reduce freedom to physical processes—swerving particles and/or machine-like natural laws—then no one *chooses* to believe or disbelieve in God—and the entire debate is reduced to the involuntary buzzing of biological machines.

2. Oughts

Consciousness deals not only with facts (what *is*) but also with values (what *ought to be*). Can normative values like good and evil come from the material world of mere descriptive facts? Can nonmaterial realities like *oughtness* sprout into existence from the soil of material *is-ness*?[6] As Don DeLillo asks in his novel *White Noise*, "They can trace everything you say, do, and feel to the number of molecules in a certain region. . . . What happens to good and evil in this system? Passion, envy, and hate? Do they become a tangle of neurons? . . . What about murderous rage? A murderer used to have a certain fearsome size to him. His crime was large. What happens when we reduce it to cells and molecules?"[7]

3. Nonphysical Laws

Physical stuff follows physical laws. Your mind, however, can operate by nonphysical laws of logic. Take, for example, the logical law of transitivity: If $A = B$ and $B = C$ then $A = C$. Is this law physical? If so, what is its chemical makeup? Is it two parts carbon and three parts helium? If the laws of logic are physical, then *where* is the law of noncontradiction (If A is true, then not-A is false)—deep in the Amazonian jungle or in a Swiss bank vault? Is the logical law of identity ($A = A$) ten years old or ten billion years old? Such questions are nonsense because the laws of logic—which exist—are not physical. What genetic mutation in our evolutionary past produced the laws of logic we use every day to recognize ourselves in the mirror, brush our teeth with a toothbrush rather than a toilet brush, and start the car with a key rather than a fork?

4. Semantics

The physical world is a world of syntax. Take this chapter, for example. It's loaded with physical syntax—black ink pixels arranged in certain squiggly shapes on a page or glowing screen, all with chemical composition and spatial location. Yet you're looking at something more than mere syntax. This book is full of what philosophers call "semantics"—the meaning conveyed through but not reducible to the physical syntax. All the syntax could change in an instant—the font altered, changed from English to Spanish, transported to a different page or screen—yet the semantics would remain intact. The nonphysical *message* is something more than the physical *medium*; therefore, there is more to existence than the physical.[8]

5. Creativity

Whether the dark beauty of Van Gogh's *Starry Night* or a child's Crayola orange sun, consciousness exhibits the power of creativity. Is every masterpiece on canvas or construction paper and every painting, song, poem, novel, play, dance, or dinner merely the mechanistic by-product of matter in motion? Is the artist no more than a bundle of swirling chemicals? Did randomly firing synapses generate Michelangelo's Sistine ceiling, the Beatles' "A Day in the Life," Maya Angelou's "Still I Rise," Dostoyevsky's *Brothers Karamazov*, Shakespeare's *A Midsummer Night's Dream*, Michael Jackson's moonwalk, and Gordon Ramsay's beef Wellington? Are we prepared to say that all beauty—whether visual, audible, cerebral, or edible—is a mere illusion, an epiphenomenon, a parlor trick of colliding neurons?

6. Intentionality

Think about the planet Mars for a moment. You can do so without the excruciating headache of the red planet materializing in your brain matter. You're not thinking Mars, but thinking *about* Mars. Consciousness has the power to be *about* things—what philosophers call "intentionality"—and it's a good thing too; otherwise we would all die of literal splitting headaches. Could genetic mutations in the concrete world of matter produce something nonphysical like an abstract thought?

7. Owned Experience

The physical world can be described in the "It" objective categories of science. But there's not only an *it-ness* but also an irreducible *I-ness* to consciousness: a subjectivity, a first-person perspective. Imagine, for example, a scientific tome about bats that explains everything that can be known scientifically about these winged creatures. What's one question such a scientific tome wouldn't answer? It wouldn't answer philosopher Thomas Nagel's famous question: "What is it like to be a bat?"[9] What does it *feel* like to fly blind through the darkness, sending out sonar shrieks to swoop full speed at an unassuming insect dinner? How do we achieve *I-ness* and *what-it's-like-ness* from the unconscious "It" of the physical world?

8. Underlying Purposes

The "It" of the physical world is what philosophers call nonteleological. Physical stuff doesn't think about underlying purposes. A beaker of mercury doesn't think, *My goal is to boil at 674.1 degrees.* It just does it. Consciousness, however, is teleological. We think purposefully, toward goals, acting *for* some reason, for instance, this very moment to choose to shift your eyeballs left to right for the purpose of reading the next sentence, for the still greater purpose of completing a truly incredible and groundbreaking theology book. Can the purposeless *it-ness* of the physical world generate the teleological *for-ness* of our conscious world?

9. Significance

Consciousness can tap into real meaning. There's something truly significant about people giving and receiving love, something of transcendent value that cannot be reduced to interacting particles or the biological quest for survival. If there is no creator God who bestows objective significance on our existence, then we are the unintended by-products of a universe that, in Richard Dawkins's words, has "no design, no purpose, no evil, no good, nothing but pitiless indifference."[10] Dawkins's fellow atheist Alex Rosenberg has the intellectual integrity to draw out the inconvenient implications:

The answer to the persistent question, What is the purpose of the universe? is quite simply: There is none. . . . No moral code is right, correct, true. That's nihilism. And we have to accept it. . . . When it comes to making life meaningful, what secular humanists hanker after is something they can't have and don't need. What they do need, if meaninglessness makes it impossible to get out of bed in the morning, is Prozac.[11]

Recall Darwin's "horrid doubt" from chapter 2: "Would anyone trust in the convictions of a monkey's mind, if there are any convictions in such a mind?"[12] With progress in the field of philosophy of mind since Darwin's day, especially over the last fifty years, we have found at least nine profound reasons that his horrid doubt is justified. How could a material "It" possibly account for nonmaterial realities you experienced ten thousand times today—realities like I-ness (first-person consciousness, known as "indexicality"), about-ness (the ability to think abstractly, known as "intentionality"), what-it's-like-ness (the phenomenological texture of subjective experience, known as "qualia"), for-ness (the ability to think toward goals, known as "teleology"), therefore-ness (the laws of logic), this-or-that-ness (choice-making power), awe-ness (creativity and aesthetics), what-ness (the meaning in language that transcends its physical medium, known as "semantics"), and ought-ness (moral values)?

> The existence of God, a supreme, creative Mind, makes sense of our consciousness, including . . .
>
> **C**hoice-making
> **O**ughts
> **N**onphysical laws
> **S**emantics
> **C**reativity
> **I**ntentionality
> **O**wned experience
> **U**nderlying purposes
> **S**ignificance

If we originate from mindless matter alone, then we—hunks of sophisticated steak that we are—must make faith leap after faith leap to pretend we have a reason to trust

If our origin points to a supreme Mind, then our minds are at home in reality.

reason. If, however, our origin points to a supreme Mind, then our minds are at home in reality. In him, we find a reason to reason. Our freedom, morality, logic, meaning, creativity, individuality, experience, and purpose are no longer explained out of existence, but are nourished and expanded.

Reason and imagination are not reduced to mere survival mechanisms. They are truth-knowing and beauty-making mechanisms gifted to us by a God of truth and beauty. Your reasoning and creative powers are not the product of dumb forces. They come from God. Don't waste them.

STARMAKER

IN C. S. LEWIS'S *VOYAGE OF THE DAWN TREADER*, WE MEET "A BOY CALLED EUSTACE Clarence Scrubb, and he almost deserved it."[1] While in Narnia, Eustace remarks, "In our world a star is a huge ball of flaming gas." A mysterious silver-haired character named Ramadu quips, "Even in your world, my son, that is not what a star is but only what it is made of."[2]

That a black sky would reveal flickering pinheads of white light has been a source of wonder to everyone with functioning eyeballs. Big screen sagas like *Star Wars, Star Trek, Stargate, Ad Astra* (to the stars), and *Interstellar* (between stars) tap into our shared sense of awe. (There is a reason we use the word *stars* to describe people whose talents leave us awestruck.) Stars hold a kind of promise of adventure and intrigue and exploration. Just ask Elon Musk. Nearly three millennia ago, King David, looking up, said, "The heavens declare the glory of God, and the sky above proclaims his handiwork" (Ps. 19:1).

Two and a half millennia ago, Plato asked, "[What] lead[s] men to believe in the gods?" and answered, "The order of the motion of the stars."[3] Plato's protégé Aristotle asked us to imagine that humanity has been trapped underground for generations, finally to emerge and look up. "When the night had darkened the lands and they should behold the whole of the sky spangled and adorned with stars," Aristotle said, "most certainly they would have judged both that there exist gods and that all these marvelous works are the handiwork of the gods."[4]

Neil deGrasse Tyson is a celebrity astrophysicist and torchbearer of Carl Sagan's show *Cosmos*. Like Sagan, he is an unblushing atheist. When pressed about what meaning he can possibly find in a godless universe, he gave an answer increasingly popular among atheists:

> Consider that the atoms in your body were manufactured in the cores of stars billions of years ago. Stars that exploded. . . . Scattering that enrichment around the galaxy. . . . And out of that enrichment forms planets, life, people. And so when you look up in the night sky, if you feel small and lonely, the knowledge that you're connected this way to the stars, that we are not just figuratively, we are literally stardust can give you a sense of belonging in what might otherwise come across to you as a cold and heartless universe.[5]

This would certainly make the universe less cold, as the temperature in the core of a collapsing star must reach a minimum of one hundred million degrees to surpass the Coulomb barrier and make nuclear fusion possible. It is not obvious that such an account of our chemical origins makes the universe any less heartless.

None of the estimated two hundred billion trillion stars in the known universe have shed a single tear at a cancer diagnosis or a miscarriage. Why should believing ourselves to be hunks of heavy elements—unfeeling, unknowing, unintended elements cooked up 40,208,000,000,000 kilometers away—bestow any real meaning or purpose to our lives? If I emerged from a petri dish in a lab down the freeway or from a collapsing gaseous mass ten light-years away, I am still a mere combination of elements on the periodic table. No possible combination of those two-letter symbols could possibly bestow meaning.

I am not knocking being awestruck at stars. I'm with the old hymn—"I see the stars . . . Thy power throughout the universe displayed." I'm not even knocking the impulse to look to stars for meaning. Though I question the method, I can at least understand why an atheist like Carl Sagan—Tyson's predecessor—would launch the SETI project to search for messages from space. Sagan's *Voyager Golden Record* and *Pioneer* plaques, with greetings from and directions to Earth—were affixed to spacecraft and hurled into space like prayers. I get why folks would check the newspaper to see what meaning the cosmos can bestow on their Leo, Virgo, or Capricorn selves.

My critique is against the exploitation of stars, using their fantastical allure as a kind of emotive sleight of hand to dodge the Starmaker and duck the meaning only he can bestow on us. Long before the Hubble Space Telescope or James Webb Space Telescope pierced our atmosphere and started relaying pictures back to us, prompting human beings to ooh and aah over them, the stars and nebulae they photographed were already beautiful and awesome. They were beautiful and awesome not because a two-hundred-pound mass of sophisticated space dust projected an artificial, epiphenomenal construct of beauty into the sky, but because God made them that way. As the ancient psalmist sang, the heavens declare *God's* glory, not their own.

As the ancient psalmist sang, the heavens declare God's glory, not their own.

So let us not confuse signposts for the destination, windows for walls, premises for conclusions. Let our sense of awe at the stars do its proper work on our souls and not become a cop-out for avoiding their Maker. Follow the two hundred billion trillion burning will-o'-the-wisps to their transcendent source. In him and in him alone, meaning is not fantasy, but reality.

SHADOW, STREAM,
AND SCATTERED BEAM
APOLOGETICS

THERE ARE MANY SO-CALLED EVIDENTIAL ARGUMENTS FOR GOD'S EXISTENCE. THE universe's beginning points to its beginner. Design in the universe points to its designer. Moral laws point to the moral lawgiver, and so on. This is standard fare in apologetic literature. Such arguments compute well with how certain minds are wired, particularly the more philosophic brainiac types who (like me) enjoy sipping a fine beverage around a firepit contemplating the mysteries of existence.

There is another style of case for Christianity, one that touches those without pipes in their teeth or five-syllable words on their tongues. There are arguments, if they can even be called that, which address more of our humanity. They address us not as cerebrums on sticks but as the artists, lovers, dreamers, hypocrites, heroes, loners, romantics, dullards, worshipers, adventurers, failures, jokesters, and weirdos that we are.

These arguments are something more like invitations, signposts, pointers, and clues. They are like keys that open doors to wider vistas of human experience, EnChroma glasses that open the color-blind to a more vivid Technicolor world, or lighthouse beacons that guide us out of churning black ocean chaos to safer shores. They are something like Jonathan Edwards understood. Describing the searching soul, Edwards said,

It sees that till now it has been pursuing shadows, but that it now has found the substance; that before it had been seeking happiness in the stream, but that now it has found the ocean. . . . How great a happiness must it be to be the object of love of him who is the Creator of the world. The enjoyment of [God] is the only happiness with which our souls can be satisfied. Fathers and mothers, husbands, wives, or children, or the company of earthly friends, are but shadows; but God is the substance. These are but scattered beams, but God is the sun. These are but streams. But God is the ocean.[1]

Let's talk shadows, streams, and scattered beams. Back in my seminary days, I would host what we called "neo-beatnik nights" in my dingy Laguna Niguel apartment. The drywall would be cracking at the seams with legions of college students performing odes to peanut butter, acoustic emo ballads, raw sermonettes, comedy sketches, djembe jams, and poetry. (I told you we're weirdos.) Of all the neo-beat artists, one poet—my friend Derrick Brown—knew how to hold a room in his palm—evoking at will either audible sighs of existential longing or the kind of laughter he would describe as "zip zang zowie." Derrick was one of the type that Jack Kerouac describes in *On the Road*, "the ones who never yawn or say a commonplace thing, but burn, burn, burn, like fabulous yellow roman candles exploding like spiders across the stars and in the middle you see the blue centerlight pop and everybody goes 'Awww!'"[2]

One poem in particular—called "A Finger, Two Dots, Then Me"—felt like a fireworks finale in my living room. There were plenty of awwws. "At that moment," Brown recited,

> the planets begin to spin and awaken
> and large movie screens appear on Mars, Saturn and Venus
> each bearing images I have witnessed throughout my life
> and over each and every clip flashes the word *holy*.
> armadillos—holy
> cows' tongues—holy
> magic tricks—holy
> snowballs upside the head—holy
> clumsy first kisses—holy
> sneaking into movies—holy
> your mother teaching you to slow dance

the fear returning
but the fear overcome—holy
eating top ramen on upside-down frisbees
'cause it was either buy plates or more beer—holy
beach cruisers at night
the $5.00 you made in Vegas
but the $450.00 you lost, all of it—holy
the last time you were nervous holding hands
feeling God at a pool hall but not church—holy
sleeping during your uncle's memorized dinner prayer—holy
losing your watch in the sea and all that that signifies—holy
the day you got to really speak to your father because the television
    broke—holy
the day your grandmother told you something meaningful 'cause
    she was dying—holy
all of the medicine
the hope
the fear
the trust
the crush
the work
the loss
the love
the test
the birth
the end
the finale
the design
the design
the design in the stars
is the same
in our hearts
the design
in the stars
is the same
in our hearts
in the rebuilt machineries of our hearts.[3]

In fairness, the list of thirty-two wonders Brown cites could stretch on for days. Dusk, magnolias, pipe smoke, ground-rule doubles, snuggles, vows, oak trees, dandelion fluff, thunder, baptisms, laughter-induced side cramps, the sudden volume spike of rain from a pitter-patter to a torrent, the conversation with a homeless man, the wrestling match with a toddler, the eighteen-year single malt, the green lights, the cool pillowcase, the Lord's Table, and on and on we could go *ad infinitum ad reverentia*. Try to wipe God from the horizon and such miracles lose their wonder. In the words of atheist Michael Ruse, they become nothing but "illusions fobbed on us by our genes."[4] To blot out God is to blacken the sun and drain the ocean; all rays of meaning go dark and all rivers of joy run dry.[5]

Every day you are bombarded with more arguments for God's existence than your five senses can possibly take in or appreciate.

Some books on my shelf list five arguments for God. Others document a dozen. Philosopher Peter Kreeft lists twenty.[6] One YouTuber boasts 150 arguments for God in a four-hour video. What is the true number? It's closer to how many drops are in the Pacific Ocean or how many subatomic particles exist. Every day you are bombarded with more arguments for God's existence than your five senses can possibly take in or appreciate.

Lord, give us eyes to see, noses to smell, buds to taste, fingertips to touch, ears to hear, and souls to sense the moment-by-moment grand case for You. Help us follow shadows to the substance, streams to the sea, sunbeams to the Sun. Amen.

MASTERPIECES

IN OUR BRIEF FORAY INTO THE CREATIVITY OF GOD, WE HAVE YET TO SET OUR SIGHTS on one of his most breathtaking masterpieces. It would be like walking the Louvre and walking right past Leonardo da Vinci's *Mona Lisa*[1] or getting so enamored with the circular floor tiles of the Sistine chapel that you forget to look up. You could peer through high-powered telescopes, walk exotic zoos, stroll lavish gardens, hike the highest mountains, and survey ten thousand beach sunsets. You could join Wheeler, Emerson, Thoreau, and the other transcendentalists, build a shanty in the woods, and spend your days breathing crisp air, communing with the elements, and earning your hipster street (or forest) cred. You would still be missing out on God's pièce de résistance. Thankfully, it does not require any pricy stargazing equipment, a ticket to the Alps, or ocean access. All you need is a mirror.

Humans are not interchangeable, xeroxed, or cookie cut.

The Jewish psalmist David said that he was "fearfully and wonderfully made" (Ps. 139:14). *Pala*—Hebrew for "wonderfully made" in this text—carries the sense of being set apart, custom designed, one of a kind, special. Humans are not interchangeable, xeroxed, or cookie cut. We are less like a stack of identical prints of, say, Van Gogh's *Starry Night* rolling off the press. We are more like the entire catalog of the great Dutchman's work, each one distinct and carefully handcrafted (but God is still alive and makes roughly 650,000 unique image-bearing artworks per day).[2] As the great theologian Dr. Seuss put it in his treatise *Happy Birthday to You!*:

Today you are you! That is truer than true!
There is no one alive who is you-er than you![3]

The psalmist also speaks of being "fearfully" made, a shocking word choice. It is the same Hebrew word—*yirah*—used over a hundred times in Scripture as the command that we, the creatures, are to fear/revere/be awestruck at God our Creator. Psalm 139:14 opens up an astounding possibility. One plausible reading of the text is that it is not the creature expressing *yirah*, but the Creator. If this is how we read the accusative adverb "fearfully," then we have found the only place in all of Scripture in which fear/reverence/awe is ascribed to God himself as he acts.[4] This is not fearfully making in the way Mary Shelley's Dr. Frankenstein might fearfully piece together his monster, trembling at all that could go wrong. Perhaps Dr. Seuss is again closer to the mark:

Thank goodness
[or, as I read it to each of my kids once a year, "Thank God"]
I'm not just a clam or a ham
Or a dusty old jar of sour gooseberry jam!
I am what I am! That's a great thing to be![5]

The Creator in Psalm 139 is making a being who, unlike clams, hams, and gooseberry jams, bears his own awesome image; hence, God's reverence for the human creature. As C. S. Lewis said, "There are no ordinary people. You have never talked to a mere mortal. Nations, cultures, arts, civilizations—these are mortal, and their life is to ours as the life of a gnat. But it is immortals whom we joke with, work with, marry, snub and exploit—immortal horrors or everlasting splendors."[6]

Paul built on the insights of Psalm 139 when he said, "We are his workmanship, created in Christ Jesus for good works, which God prepared beforehand, that we should walk in them" (Eph. 2:10). Paul infused the whole passage with the language of God as the artist, the craftsman, and the author, and we as the artworks.[7] Some translations appropriately render the word for "workmanship"—*poiema*—as "masterpiece." Perhaps Paul had in the back of his mind the Master-and-his-medium language of Isaiah 29:16, in which God is "him who formed" (*poiesanti* in the LXX) and Isaiah 64:8: "We are the clay, and you are our potter; we are all the work of your hand."[8]

In Ephesians 2, masterpieces are not merely created; we are created "in

Christ Jesus for good works" (v. 10). In Paul's theology, being *"in* Christ Jesus" cannot be separated from becoming *like* Christ Jesus. The Father predestines us to be conformed to the image of his Son (Rom. 8:29). We are to have the mind of Christ (1 Cor. 2:16). We must imitate him (Phil. 2:5–8; 1 Thess. 1:6). We are "being transformed into the same image [that is, the image of Christ] from one degree of glory to another" (2 Cor. 3:18).[9]

How do we square Psalm 139's claim that a human being is *pala*— that is, set apart, distinguished, uniquely designed—with all this New Testament business about conforming, imitating, and being transformed to the image of only one person, Jesus? Wouldn't we only be xeroxed copies with Christ as the original? Are we identical prints and Christ the original *Starry Night?* Doesn't the call to lose ourselves in Christ mean that we are no longer unique masterpieces? C. S. Lewis again comes to our aid. He is worth quoting at length.

> Out of our selves, into Christ, we must go. His will is to become ours and we are to think His thoughts, to "have the mind of Christ" as the Bible says. And if Christ is one, and if He is thus to be "in" us all, shall we not be exactly the same? It certainly sounds like it; but in fact it is not so. . . .
>
> Suppose a person who knew nothing about salt. You give him a pinch to taste and he experiences a particular strong, sharp taste. You then tell him that in your country people use salt in all their cookery. Might he not reply, "In that case I suppose all your dishes taste exactly the same: because the taste of that stuff you have just given me is so strong that it will kill the taste of everything else." But you and I know that the real effect of salt is exactly the opposite. So far from killing the taste of the egg and the tripe and the cabbage, it actually brings it out. They do not show their real taste till you have added the salt. (Of course, as I warned you, this is not really a very good illustration, because you can, after all, kill the other tastes by putting in too much salt, whereas you cannot kill the taste of a human personality by putting in too much Christ. I am doing the best I can.)
>
> It is something like that with Christ and us. The more we get what we now call "ourselves" out of the way and let Him take us over, the more truly ourselves we become. There is so much of Him that millions and millions of "little Christs," all different, will still be too few to express Him fully.[10]

To be masterpieces "in Christ" makes us more truly, uniquely, and wonderfully ourselves. To "Seussify" Paul's theology, there is no you that is you-er than the you that you are "in Christ." Van Gogh's *Starry Night* is not his *Café Terrace at Night*, which is not his *Bedroom in Arles*; rather, each masterpiece shows something of Van Gogh's genius in a way that no other masterpiece can. You, then—masterpiece in process that you are—have a capacity to reflect Jesus like literally no other human being in the history of the world ever has or ever could.

How, then, do we revere God the Father? We revere him by reflecting his Son, Jesus—the serpent-crushing seed of woman (Gen. 3:5); God with us (Isa. 7:14); the wonderful counselor, mighty God; everlasting father; prince of peace (Isa. 9:6); the suffering servant (Isa. 53); the atoning messiah (Dan. 9:24–27); the virgin-born (Matt. 1:20–23), storm-breaking (Mark 4:35–39), broken body–mending (Luke 17:11–19), wave-walking (John 6:16–24), grave-defeating (John 20:1–29) reigning king (Eph. 2:6); the bread of life (6:35); the light of the world (8:12); the "I AM" (John 8:58), the only door (10:7); the good shepherd (10:11); the resurrection and the life (11:25); the way, the truth, and the life (14:6); the vine (15:1); the *logos* (John 1:1); the *agapetos* (Mark 1:11); the *telos* (Rom. 10:4); the very form of God (Phil. 2:6); the image of the invisible God, by whom and for whom the universe was made and sustained (Col. 1:15–17), eternally enthroned, worshiped by angels (Heb. 1:6, 8); the author and perfecter of our faith (Heb. 12:2); the slain lamb of God (Rev. 5:6); the returning bridegroom (Rev. 19:6–9); the King of kings and Lord of lords (Rev. 19:16); the Alpha and Omega, the first and the last, the beginning and the end (Rev. 22:13)— that is the Jesus we are to reflect to become the most God-revering and, therefore, the most glorious versions of ourselves.[11]

> **There is no you that is you-er than the you that you are "in Christ."**

JONI EARECKSON TADA ON THE EXPRESSIVE ARTISTRY OF GOD

Joni Eareckson Tada is an author, a speaker, and an international advocate for people with disabilities. Painting with her mouth from a wheelchair, she is also a celebrated artist. Her ministry, Joni and Friends (http://www.joniandfriends.org), provides programs for special needs families, as well as training for churches worldwide. She is also a woman who reveres God. This is her story of how the expressive creativity of God has impacted her life.

My husband, Ken Takeshi Tada is sansei, that is, third-generation Japanese-born in America. Even though Ken is as American as they come, his heart is rooted in the Japanese culture. And, in a way, so is mine. Especially when it comes to art.

In pondering how God's creativity has shaped my life over the decades, I am reminded of a Japanese art form known as kintsugi. It is a method of repairing broken pottery. Rather than throw a shattered ceramic in the trash because it's useless, a kintsugi artist gathers all the broken shards together on his work area. He then mixes a special lacquer of gold or platinum and uses it as a bonding agent to adhere the broken pieces together. The artist fills each crack with the expensive lacquer, putting each shard in its place. The result is a stunning work of art.

The point behind kintsugi is to showcase the object's brokenness yet to visibly highlight its repair into an entirely new piece. Rather than working to conceal its brokenness or disguise the injury, the artist intends for you to delight in his repair work. He creates a restored masterpiece that is far more unique than the original piece of ordinary pottery. The end result is not only beautiful but more valuable, and radiant with gold and platinum.

I can scarcely think of a more fitting image for what God has done in my life. I was quite literally broken by a diving accident as a teenager that has left me quadriplegic for more than five decades. Early on I found dark companions who helped me numb my depression with scotch-and-cola. I just wanted to disappear. I wanted to die. Since then I have dealt with seasons of darkness, chronic pain, and multiple bouts with cancer. I am in many ways the human version of broken pottery, and God has been my great kintsugi artist.

I have learned by experience that our fragile bodies, as 2 Corinthians 4:7 says, are jars of clay. We know clay can easily break, but Psalm 147:3 says God binds up our wounds. He is near to the brokenhearted, Psalm 34:18 says, and he saves those who are crushed in spirit. God never tosses aside or trashes a broken life. He is too loving, kind, and creative for that. As the Master Artist, God has applied the gold of his grace to my broken life. He has a masterful and tender way of putting us back together again in a way that does not conceal our pain but reveals his grace in and through it. Rather than disguise the shattered pieces of our life, God accentuates them as the very places where his grace is on display.

Another word for kintsugi is "golden joinery." There's a reason for naming it golden! Japanese artists spare no expense in choosing precious metals as bonding agents. And God is the same! Just look at the enormous expense God undertook to redeem us! God applies the priceless blood of his own Son to our broken lives. As kintsugi glorifies the artist—it shows him to be utterly masterful—so God's redemptive mastery is on display through us. Nothing is a surprise to God; nothing is a setback to his plans; nothing can thwart his purposes; and nothing is beyond his control. His sovereignty is absolute, and he uses it to bring beauty from our brokenness. Every winsome, lovely attribute of God comes shining through when he redeems and restores lives. Our redeemed lives then make others hungry and thirsty for that same godly compassion in brokenness. My wheelchair was the key to seeing all this happen—especially since God's creative grace and power show up best in weakness.

Our often despairing world needs authentic testimonies of people who, like me, have found hope, life, and dignity in Christ through despair, darkness, and death. The world will then sit up and take notice; they will look on in amazement that hope really can be found in hardship. They will see heaven-sent beauty as we show courage, perseverance, endurance, and hope in our hardship. God then intends that we pass on the hope we've found to others—God's redemptive creativity is *never* a private matter. It's what can happen when we yield all our brokenness to God so he can administer his "golden joinery," the precious platinum of his grace.

So when your life is shattered by deep disappointment or pain, as mine has been, allow God to "put you back together" in a way that is far more beautiful than before the trial. Rather than conceal the damage done, invite him to accentuate the gold of his grace through the broken pieces of your life—it's a way of highlighting his magnificent handiwork in you so that people can't help but admire the elegance of his glorious design in your life and, in turn, praise the Master Artist.

A PRAYER TO REVERE THE EXPRESSIVE GOD

Father, you are the Maker of the heavens and the earth, the master craftsman of the universe, the grand artist who did not have to, but chose to infuse your cosmos with beauty for beauty's sake. Awaken our five senses to better behold the beauties of your creation, and that in beholding we would be drawn not to worship creation but you, its Creator. Yes, ever since Genesis 3, the world has groaned under the weight of corruption and futility, but thank you for preserving enough beauty to intensify our longing for cosmic redemption, the untainted beauty of the new heavens and the new earth. Continue, Divine Artist, to conform us to the image of Christ, that day by day we become more radiantly the masterpieces you created and redeemed us to be. Amen.

REFLECT

Ponder these questions for personal study or group discussion:

1. See if you can recall the six leaps required to deny the existence of the Creator. Which of these leaps do you find to be the biggest, and why?

2. What specific aspects of the created world do you find most beautiful? Share your top three to five. Thank the Divine Artist.

3. If we don't find our self-perception in how God sees us, namely, as his masterpieces, then we will turn elsewhere to define ourselves. What do you see as some of the most powerful and destructive alternatives to God that people resort to and that warp their perceptions of themselves?

4. Believing that human beings bear God's image is one thing. Treating them like it is another. What are three practical steps we could take this week to better love our neighbors as the divine image bearers they are?

REPENT

In the left column, write down ways that you revere God in his expressive artistry. In the right column, list ways that your life does *not* revere him. We often wear rose-colored glasses when we introspect, so pray with the psalmist, "Search me, O God, and know my heart! Try me and know my thoughts! And see if there be any grievous way in me, and lead me in the way everlasting!" (Ps. 139:23–24). Ask yourself honestly: *Do I stop to stand and admire God's creation? Do I follow the beautiful signposts in creation to their divine source and worship God for expressing beauty? Is my creative life integrated with my spiritual life?*

Pray your way down the left column. Thank God for any ways that you are living out his expressive artistry. Recognize that any ways in which you actually revere him are not from your own willpower but from his grace so he gets the praise and thanks. Then pray down the right column, confessing any ways in which you are not living in sync with God's creativity. Ask him for a supernatural dose of faith.

HOW I AM REVERING	HOW I AM *NOT* REVERING

RESOURCES

Here are great theological resources to take your reverence for the expressive artistry of God to the next level:

Mike Cosper, *Recapturing the Wonder: Transcendent Faith in a Disenchanted World* (IVP, 2017).

Makoto Fujimura, *Art and Faith: A Theology of Making* (Yale, 2021).

Malcolm Guite, *Lifting the Veil: Imagination and the Kingdom of God* (Square Halo Books, 2021).

Madeleine L'Engle, *Walking on Water: Reflections on Faith and Art* (Convergent, 2018).

Nancy Pearcey, *Saving Leonardo* (B&H, 2010).

Marilynne Robinson, *Gilead* (Picador, 2020).

Hans Rookmaaker, *Modern Art and the Death of a Culture* (Crossway, 1994).

Dorothy Sayers, *The Mind of the Maker* (Continuum, 2005).

Francis Schaffer, *Art and the Bible* (IVP, 2006).

Andrew Wilson, *God of All Things: Rediscovering the Sacred in an Everyday World* (Zondervan, 2021).

EPILOGUE

SIMPLICITY AND THE SOUL-ARTIST

MY FIRST JOB INTERVIEW WAS AROUND AGE NINE. I APPROACHED A PROFESSIONAL caricature artist at the Orange County Fair—you know, the ones who draw gigantic heads on top of tiny waterskiing, kung-fu-fighting, or guitar-strumming bodies. In hopes of a job, I offered him some of my best carica-tures of my favorite late-1980s sports stars—Michael Jordan, Magic Johnson, Walter Payton, Jerry Rice, Rickey Henderson, and Kirk Gibson. Whether it was California's silly progressive "child labor laws" or the threatening superiority of my nine-year-old drawings against the pro-artist's livelihood in a capitalist free market, I will never know. But, alas, I did not get the job. I consoled myself with a cinnamon roll bigger than my face and a nauseous ride on the Gravitron, a heap of sophisticated creaking metal operated by a leather-skinned carney with bloodshot eyes and a yellow mustache, who was either a twenty-five or seventy-five-year-old probably named Jim, blasting Guns N' Roses on the stereo behind a plume of Marlboro smoke. Oh, the 1980s. God bless you.

Imagine, a skilled caricature artist (yes, even better than 80s Thad) so talented that he can draw not just people's looks but also their souls. Some people turn out like brains floating in a vat—the overanalytical thinker-types. Others have gigantic chests with bright-red, beating hearts. They live mostly in their emotions. Still others would have ridiculously oversized hands. They are all about action. Some (myself included, though in good company with Chesterton and Spurgeon) would have robust bellies. They are about consuming anything that once oinked or mooed.

If our soul-searching caricature-artist were to capture your soul in ink, what would it look like? Would certain aspects of you appear disproportionately huge and others hilariously small? Put that mental image on hold for a moment.

SIMPLICITY

We have covered many truths about God so far: his reliability, his enjoyability, his victorious sovereignty, eternal love as Father, Son, and Spirit, his redemptive grace, and expressive artistry. There is another truth about God that touches how we think of all these other divine truths. It is the attribute of divine simplicity.

Divine simplicity does *not* mean that God is easy to understand, far from it. The opposite of simplicity in the theological world is not difficult-to-understand, but made-up-of-parts. A mousetrap may be simple to understand but is not simple in the theological sense of the word. A mouse trap requires parts—a spring-loaded metallic trapper and trigger affixed by nails to a wooden base. God is not the sum of parts all working together. It is not as if you add the free-floating attributes of omniscience, omnipotence, and omnipresence together with a mix of other great-making properties and end up with God at the end of the equation.

Divine simplicity means that God is without parts, a total unity.[1] Back in the second century the church father Irenaeus said it better. "God is not as men are. . . . He is a simple uncompounded Being, without diverse members, and altogether life, and equal to Himself, since he is wholly understanding, and wholly spirit, and wholly thought, and wholly intelligence, and wholly reason . . . wholly light, and the whole source of all that is good."[2]

Note well: God is not *unified*; he is a *unity*. *Unified*—a passive adjective—implies that different parts have been brought together, like a ragtag group of kids to form a baseball team, a selection of metals to form a wristwatch, or fifty different states to form a nation. Again, God is not unified; he is a unity: "Behold, O Israel, the LORD our God, the LORD *is* one" (Deut. 6:4, emphasis added), not the Lord *became* one. If God were not a unity but unified, we'd have two problems, which would lead to a massive third problem.

First, it would mean that properties like goodness, love, wisdom, and power could somehow exist above and beyond God, and that "God" is what happens when those properties are cooked into just the right God-recipe. But God is not the sum or combination of properties above and beyond himself. He does not *have* goodness, love, wisdom, and power. He *is* goodness. He *is* love. He *is* wisdom. He *is* power. He is not the sum of, he is the very substance of everything True, Good, and Beautiful (and in him, his Truth *is* his Goodness, his Goodness *is* his Beauty, his Beauty *is* his Truth—a thought we could spend a lifetime thinking about and still be awestruck. Just picture everything true, good, and beautiful in anything or anyone you've ever encountered as one glorious singularity, then multiplied by infinity!). Why then, you may ask yourself, do God's attributes appear to us differently? The short answer is that we stand on the other side of the glass. Borrowing the imagery of Puritan George Swinnock, God is like a sunbeam—a single, indestructible, powerful ray of light—striking a stained glass window. "When the sunbeams shine through a yellow glass they are yellow, a green glass they are green, a red glass they are red, and yet all the while the beams are the same."[3]

Second, if God were unified rather than a unity, that would imply there was someone or something above and beyond God that drew all those properties together to form God. In that case, God would no longer be God. He would no longer be the supreme Creator, but another creation. Whatever force or being arranged his properties together would be what's really supreme—some chef who arranged all the ingredients just right to cook up a deity. Anything made of parts—a Tesla Model 3 electric car, a Gibson Les Paul electric guitar, or a human being—anything composite, requires a composer,[4] an Elon Musk and his team of brilliant engineers for a Tesla, Les Paul and a legacy of skilled luthiers for a Gibson, and a triune God for a human being. But there is an infinite divide between Musk, Paul, and God. Elon Musk and Les Paul are made-makers. They owe their existence to parents and properties beyond themselves.

God and God alone is the unmade Maker. He has no engineer, no designer, no parents. No preexisting properties combined to make him. God is the only being in existence with no origin story. He doesn't say "I *became* who I am" but "I *am* who I am" (Ex. 3:14, emphasis added). To borrow Thomas Aquinas's categories from a thousand years ago, part of what we mean when we say "God" is the ultimate Composer; no one and nothing composes him, or he would cease to be God.

"Who cares?" you may think. This leads us to the massive third problem. If God is not simple, then he is not worth worshipping or centering your life on. If you care about worshipping the most supreme Being who could possibly exist—in other words, if you are a theist—then the doctrine of divine simplicity should be precious to you. A God who depends on properties beyond himself to be God or some entity beyond himself to arrange him into proper God-formation, then he isn't really worthy of the title "God," and deep down we all long to worship someone worthy of the title "God." Only a simple God merits the title "God."

BECOMING "SIMPLE"

Theologians are quick to point out that the simplicity of God is an unshared attribute. God has it; we don't, and never will. We are made up of parts, God is not. That much is true, true in a way that highlights the Creator-creature distinction, and draws creatures like us to worship. But what if there is a different sense in which image-bearing creatures like us can share in something *resembling* but never the same as divine simplicity? Before branding me with a scarlet *H* for heresy, hear me out.

Considering again our talented soul-artist, most of us would have rather silly looking soul-caricatures. I know I would. But some people's hearts, heads, and hands seem to have grown together in a way that makes their humanity truly imposing and something to marvel at. They are not simple in the divine sense, but the more they have centered their lives on God, the more integrated they become. They are not *merely* loving, *merely* creative, or *merely* powerful. They are *lovingly* creative, *creatively* loving, *powerfully* loving and creative, *lovingly* powerful and creative, and so on. In short, they are integrated. Their soul-caricatures would not look silly, but substantial and charged with glory.

Consider the Bible's commands to be integrated selves centered on Christ.

> Make every effort to supplement your faith with virtue, and virtue with knowledge, and knowledge with self-control, and self-control with steadfastness, and steadfastness with godliness, and godliness with brotherly affection, and brotherly affection with love. For if these qualities are yours

and are increasing, they keep you from being ineffective or unfruitful in the knowledge of our Lord Jesus Christ. (2 Pet. 1:5–8)

The Christian life here is not a matter of a gigantic cranium packed with theological buzzwords. It expands the whole person. It is marked by increasing faith, virtue, knowledge, self-control, steadfastness, godliness, brotherly affection, and love.

The fruit of the Spirit is love, joy, peace, patience, kindness, goodness, faithfulness, gentleness, self-control. (Gal. 5:22–23)

"Fruit" in the original Greek (*karpos*) is a singular noun. The singular fruit produced by the Spirit in our lives manifests itself in diverse ways, as love, joy, peace, and so on.

It is my prayer that your love may abound more and more, with knowledge and all discernment, so that you may approve what is excellent, and so be pure and blameless for the day of Christ, filled with the fruit of righteousness that comes through Jesus Christ, to the glory and praise of God. (Phil. 1:9–11)

The goal of the God-glorifying life is not merely to mirror his love. Rather, we are to become loving in a *knowing* and *discerning* way, in a way that makes us *pure* and *blameless*, and fills us with *righteousness*.

That's how Jesus lived his life. His every movement was *simultaneously* an expression of faith, virtue, knowledge, self-control, steadfastness, godliness, brotherly affection, love, discernment, purity, blamelessness, righteousness, joy, peace, patience, kindness, goodness, faithfulness, gentleness, and self-control. *Simple God, help us reflect Jesus.*

ACKNOWLEDGMENTS

THIS BOOK WOULD NOT BE POSSIBLE WITHOUT THE STIMULATING CONVERSATIONS OF my beloved Biola students; the hard work of my TAs Colton Jones and Tommy Maroon; the support of my theology department and university leaders Uche Anizor, Doug Huffman, Scott Rae, Ed Stetzer, and Barry Corey; the red pens of my talented editors Kim Tanner and Taylor Landry; the teamwork of Ryan Pazdur, Emily Voss, Amy Bigler, and the whole Zondervan team; the insights of my contributors Vishal Mangalwadi, John Perkins, Michael Horton, Fred Sanders, Erik Thoennes, and Joni Eareckson Tada; the theological musings of friends Joseph Mellema, Trevor Wright, Aron McKay, James Petitfils, Ben Carmona, Sean Maroney, and Josiah Solis; the prayers and encouragement of my parents and in-laws; the sacrifices of my wife Jocelyn; the life-giving silliness of our kids Gracelyn, Holland, Harlow, and Henry; and most of all the grace and sovereignty of God by which an idiot like me can help others know him better. Thank you!

NOTES

How to Read This Book

1. Vishal Mangalwadi, "A Different Kind of Guru," *Christianity Today*, January 12, 1998, https://www.christianitytoday.com/ct/1998/january12/8t1042.html.
2. See Paul Piff, Pia Dietze, Matthew Feinberg, Daniel Stancato, and Dacher Keltner, "Awe, the Small Self, and Prosocial Behavior," *Journal of Personality and Social Psychology* 108, no. 6 (2015): 883–99, https://www.apa.org/pubs/journals/releases/psp-pspi0000018.pdf; Michelle Shiota, Dacher Keltner, Amanda Mossman, "The Nature of Awe: Elicitors, Appraisals, and Effects of Self-Concept," *Cognition and Emotion* 21, no. 5 (2007): 944–63, https://greatergood.berkeley.edu/dacherkeltner/docs/shiota.2007.pdf; and Kevin Corcoran, "Happiness on the Brain: The Neuroscience of Happiness, Part 1," *The Table*, October 21, 2015, https://cct.biola.edu/happiness-on-the-brain-neuroscience-happiness-part-1/.
3. Michelle Lani Shiota, "How Awe Sharpens Our Brains," *Greater Good*, May 11, 2016, https://greatergood.berkeley.edu/article/item/how_awe_sharpens_our_brains.
4. *The Westminster Shorter Catechism*, Q. 1.

What Is a Theologian?

1. G. K. Chesterton, *Orthodoxy* (New York: John Lane Company, 1908), 223.
2. Cited in J. I. Packer, *Knowing God* (Downers Grove, IL: InterVarsity, 2018), 22.
3. In Roland Bainton's definition of *Anfechtung*, "It is all the doubt, turmoil, pang, tremor, panic, despair, desolation, and desperation which invade the spirit of man." *Here I Stand: A Life of Martin Luther* (New York: Abingdon, 1950), 42.
4. Haynes used the language of "spiritual watchmen" rather than theologian,

which is, in itself, an illuminating title for those engaged in the sacred task of theology.

5. Lemuel Haynes, "The Character and Work of a Spiritual Watchman Described," in *Selected Sermons* (Wheaton, IL: Crossway, 2023), 34–36.

6. Herman Bavinck, *The Doctrine of God* (Carlisle, PA: Banner of Truth, 1978), 126.

7. Charles Octavius Boothe, *Plain Theology for Plain People* (Bellingham, WA: Lexham, 2017), 4.

8. Augustine, "Prayers by Saint Augustine of Hippo," Theology of the Heart: Teachings of the Saints, accessed November 13, 2023, https://www.pierced hearts.org/theology_heart/wisdom_heart/augustine_prayers.htm.

9. Anselm, *Proslogion*, trans. Thomas Wilson (Indianapolis, IN: Hackett, 2001), 6.

10. Cited in A. W. Tozer, *The Pursuit of God* (Harrisburg, PA: Christian Publications), 15.

11. Cited in *Piercing Heaven: Prayers of the Puritans*, ed. Robert Elmer (Bellingham, WA: Lexham, 2019), 218.

12. Amy Carmichael, "Make Me Thy Fuel," in *Mountain Breezes* (Fort Washington, PA: Christian Literature Crusade, 1999), 223.

13. Cited in *Piercing Heaven*, 54.

14. Charles Spurgeon, "Charles Spurgeon's Prayers," Spurgeon Gems, accessed November 13, 2023, https://www.spurgeongems.org/spurgeon-prayers/#4.

15. Søren Kierkegaard, *The Prayers of Kierkegaard*, ed. Perry LeFevre (Chicago: University of Chicago Press, 1956), 31.

16. Tozer, *Pursuit of God*, 20.

17. Allen Frances, "Inside the Mind of a Fanatic," *Huffpost*, November 13, 2017, https://www.huffpost.com/entry/inside-the-mind-of-fanaticism_b_5a07205 9e4b0ee8ec36941e1.

18. Anselm, *Proslogion with the Replies of Gaunilo and Anselm*, tr. Thomas Williams (Indianapolis, IN: Hackett, 2001), 7.

19. Augustine, *Exposition of the Psalms*, Psalm 134(135):3 (New York: New City Press, 2004), 6:192.

20. Jonathan Edwards, *The Works of Jonathan Edwards, Vol. 17, Sermons and Discourses*, ed. Mark Valeri (New Haven, CT: Yale University Press, 1999), 437–438.

21. Herman Bavinck, *Our Reasonable Faith* (Grand Rapids, MI: Eerdmans, 1956), 139.

22. Packer, *Knowing God*, 22.

23. Jamie R. Love, "Responding to God's Mercies," in *His Testimonies, My Heritage: Women of Color on the Word of God*, ed. Kristie Anyabwile (Charlotte, NC: The Good Book Company, 2019), 74, 78.

24. George Barna, *Index of Leading Spiritual Indicators* (Nashville, TN: W Publishing Group, 1997), 77–82.
25. Quina Aragon, "A Final Plea," in *His Testimonies, My Heritage*, 227.
26. Helmut Thielicke, *A Little Exercise for Young Theologians* (Grand Rapids: Eerdmans, 2016), 118.
27. This research became the book *God Reforms Hearts: Rethinking Free Will and the Problem of Evil* (Bellingham, WA: Lexham Academic, 2022).
28. John Owen, *The Mortification of Sin* (Rosshire, UK: Christian Focus, 2012), 50.
29. "Gotta Serve Somebody," track 1 on Bob Dylan, *Slow Train Coming*, Columbia, 1979.
30. Several of these studies are cited in Linda and Charlie Bloom's "Want More and Better Sex? Get Married and Stay Married," *Huffpost*, July 13, 2017, https://www.huffpost.com/entry/want-more-and-better-sex-get -married-and-stay-married_b_5967b618e4b022bb9372aff2.
31. See Thaddeus Williams, "The Scandalous Seven: Who's Really Teaching Our Children about Sex?," *World*, September 26, 2023, https://wng.org /opinions/the-scandalous-seven-1695727432.
32. "American Worldview Inventory 2022: Release #5," Culture Resource Center, May 10, 2022, https://www.arizonachristian.edu/wp-content /uploads/2022/05/AWVI2022_Release05_Digital.pdf. The Cultural Research Center measures a Christian worldview in eight categories: 1. Bible, Truth, and Morals, 2. Faith Practices, 3. Family and the Value of Life, 4. God, Creation, and History, 5. Human Character and Nature, 6. Lifestyle, Behavior, and Relationships, 7. Purpose and Calling, and 8. Sin, Salvation, and God Relationship. "What Is a Biblical Worldview?," https://www.arizonachristian.edu/wp-content/uploads/2022/06/CRC-Brief -What-is-Worldview_Biblical-Worldview_Digital.pdf. For the specific basic Christian beliefs and behaviors measured under those eight headings, see "American Worldview Inventory 2022: Release #3" April 12, 2022, https:// www.arizonachristian.edu/wp-content/uploads/2022/04/AWVI2022 _Release_03_DigitalVersion.pdf.
33. "American Worldview Inventory 2022: Release #5."
34. "The State of Theology," Ligonier Ministries and LifeWay Research, 2022, https://thestateoftheology.com.
35. "American Worldview Inventory 2022: Release #3."
36. "American Worldview Inventory 2022: Release #3."
37. "American Worldview Inventory 2022: Release #3."
38. "Almost Half of Practicing Christian Millennials Say Evangelism Is Wrong," Barna, February 5, 2019, https://www.barna.com/research /millennials-oppose-evangelism/.

39. See Thaddeus Williams, "Disagreement Equals Hate? The False Assumption Sweeping the Nation," *World*, February 8, 2022, https://wng .org/opinions/disagreement-equals-hate-1644321035.

40. Some may bristle at my use of negative terminology to define the theologian. Since the theologians who wrote the Bible didn't hesitate to identify themselves as "fools," "wretches," "slaves," and "chiefs of sinners," we're in good company. If, however, we seek positive terms, we may describe the theologian as a humble, intensely God-focused, avid student of God's Word, aware of their inadequacy, committed to personal holiness, a servant, who stands in awe of the Creator.

41. Augustine, *Confessions* (San Francisco, CA: Ignatius Press, 2012), 3.

Chapter 1: Out of the Silent Universe

1. Quoted in Howard Mumma, *Albert Camus and the Minister* (Brewster, MA: Paraclete, 2000), 12.

2. Mumma, *Albert Camus and the Minister*, 12.

3. Mumma, *Albert Camus and the Minister*, 14.

4. Mumma, *Albert Camus and the Minister*, 12–13, 14.

5. Mumma, *Albert Camus and the Minister*, 95.

6. "2022 Global Scripture Access," Wycliffe Global Alliance, accessed July 30, 2023, https://www.wycliffe.net/resources/statistics/.

7. Arnold Cole and Pamela Caudill Ovwigho, "Understanding the Bible Engagement Challenge: Scientific Evidence for the Power of 4," Center for Biblical Engagement, December 2009, https://bttbfiles.com/web/docs/cbe /Scientific_Evidence_for_the_Power_of_4.pdf.

Chapter 2: The Source of Reason

1. "Michelangelo: To Giovanni Da Pistoia When the Author Was Painting the Vault of the Sistine Chapel (1509)," in Gail Mazur, *Land's End: New and Selected Poems* (Chicago: University of Chicago Press, 2020), 149.

2. "Michelangelo: To Giovanni Da Pistoia When the Author Was Painting the Vault of the Sistine Chapel (1509)," 149.

3. John Wimber, "History and Vision of Vineyard Christian Fellowships," Vineyard Christian Fellowship, Anaheim, CA, May 18, 1980, audiotape.

4. Paul Crouch, "Praise-a-Thon," TBN, April 2, 1991.

5. Lindell Cooley, "1997 Conference on the Ministry" brochure, First Assembly of God, Grand Rapids, 1997.

6. Galileo Galilei, "Letter to the Grand Duchess Christina of Tuscany: 1615," 5, Internet Modern History Sourcebook, August 1997, https://web.stanford .edu/~jsabol/certainty/readings/Galileo-LetterDuchessChristina.pdf.

7. On the role good theology played in sparking the scientific revolution, see

Ian Barbour, *Religion and Science: Historical and Contemporary Issues* (New York: HarperCollins, 1997), 3–32.

8. Os Guinness, quoted in Mark Noll, *The Scandal of the Evangelical Mind* (Grand Rapids: Eerdmans, 1995), 23.

9. In describing God as a "thinking God," I speak analogically. I do not mean that God thinks in the same way that humans think. Given God's pure actuality and perfect exhaustive knowledge, he has no need to reason, deliberate, or analyze his way toward true knowledge as we do.

10. In the words of the late Jaegwan Kim, once Brown University's premier philosopher of mind, "To think that one can be a serious physicalist and at the same time enjoy the company of things and phenomena that are nonphysical, I believe, is an idle dream. . . . [T]his is what we should expect from physicalism. . . . Physicalism cannot be had on [the] cheap." Jaegwan Kim, *Mind in a Physical World: An Essay on the Mind-Body Problem and Mental Causation* (Cambridge, MA: MIT Press, 2001), 120.

Put differently, if we reduce minds to matter, then what, we may ask, would we use to justify such a conclusion—"minds" that turn out to be a logic-less, freedom-less, goal-less buzzing of brain matter? Is the argument that there are no minds merely the physical by-product of non-minds? How then could such conclusions possibly be logically valid? The materialist (what Kim called a "physicalist") must make use of the very thing he is denying, a mind to argue there are no minds, landing him in the same self-refuting plight as the person who states that "there is no such thing as a sentence with more than three words in it."

11. Charles Darwin, "Letter to William Graham" in *The Life and Letters of Charles Darwin* (n.p.: D. Appleton and Company, 1887), 1:255. As C. S. Lewis observed,

> It follows that no account of the universe can be true unless that account leaves it possible for our thinking to be real insight. A theory which explained everything else in the whole universe but which made it impossible to believe that our thinking was valid, would be utterly out of court. For that theory would itself have been reached by thinking, and if thinking is not valid that theory would, of course, be itself demolished. It would have destroyed its own credentials. It would be an argument which proved that no argument was sound—a proof that there are no such things as proofs—which is nonsense. . . . Evolution gave us a reason for everything, but made it impossible for us to believe that our reasoning was correct. *Miracles* (New York: HarperCollins, 2001), 21–22.

12. I am not saying that one has to *consciously* rely on God in order to draw

sound conclusions and make genuine intellectual breakthroughs. Thomas Edison didn't have to be a devout believer to invent the first incandescent light bulb, phonograph, or microphone. But he did depend on laws of physics and the laws of logic that neither he nor any other scientific visionary invented. There was an unconscious reliance on the Original Inventor.

Chapter 3: The Standard of Reason

1. And why would they? The faith-at-war-with-science interpretation neatly fits a narrative in which many people's entire lives are invested.
2. King Solomon even started what could be thought of as the first school of science and technology right beside his famous temple, a place to study various animal and plant species, a place where irrigation technologies could be developed, agricultural techniques pioneered, and God's creation explored and enjoyed. If God were as anti-knowledge as some forms of faith might lead us to believe, then he could have made humanity with the collective IQ of a dead goldfish. But he didn't.
3. Some have taken "knowledge" here to mean personal knowledge as opposed to mere abstract knowledge. Before they fell into temptation, Adam and Eve could only know the difference between good and evil *theoretically*. Eating the forbidden fruit showed our first parents the difference between good and evil *by firsthand experience*, by what theologians have dubbed *cognitio experimentalis*. Adam and Eve would not only *know about* evil but would *know evil*, having perpetrated it themselves. The abstract became painfully personal.

   There are several problems with this reading, not the least of which is that the text says, "You will be *like God*, knowing good and evil" (Gen. 3:5, emphasis added). The God of the Bible certainly doesn't know evil by *cognitio experimentalis*. He never has and never will have firsthand experience of perpetrating injustice.
4. As Abraham Kuyper put it, Adam

   > decided to evaluate for himself, and came to a conclusion opposite God's conclusion, and as independent evaluator of good and evil, he placed himself over against God and through this he fell away from God. He wanted to stand beside God as a second god, just as Satan had suggested. God and man thus would both independently and sovereignly evaluate what was good and what was evil, and this unlocked all depths of sin. Thus we see exactly how it was this arbitrary probationary command of the tree of knowledge that became the effective means to bring man to the decision whether he wanted to leave to God the knowledge, that is, the assessment of good and evil or take it to himself. . . . Knowledge of good and evil means that man himself sovereignly evaluates, determines,

and decides what is good and what is evil for him. *Common Grace: God's Gifts for a Fallen World* (Bellingham, WA: Lexham, 2015), 1:240, 242.

5. It is similar to the ancient Egyptian term *evil-good*, which meant everything, or the line from Homer's *Odyssey* that says, "I know all things, the good and the evil."

6. In the words of Charles Octavius Boothe, the tree "had in itself, it appears, no extra virtue; it was a peculiar tree only because it was guarded by a peculiar command from God. God must needs begin at some point to teach and to enforce his authority upon Adam, and he chooses to begin with the command in regard to this one tree." *Plain Theology for Plain People* (Bellingham, WA: Lexham, 2017), 25.

7. As the *English Standard Version Reformation Study Bible* comments on Genesis 2:9, "A figure for potentially unlimited knowledge. It is a good tree but man must not seize it. The illicit taking of this fruit involved the assertion of human autonomy, the attempt to know all apart from God. Man must live by faith in God's word and not by a professed self-sufficiency of knowledge." R. C. Sproul, *English Standard Version Reformation Study Bible* (Phillipsburg, NJ: P&R, 2005), 11.

Chapter 4: The Savior of Reason

1. I have found by experience that there are essentially two ways to become an idiot: (1) Thinking too much and thinking that our thinking is the final word on reality. That is called "hubris." (2) Thinking too little and thinking that lack of thinking is some mark of great faith. That is called "hysteria." Reverence for God is an illuminated path between the two.

2. As art historian James Romaine points out,

> The prophets, sibyls, ancestors, and other figures surrounding the ceiling are visually and theologically connected to the nine central scenes by the illusion of a single light source—not the natural light from the windows along the chapel's side walls—emanating from the scene of God separating the light from the darkness directly above the altar. This light not only unifies the entire ceiling, it also symbolizes how the light of God that now flows out of the church and its sacraments connects Jew and Gentile, East and West, man and woman—all who live in the light of the gospel. "Scripture on the Ceiling," *Christian History* 91 (2006), https://christianhistoryinstitute.org/magazine/article/scripture-on-the-ceiling.

3. Herman Bavinck added, "Implied in the designation 'light' is that God is perfectly conscious of himself, that he knows his entire being to perfection, and that nothing in that being is hidden from his consciousness." *Reformed Dogmatics, Vol. 2: God and Creation* (Grand Rapids: Baker, 2004), 151.

4. See Francis Schaeffer, *He Is There and He Is Not Silent*, 30th anniversary ed. (Carol Stream, IL: Tyndale Elevate, 2001), for deeper insight.

5. It is worth noting that Noah shows up again in *The Last Judgment*, only this time he is not naked and unconscious before his sons but dressed in red with eyes wide open under the right hand of the Son of God.

6. John 1:18 adds, "No one has ever seen God; the only God, who is at the Father's side, he has made him known."

7. Quoting from Isaiah 9:2.

8. For nine ways that Jesus does just that, see chapter 1 of my work *Reflect: Becoming Yourself by Mirroring the Greatest Person in History* (Bellingham, WA: Lexham, 2021).

Chapter 5: The Shadow of Reason

1. If God made no shadows, if we could see and understand everything, we would have no reason to trust him, no need to be relational. And God wanted to fill his world with image bearers, not computers. Allow me to elaborate. I have often heard atheist friends protest what they perceive as a lack of evidence for God's existence. Bertrand Russell famously quipped that if he stood before his Maker one day and was asked why he did not believe, his response would be, "Not enough evidence." Why doesn't God chisel "Made by God" on every rock formation or arrange the stars to spell "God exists" in the night sky? If God is indeed running the cosmos moment by moment, directing each subatomic particle on his providential pathway, why does so much of the universe seem so willy-nilly to us? It has something to do with God's original vision for what kinds of beings he wished into existence, what kind of cosmic conditions would achieve his intentions. God wished image bearers, humans who would reflect him, into existence. If God was merely intellect, some kind of super knower with an IQ of infinity, whose sole delight was possessing a complete set of justified true propositions in his mind, then, indeed, it would make sense to hardwire humanity so that we spring from the womb primed to crack the mysteries of quantum mechanics in our toddler years, articulate the grand unified theory by adolescence, and achieve philosophical omniscience by our teen years. But God is not mere intellect. God is also (and I say "also," not "instead") love. He delights not merely in knowing propositions but in knowing persons and in being known by persons. If we knew everything, then why bother trusting anyone? Why bother moving a single inch beyond our own skulls? We would become prisoners inside our own heads. Instead, God willed image bearers into existence. We are made not only to reason but also to rely. The only way for us to enjoy something like the triune God has always enjoyed is within the rational relationality that is God, that is, in a state of trust.

2. First Corinthians 1:20 adds, "Where is the one who is wise? Where is the scribe? Where is the debater of this age? Has not God made foolish the wisdom of the world?"

3. As Herman Bavinck said in the opening lines of *The Doctrine of God*, "The truth which God has revealed about himself in nature and in Scripture far surpasses human conception and comprehension. In that sense Dogmatics is concerned with nothing but mystery, for it does not deal with finite creatures, but from beginning to end raises itself above every creature to the Eternal and Endless One himself" (Carlisle, PA: Banner of Truth, 1978), 18.

4. Herman Bavinck, *The Doctrine of God* (Carlisle, PA: Banner of Truth, 1978), 126.

5. Jesus famously said that it's easier for a camel to fit through the eye of a needle than for a rich man to enter God's kingdom (Matt. 19:24). We might add, that camel also has an easier time than the theologian who tries to fit God through the pinhole of his own mind. The theologian's system must never be mistaken for the Substance, or that which should be the source of wonder, joy, and inspiration will evoke no more awe than the sight of a Greek verb paradigm, the periodic table, or long lines of computer code. When the theologian mistakes his system for the Substance—the living, breathing God around whom that entire system, if it be a good system, centers—then his situation becomes absurd. He thinks he is thinking of God—the infinite source of joy, satisfaction, and purpose—but he is locked behind his own concepts, or his access to God is only channeled through those concepts. The infinite oasis is bottlenecked for him. He tries to drink it in through a straw, the tiny straw of his own intellect. And so he is not refreshed, while knowing he is sipping at the very source of all true refreshment. He grows thirsty on the banks of infinite quenching. His solution? Drop the straw and plunge in.

6. The Bible says as much: "For my thoughts are not your thoughts, neither are your ways my ways, declares the LORD. For as the heavens are higher than the earth, so are my ways higher than your ways and my thoughts than your thoughts" (Isa. 55:8–9). This has something to do with the Greatest Commandment to love God with *all* of our minds. *"All"* entails both the baffled and the comprehending aspects of the intellect, the cognitive and the confounded.

7. If you make how much you know and how well you know it your source of safety and security, then you will never feel safe and secure. There are just too many unknowns. When the Apollo 13 spacecraft left our atmosphere, how could the astronauts have known that a defective oxygen tank would burst 321,860 kilometers from Earth? They couldn't.

8. Part of the futility of our attempts at omniscience has to do with our

relation to time in contrast to God's relation to time. Our time-boundedness means that certain peace-bestowing conclusions are simply impossible, metaphysically and epistemically, for us to reach. The Israelites stuck in the moment on the Red Sea shores could hardly have seen what God was on the brink of pulling off for their deliverance. Thus, time-bound logic becomes notorious for drawing premature and eventually false conclusions that nevertheless, in the moment, seem totally logical, but which are mocked for their absurdity again and again by the unfolding of providence. Part of trusting the Father, so that real gladness can be experienced, is trusting an eternal Father, a Father who made time and is therefore unbound by time.

9. Take the crucial biblical plot point that you are loved by God with the full weight of his divine perfections. The claim is an assault on reason. There is no tidy logical syllogism that will render this conclusion with the force of Cartesian certainty. There is no scientific experiment that can demonstrate it empirically. And even if we resort to experience, we could marshal all kinds of heartaches and seasons of divine absence as evidence against it. But it is true, and not merely true but True with a capital *T*, a meta-Truth that opens up a million others truths to which we otherwise would be oblivious. You are not merely loved. The Father loves you "even as" he loves the Son (John 17:23).

10. It leaves us in the same logical and sad state that Andrew Bird captures so well in the lyrics of his song "Master Fade": "Well, you sure didn't look like you were having any fun with that heavy-metal gaze they'll have to measure in tons. And when you look up at the sky, all you see are zeroes, all you sees are zeroes and ones."

This is something like David Hume experienced when he wrote,

> "I am first affrighted and confounded with that forelorn solitude, in which I am plac'd in my philosophy, and fancy myself some strange uncouth monster . . . utterly abandon'd and disconsolate. . . . When I look abroad, I foresee on every side, dispute, contradiction, anger, calumny and detraction. When I turn my eye inward, I find nothing but doubt and ignorance. . . . Every step I take is with hesitation, and every new reflection makes me dread an error and absurdity in my reasoning. Most fortunately it happens, that since reason is incapable of dispelling these clouds, nature herself suffices to that purpose, and cures me of this philosophical melancholy and delirium, either by relaxing this bent of mind, or by some avocation, and lively impression of my senses, which obliterate all these chimeras. I dine, I play a game of backgammon, I converse, and am merry with my friends; and when after three or four hours' amusement, I wou'd return to these speculations, they appear so cold, and strain'd, and ridiculous, that I

cannot find in my heart to enter into them any farther." *A Treatise of Human Nature*, pt. 4., sec. 7 (1739).

11. G. K. Chesterton added, "A man cannot think himself out of mental evil; for it is actually the organ of thought that has become diseased, ungovernable, and, as it were, independent. He can only be saved by will or faith. The moment his mere reason moves, it moves in the old circular rut; he will go round and round his logical circle." *Orthodoxy* (Walnut, CA: MSAC Philosophy Group, 2008), 13.

12. J. I. Packer, *Knowing God* (Downers Grove, IL: InterVarsity, 2018), 91–92.

13. In an interview with Robert Persig, Tim Adams comments, "He says that ever since he could think he had an overwhelming desire to have a theory that explained everything. As a young man—he was at university at 15 studying chemistry—he thought the answer might lie in science, but he quickly lost that faith. 'Science could not teach me how to understand girls sitting in my class, even.'" "The Interview: Robert Persig," *The Guardian*, November 18, 2006, https://www.theguardian.com/books/2006/nov/19/fiction.

14. Packer, *Knowing God*, 94–95.

15. Psalm 33:21. According to this psalm, gladness and trust exist in parallel ratio to one another. When we don't trust an omniscient being, we try to become the omniscient being. And that quest for omniscience (which often gets expressed in a cavalier way as "I'm an overthinker," "I overanalyze," etc.) is anything but glad. For every eventuality pondered, there are five million more unpredictable plot twists and turns that make reasoning our way to peace of mind impossible, draining, frustrating, even maddening. The trust the psalmist has in mind is the kind of trust that says, I know someone who understands every plot twist, who comprehends what to me is the vast unknown, whose IQ can process the whole sum of existence in an instant, and that God, the only wise God, knows me, cares for me, works all things for my good and his glory. And so insecurity is no longer the fuel that drives the pursuit of knowledge. Building the "ready defense for the hope that lies within" does not become a ridiculous defense mechanism for the fears that lie within. I no longer have to be threatened by the unknown (because part of God's infinite wisdom is letting me know what I need to know precisely when I need to know it so the threat of some yet-to-be-thought insight that I am missing and that would demolish my joy and confidence in the present becomes an absurd, nonexistent threat. I now know precisely what the All Wise now wants me to know, and in the likely event that I now know in part, or think I know what may turn out to be a flat-out falsehood, is itself an ignorance preordained wisely for my good, that I may know more truly at some future point in precisely the kind of way that it can be known best, result in the most good for me and others and in the most glory for God).

That liberation from the need for omniscience is part of what it means to have gladness in the biblical sense.

In this light, we can see many forms of liberation from the need for omniscience as cheap substitutes for the real thing, a trust-based relationship with an all-knowing beneficent Father. For example, booze is often used to help people feel glad insofar as it chemically helps to inhibit the cognitive capacities that hopelessly pursue omniscience to relieve stress. It gives the boozer an artificial sense of gladness, artificial insofar as, rather than gladness being relationally anchored in an objective reality, that is, that an all-knowing being is purposing all things for his glory and my good, the booze-induced gladness has no such assurance. It only shuts down the mechanism by which we seek such assurance and gives us a temporary flight from reality. Entertainment can function in a very similar way, as a substitute for true relief by distracting our cognition.

Without prayerful reliance on the all-wise Father, without consciously bringing our minds before the Father, unloading their stress-inducing finite and usually false conclusions down at his feet, "casting our anxieties on him," renouncing our epistemic claim as the final word on reality for my emotions to follow, asking humbly for an enlarged trust capacity, without all that, then two great gifts, like alcohol and entertainment, can quickly twist and morph into destructive gods, false idols that promise us gladness and ultimately deliver emptiness. If, on the other hand, we are regularly and actively trusting, then we are not only freed up to be lighthearted and glad, but we are actually able to enjoy things like alcohol and entertainment without them ripping us apart. When the Father is our ultimate thing, then these no longer have to be sought as ultimate things and can thereby be enjoyed as good things.

16. Packer, *Knowing God*, 96–97.
17. John 1:18 adds, "No one has ever seen God; the only God, who is at the Father's side, he has made him known."
18. See also Psalm 111:10; Proverbs 1:7; 15:33; Eccl. 12:13.
19. *The Sayings of the Fathers*, III, 21, cited in Abraham Heschel, *God in Search of Man: A Philosophy of Judaism* (New York: Noonday, 1976), 78.
20. Ayanna Thomas Mathis, "God's Statutes, Our Rewards," in *His Testimonies, My Heritage: Women of Color on the Word of God*, ed. Kristie Anyabwile (Charlotte, NC: The Good Book Company, 2019), 67.

Chapter 6: Be Boring

1. Veronica Ruckh, "The Official Ranking of the Most Boring Schools in Each State," *Total Sorority Move,* accessed October 9, 2022, https://

totalsororitymove.com/the-official-ranking-of-the-most-boring-schools
-in-each-state/.
2. "Things to Do in Lynchburg," Tripadvisor, accessed August 15, 2023,
https://www.tripadvisor.com/Attractions-g57919-Activities-Lynchburg
_Virginia.html.
3. Epicurus preferred mental pleasures to physical pleasures, criticizing the
latter as short-lived. Aristippus was the true Greek father of physical
hedonism.
4. C. S. Lewis, *The Weight of Glory* (New York: HarperOne, 1949), 26.
5. Trillia Newbell, "Godly Sorrow and the Freedom of Grace," in *His
Testimonies, My Heritage: Women of Color on the Word of God*, ed. Kristie
Anyabwile (Charlotte, NC: The Good Book Company, 2019), 58.

Chapter 7: In an Elevator with a Sociopath

1. J. I. Packer, *Knowing God* (Downers Grove, IL: InterVarsity, 2018), 214.
2. Packer, *Knowing God*, 207.
3. Blair Linne, "Finding God as Your Father," *Wonderfully Made* podcast,
June 13, 2022, https://wonderfullymade.org/2022/06/13/finding-god-as
-your-father-with-blair-linne/.
4. Packer, *Knowing God*, 207.
5. *Joker*, directed by Todd Phillips (Hollywood, CA: Warner Bros. Pictures,
2019), DVD.
6. *Joker*, directed by Todd Phillips.
7. *Joker*, directed by Todd Phillips.
8. *The Dark Knight*, directed by Christopher Nolan (Hollywood, CA: Warner
Bros. Pictures, 2008), DVD.
9. *The Westminster Confession of Faith*, ch. 12.

Chapter 8: No, You Are Not a Freak

1. Technically, in the field of ethics, *hedonism* conveys a theory of value in
which pleasure is the only good in existence. I do not, nor does Piper
who coined the term *Christian hedonism*, mean the term in the technical
philosophical sense, but rather to capture something of the Bible's many
commands (not suggestions) to enjoy God as the ultimate Good.
2. Throughout the Bible, joy stands in an asymmetrical relationship above
other emotions. We climb through sorrow and suffering as a means to
reaching more profound joy (see 2 Cor. 4:17–18; Heb. 12:2; and James 1:2),
but joy in Scripture is not a means to reaching greater pain and despair.
3. Likewise, David asked "Why, O Lord, do you stand far away? Why do you
hide yourself in times of trouble?" (Ps. 10:1; cf. 9:1).
4. St. John of the Cross described how through "this arid and dark night, [the

soul] cannot experience spiritual pleasure and good, but only aridity and lack of sweetness, since it misses the pleasure which aforetime it enjoyed so readily." He spoke of how many Christians "fear of being lost on the road, thinking that all spiritual blessing is over for them and that God has abandoned them since they find no help or pleasure in good things." *The Dark Night of the Soul*, trans. E. Allison Peers (Garden City, NY: Image Books, 1959), 55–56.

5. Roland H. Bainton, *Here I Stand: A Life of Martin Luther* (New York: Abingdon-Cokesbury Press, 1950), 361.

6. *Piercing Heaven: Prayers of the Puritans*, ed. Robert Elmer (Bellingham, WA: Lexham, 2019), 76.

7. *Piercing Heaven*, 28.

8. *Piercing Heaven*, 63.

9. "The Life of David Brainerd," in *The Works of Jonathan Edwards*, ed. Norman Pettit (New Haven, CT: Yale University Press, 1984), 7:285.

10. Gilbert Thomas, *William Cowper and the Eighteenth Century* (London: Allen & Unwin, 1948), 225.

11. C. H. Spurgeon, *Lectures to My Students: A Selection from Addresses Delivered to the Students of the Pastors' College, Metropolitan Tabernacle* (London: Passmore and Alabaster, 1875), 1:1–9.

12. C. S. Lewis, *A Grief Observed* (New York: Bantam, 1988), 4.

Chapter 9: The Hiding Chef

1. See also Pss. 4:7; 9:2; 17:15; 51:10, 12; 73:25–26.

2. John Piper, "Your Love Is Better Than Life: Savoring the Vision," desiringGod, September 13, 1987, https://www.desiringgod.org/messages/your-love-is-better-than-life.

Chapter 10: The Wisdom of a Nine-Year-Old

1. This chapter draws heavily on material from Thaddeus Williams, *Don't Follow Your Heart: Boldly Breaking the Ten Commandments of Self-Worship* (Grand Rapids: Zondervan, 2023).

2. Steve Jobs, "How to Live Before You Die," Stanford University commencement speech, TED, 2005, https://www.ted.com/talks/steve_jobs_how_to_live_before_you_die.

3. This and the next few quotes are from "The End of Absolutes: America's New Moral Code," Barna, May 25, 2016, https://www.barna.com/research/the-end-of-absolutes-americas-new-moral-code/. This is not new. Back in 1831, Alexis de Tocqueville made the transatlantic voyage to research his celebrated opus *Democracy in America*. What he found was "an innumerable multitude of men constantly circling around in the pursuit of petty and banal

pleasures with which they glut their souls. Each one of them, withdrawn into himself, is almost unaware of the fate of the rest. He touches them but feels nothing. He exists in and for himself." *Democracy in America*, trans. Henry Reeve, ed. Bruce Frohnen (Washington, DC: Regnery, 2002), 268.

4. "Anxiety Disorders: Facts & Statistics," Anxiety & Depression Association of America, accessed August 9, 2023, https://adaa.org/understanding -anxiety/facts-statistics.

5. Psychologist Barry Schwartz captures the irony of our age: "We have more choice, and thus more control, than people have ever had before. . . . [This] might lead you to expect that depression is going the way of polio, with autonomy and choice as the psychological vaccines. Instead, we are experiencing depression in epidemic numbers." Barry Schwartz, *The Paradox of Choice: Why Less Is More* (New York: HarperCollins, 2005), 109–10.

6. David Foster Wallace, "This Is Water," Kenyon College commencement speech, 2005, https://fs.blog/david-foster-wallace-this-is-water/.

7. C. S. Lewis, *The Abolition of Man*, in *The Complete Lewis Signature Classics* (New York: HarperCollins, 2007), 710.

8. *The Incredibles*, directed by Brad Bird (Burbank, CA: Buena Vista Pictures, 2004), DVD.

9. Jean-Jacques Rousseau, *Il n'y a point de perversité originelle dans le cœur humain Émile, ou De l'éducation/Édition* 1852/Livre II; *Letters to Malesherbes*, in *The Collected Writings of Rousseau*, ed. Christopher Kelly, Roger D. Masters, and Peter G. Stillman, trans. Christopher Kelly (Hanover, NH: University Press of New England, 1995), 5:575; *Oeuvres Complètes*, ed. Bernard Gagnebin and Marcel Raymond (Paris: Gallimard, Bibliothèque de la Pléiade, 1959–95), 1:1136.

10. Celine Dion, "If you follow your dreams, it means you follow your heart," May 22, 2001, YouTube video, 1:17, https://www.youtube.com/watch?v= y5JiQEaQD30.

11. Joel Osteen, *Becoming a Better You: 7 Keys to Improving Your Life Every Day* (New York: Free Press, 2007), 56, 87, 91, 129.

12. David Meyers, "A New Look at Pride," in *Your Better Self*, ed. C. W. Ellison (San Francisco: Harper & Row, 1983), 83.

13. Visit jointheheretics.com to view and sign "A Heretic's Manifesto" and find additional resources on resisting the flow of expressive individualism.

Interstitial – John M. Perkins

1. Some of this material was adapted from John M. Perkins with Karen Waddles, *Count It All Joy: The Ridiculous Paradox of Suffering* (Chicago: Moody Press, 2021).

2. R. H. Cornelius, "O I Want to See Him," public domain.

Chapter 11: The Sovereignty Circle

1. Perry Miller, *Jonathan Edwards* (Lincoln: University of Nebraska Press, 2005), 225.
2. Jonathan Edwards, "An Autobiography, a Personal Narrative," APM, accessed November 11, 2023, https://www.apuritansmind.com/puritan-favorites/jonathan-edwards/biographical-writings/edwards-personal-narrative/.
3. Jonathan Edwards, *The Life of the Rev. David Brainerd* (London: Burton and Smith, 1818), 299.
4. R. C. Sproul, *Chosen by God* (Carol Stream, IL: Tyndale Elevate, 2021), 11, 12.
5. Edwards described his transformation on the doctrine of divine sovereignty as follows:

> From my childhood up, my mind had been full of objections against the doctrine of God's sovereignty, in choosing whom he would to eternal life, and rejecting whom he pleased; leaving them eternally to perish, and be everlastingly tormented in hell. It used to seem like a horrible doctrine to me. But I remember the time very well, when I seemed to be convinced, and fully satisfied, as to this sovereignty of God and his justice in eternally dealing with men according to his sovereign pleasure . . . my mind rested in it; and it put an end to all those cavils and objections. And since then, there has been a wonderful transformation in my mind, in respect to the doctrine of God's sovereignty; so that I hardly ever have found so much as the rising of an objection against God's showing mercy to whom he will show mercy, and hardening whom he will. God's absolute sovereignty and justice, with respect to salvation and damnation, is what my mind seems to rest assured of, as much as of any thing that I see with my eyes. . . . But I have often, since that first conviction, had a whole new sense of God's sovereignty than I had then. I have often since had not only a conviction, but a delightful conviction. The doctrine has very often appeared exceedingly pleasant, bright, and sweet. Absolute sovereignty is what I love to ascribe to God. ("An Autobiography, a Personal Narrative")

6. "God, I trust, brought me to a hearty disposition to exalt Him and set Him on the throne." Jonathan Edwards, *The Life and Diary of David Brainerd*, ed. Philip E. Howard Jr. (Grand Rapids: Baker, 1949), 70.
7. Sproul, *Chosen by God*, 14.
8. Martin Luther, *Martin Luther: Selections from His Writings*, ed. John Dillenberger (Albany, NY: Anchor, 1958), 179.
9. A. W. Pink, *The Attributes of God* (Grand Rapids: Baker, 1975), 29.

Chapter 12: Where Is God When the Sky Is Falling?

1. The list of Luke 4:5–6 matches the cast of characters behind Christ's arrest and execution. See τοὺς ἄρχοντας, τοὺς πρεσβυτέρους in Luke 22:52, 66, τοὺς γραμματεῖς in Luke 22:66, and ὁ ἀρχιερεύς in Luke 22:54.

2. This rare liturgical title for God occurs sporadically in the Bible (Ex. 20:11; Ps. 146:56; Job 5:8 [LXX]; Luke 2:29; Jude 4; Rev. 6:10), with some usage in Jewish prayers (Josephus, *Jewish Wars* 7.323; 3 Macc. 2:2; Wis. 6:7; 3 Sir. 36:1) and greater attestation in Greek political literature (Aelius Aristides, *Works* 37:1; Xenophon, *Anabasis* 3:2, 13).

3. For an interesting parallel to the prayer of Acts 4:24–30, see Josephus, *Antiquities of the Jews*, in *Josephus: Complete Works*, trans. William Whiston (Grand Rapids: Kregel, 1981): 40–50, 87.

4. Joseph Fitzmeyer, *The Acts of the Apostles* (New Haven, CT: Yale University Press, 1998), 310.

5. The Septuagint uses *cheir* language in the liberation accounts in Exodus 13:3, 14, and 16 (see also Ps. 55:21).

6. As the LXX of Daniel 4:32 reads, οὐκ ἔστιν ὅς ἀντιποιήσεται τῇ χειρί ("No one can hinder God's hand").

7. In Acts 2:23, the parallel of Acts 4:28, it is by God's ὡρισμένη βουλή, i.e., his "determined" and "clearly defined plan" that Jesus was delivered over to his executioners. Simon Kistemaker observed, "The expression *set purpose* [ὡρισμένη βουλή] denotes a plan that has been determined and is clearly defined. The author of this purpose is God himself." *Acts*, New Testament Commentary (Grand Rapids: Baker, 1991), 93. See also Ernst Haenchen, *The Acts of the Apostles: A Commentary* (Louisville: Westminster John Knox, 1971), 180; and I. Howard Marshall, *The Acts of the Apostles* (Grand Rapids: Eerdmans, 1980), 75.

8. From the *protoevangelium* of Genesis 3:15, in which a seed of woman would be bruised while crushing the serpent's head, to the suffering servant whom it *pleased* (βούλεται [LXX]) the LORD to bruise (Isa. 53:10), the Old Testament previews a divine plan that was in motion toward a supreme act of redemptive suffering. The Luke-Acts narrative acknowledges the Old Testament precedent for a suffering messiah (Luke 24:25–26, 46; Acts 17:3; 26:23). This ancient Hebrew motif underscores the claim in Acts 4:28 that God's "plan" was active in the sufferings of Jesus.

9. See Rom. 8:30; 1 Cor. 2:7; and Eph. 1:5, 11.

10. Theologian Greg Boyd has attempted to diminish the weight of divine sovereignty in the early church's prayer with three innovative, alternate interpretations of the Acts 4 prayer. First, he argues that God could have ordained *that* the crucifixion would occur without ordaining *who* would bring it about, thereby preserving Boyd's notion of libertarian free will.

Second, he argues that God could have ordained who would conspire to execute Jesus if those moral agents had previously chosen such conspiring characters with libertarian freedom. Third, he argues that the cross may be such a one-of-a-kind event in redemption history that God uniquely flexed his sovereign power to bring it about, but that such divine determination is an exception rather than the rule of how God acts in the universe. See Boyd's *Satan and the Problem of Evil* (Downers Grove, IL: InterVarsity, 2001), 11, 44–45, 121–122, 186, 423. I address all three of these interpretations in *God Reforms Hearts: Rethinking Free Will and the Problem of Evil* (Bellingham, WA: Lexham Academic, 2021), 107–13.

11. If the early church was right about God's sovereignty over pain, wouldn't that make God himself blameworthy for evil? Isn't this God more like the godfather, sending mobsters out to do his dirty work? The answer to this question is a clear, emphatic, and biblical "no." The Bible is clear that "his work is perfect, for all his ways are justice. A God of faithfulness and without iniquity, just and upright is he" (Deut. 32:4). Having firmly established from the Bible that God can in no way be charged with evil, Scripture throws some twists at us: "For it was the Lord's doing to harden [the Hivites'] hearts that they should come against Israel in battle, in order that they should be devoted to destruction and should receive no mercy but be destroyed, just as the Lord commanded Moses" (Josh. 11:20). "God sent an evil spirit between Abimelech and the leaders of Shechem, and the leaders of Shechem dealt treacherously with Abimelech, that the violence done to the seventy sons of Jerubbaal might come, and their blood be laid on Abimelech their brother, who killed them, and on the men of Shechem, who strengthened his hands to kill his brothers" (Judg. 9:23–24). "O Lord, why do you make us wander from your ways and harden our heart, so that we fear you not?" (Isa. 63:17).

Scripture is teeming with examples of God sovereignly ordaining agents to commit evil to carry out his own holy ends, from his hardening of Pharaoh's heart (Ex. 4:21, which happened before Pharaoh hardened his heart in 8:15) to display his power, to his predestining of Christ's crucifiers (Acts 2:23; 4:27–28) to display his redeeming love.

The question may be brewing in your mind, *Doesn't this make God blameworthy for sin?* To unravel this tangled question, we must first ask ourselves, "What makes an action evil and a person blameworthy?" Suppose man X kills man Y. A superficial look at that action won't tell us for sure if it is good or evil or if man X should be praised or punished. Why? Because we don't know man X's intentions, and intentions, which reflect character, are what make actions evil and actors blameworthy.

What if man X is a president or prime minister and man Y is a terrorist with his finger on a button to detonate explosives in highly populated cities? If man X's intention is to stop this atrocity from happening by terminating the source, then his preemptive strike is good and he is praiseworthy. If, on the other hand, man X is a sadistic serial killer with the intention of killing for killing's sake, then his action is evil and he is blameworthy. When it comes to assessing good, evil, praise, and blame, intentions are what count.

According to Judges 9, what was God's intention for sending an evil spirit? The answer: to bring the murderers of Jerubbaal's sons to justice. It should be no surprise that God's intentions are absolutely holy and righteous, as opposed to the godfather who directs his mobsters with bad intentions, because Moses was right when he confessed, "Just and upright is he" (Deut. 32:4).

Biblically, God gives spirits of stupor, hardens hearts, and even sends evil spirits. But in every case, the underlying intention coming from his character is holy, righteous, just, and self-glorifying. And God still rightly punishes the spiritually apathetic, the hard-hearted, and the evil-spirited because their intentions and resulting actions, not God's, are evil, unlike God's, so they, not God, are blameworthy and deserve God's punishment.

Chapter 13: The Counterculture in the Age of Anxiety

1. "The Cost of Freedom: How Disagreement Makes Us Civil; Robert George, Cornel West, and Rick Warren in Conversation," Biola University, May 1, 2015, https://www.youtube.com/watch?v=XNDQj8QK8Zc.
2. "Anxiety Disorders: Facts & Statistics," Anxiety & Depression Association of America, accessed August 9, 2023, https://adaa.org/understanding -anxiety/facts-statistics.
3. Jonathan Haidt and Greg Lukianoff, *The Coddling of the American Mind: How Good Intentions and Bad Ideas Are Setting Up a Generation for Failure* (New York: Penguin, 2019), 156–57.
4. "Stress in America 2020: A National Health Crisis," American Psychological Association, accessed August 9, 2023, https://www.apa.org/news/press /releases/stress/2020/sia-mental-health-crisis.pdf.
5. "The Top Ten Fears in America: Did Your Fears Make the List?" *The Voice of Wilkinson* (blog), Chapman University, October 14, 2022, https://blogs .chapman.edu/wilkinson/2022/10/14/the-top-10-fears-in-america-2022/. Chapman's research found that it is not the *fact* of fear but the *focal point* of fear that shifts by political affiliation. For example, 29.5 percent of conservatives feared the outcome of the 2020 election, compared to 74.6 of liberals. Over half of Democrats are "afraid" or "very afraid" of contracting COVID; a quarter of Republicans share that fear. Only 43.2 percent of Americans identifying as "extremely conservative" fear widespread civil unrest, compared with 75.8 percent identifying as "extremely liberal."

Of course the political left doesn't have a monopoly on fear. Fear crosses partisan lines because, well, there are human beings across the political spectrum. The bipartisan power of fear is evident in the fact that the foremost fear in the US (for the sixth year in a row) is fear of "corrupt government officials." It's a fear shared by Republicans (84.6 percent) and Democrats (77.8 percent) alike; it is such a dominant fear that the next highest-ranking fear ("people I love dying") is a full 20 points lower. There are many reasons (some valid, some irrational) why the thought of "corrupt government officials" sparks so much fear—even more than the thought of losing a loved one.

6. See Haidt and Lukianoff, *Coddling of the American Mind.*

7. Tilly is not her real name.

8. Charles Taylor, *A Secular Age* (Cambridge, MA: Belknap, 2007), 542.

9. For those who, like me, have battled intense anxiety, I highly recommend my mentor and friend J. P. Moreland's outstanding work *Finding Quiet: My Story of Overcoming Anxiety and the Practices That Brought Peace* (Grand Rapids: Zondervan, 2019).

10. See Neil Postman's classic *Amusing Ourselves to Death: Public Discourse in the Age of Show Business* (New York: Penguin, 2005).

11. If history is any teacher, then a culture-wide anxiety crisis is nothing to take lightly. It primes a culture to enter ages of political totalitarianism, ideological violence, shallow escapism, and other gloomy outcomes. Speaking of another "major watershed in history, equal in importance to the turn from the Middle Ages to the Renaissance," Alexander Solzhenitsyn closed his famous 1978 Harvard commencement speech with the poignant words, "It will demand from us a spiritual blaze. . . . No one on earth has any other way left but—upward" (Alexander Solzhenitsyn, "A World Split Apart," Commencement Speech at Harvard [1978]). Amen. Rather than watching passively as our age of feeling and anxiety devolves into ages of totalitarianism and chaos, let us look upward to a sovereign God and pray for an age of revival like the early church experienced.

Chapter 14: "This, Please, Cannot Be That"

1. See Clark Pinnock, "God Limits His Knowledge," in *Predestination and Free Will: Four Views of Divine Sovereignty and Human Responsibility*, ed. David Basinger and Randall Basinger (Downers Grove, IL: InterVarsity, 1986). See also John Sanders, *The God Who Risks: A Theology of Providence* (Downers Grove, IL: InterVarsity, 1998); and Gregory Boyd, *Satan and the Problem of Evil* (Downers Grove, IL: InterVarsity, 2001).

2. This and other quotes in this section from *Magnolia*, written and directed by P. T. Anderson, New Line Cinema, 1999.

3. *Magnolia*, written and directed by P. T. Anderson.
4. For the historicity of Luke's account over and against attempts to reduce it to fiction, see Craig Keener's "Novel's 'Exotic' Places and Luke's African Official (Acts 8:27)," *Andrews University Seminary Studies* 46, no. 1 (2008): 5–20.
5. Charles Spurgeon, *Spurgeon's Sermon Notes: 193 Sermon Illustrations and Outlines from Genesis to Revelation*, ed. David Otis Fuller (Grand Rapids: Kregel, 1990), 110.
6. Franz Delitzsch, *Biblical Commentaries on the Prophecies of Isaiah* (Grand Rapids: Eerdmans, 1954), 2:303.
7. Don't get me wrong: I think such passages are important and that on their deepest reading do point to Jesus.

Chapter 15: Letters to a Father from the Black Hole

1. On motherhood imagery for God, see Isaiah 42:14; 49:15; 66:13. On the names and images of God, see Herman Bavinck, *The Doctrine of God* (Carlisle, PA: Banner of Truth, 1977) 83–111.
2. For a helpful exegesis of these fifteen occurrences, see Goran Medved, "The Fatherhood of God in the Old Testament," *KAIROS: Evangelical Journal of Theology* 10, no. 2 (2016): 203–14. Fatherhood language for God can also be found in early extrabiblical Jewish sources, including the Babylonian Talmud Ta'anit 25b, the Mishnah in Sotah 9:15, the Midrash on Psalm 25:13; Ben Sira 51:10; and the Dead Sea Scrolls 4Q511, fragment 127, line 1.
3. J. I. Packer, *Knowing God* (Downers Grove: IL: InterVarsity, 2018), 200.
4. Packer, 201.
5. Barack Obama, "Father's Day 2008 Speech at Chicago's Apostolic Church of God," June 15, 2008, *Politico*, https://www.politico.com/story/2008/06/text-of-obamas-fatherhood-speech-011094.
6. Paul Vitz, *Faith of the Fatherless: The Psychology of Atheism* (San Francisco, CA: Ignatius, 2013).
7. Take my week, for example. Today is Thursday. On Monday I had what felt like a Samurai sword lodged in my spine. My back went out mid-lecture in front of sixty students on the first day of class. On my way out the door Tuesday morning to present my last semester's research to fellow faculty, I came downstairs to black sewage dumping through the ceiling. The next day, with my living room sealed off like a nuclear quarantine, I left again for campus. It was dumping rain. My car's electrical and brake systems decided to fail simultaneously. Add to that a three-week-plus cold, and you can see what great timing it is to be working on a chapter about the sovereignty of God over all of life.

You might think that I have a severe case of cognitive dissonance to keep writing. You might picture me shaking my fist, throwing a pity party, short-fused with my family, or making a mad scramble to restore order to my world. But I am not. I am really quite content. Has it been frustrating? Of course. But underneath that there is calm, a deep liberating sense that God remains in charge, that no inconvenience slips by him unaware, that nothing befalls me that has not been ordained for his glory and my good.

8. Guido de Bres, "Personal Letter," trans. W. L. Bradenhof, reprinted in *Biblioteca Reformatoria Neerlandica* 7 (1903): 624–28.

9. Kevin DeYoung, "The Belgic Confession and the Hero No One Remembers," TGC, February 24, 2009, https://blogs.thegospelcoalition.org /kevindeyoung/2009/02/24/belgic-confession-and-hero-no-one/.

10. Guido de Bres, "Personal Letter."

11. Guido de Bres, "Personal Letter." John Piper echoes, "When a person settles it biblically, intellectually, and emotionally, that God has ultimate control of all things, including evil . . . then a marvelous stability and depth come into that person's life." *Desiring God* (Colorado Springs, CO: Multnomah, 2011), 354.

12. Guido de Bres, "Personal Letter."

13. I read a draft of this chapter to a dear friend, Trevor Wright, as he battled aggressive cancer. These were Trevor's words of authentic tearful joy as he reflected on God's sovereignty over his own suffering: "This was purposeful and there is a sovereign and good God over the top of it. I'm astounded at how much more stable I am, even though the pain is worse. . . . There's a sovereign God over it all" (personal phone call, August 17, 2023).

Chapter 16: The Infinitely Worst God

1. Lorenzo Snow, *The Millennial Star*, 54:404.

2. Joseph Smith, *History of the Church: 1843–1844, Vol. 6* (Salt Lake City, UT: Deseret, 1978), 305–6.

3. Smith, 476. First counselor of the LDS church's first presidency concurs that "we shall go back to our Father and God, who is connected with one who is still farther back; and this Father is connected with one still further back, and so on." *Journal of Discourses, by Brigham Young, President of the Church of Jesus Christ of Latter-day Saints, His Two Counsellors, the Twelve Apostles, and Others*, 26 vols., reported by G. D. Watt (Liverpool: F. D. Richards, 1854–86), 5:19.

4. Charles Octavius Boothe, *Plain Theology for Plain People* (Bellingham, WA: Lexham, 2017), 4.

5. A. W. Pink, *The Attributes of God* (Grand Rapids, MI: Baker, 1987), 37.

6. Herman Bavinck, *The Doctrine of God* (Carlisle, PA: Banner of Truth, 1978), 149.

Chapter 17: Is God or Tod an Egomaniac?

1. Dotson Rader, "Interview with Brad Pitt," *Parade*, September 18, 2007, https://parade.com/50120/parade/interview-with-brad-pitt/.
2. Lemuel Haynes, *Selected Sermons* in Crossway Short Classics Series (Wheaton, IL: Crossway, 2023), 39.
3. John Piper, *Desiring God: Meditations of a Christian Hedonist* (Sisters, OR: Multnomah, 1996), 50.
4. John Piper, *God's Passion for God's Glory: Living the Vision of Jonathan Edwards with the Complete Text of* The End for Which God Created the World (Wheaton, IL: Crossway, 1998), 248–249.
5. C. S. Lewis, *Reflections on the Psalms* (New York: Harcourt, Brace & Co., 1958), 97.

Chapter 18: "God in Three Persons . . ."

1. Joseph Smith, *History of the Church: 1843–1844, Vol. 6* (Salt Lake City, UT: Deseret, 1978), 474.
2. See John 5:17, 19; 8:16–19; 10:30, 32, 38; 12:49–50; 14:7–11; 15:5.

Chapter 19: ". . . Blessed Trinity"

1. Sartre, *Existentialism and Human Emotion* (Secaucus, NJ: Citadel, 1957), 22. Sartre borrowed this insight from Ivan Karamazov in Fyodor Dostoyevsky's *Brothers Karamazov*.
2. Michael Ruse and E. O. Wilson, "The Evolution of Ethics," *Religion and the Natural Sciences*, ed. J. E. Huchingson (Orlando: Harcourt Brace, 1993), 310.
3. Michael Ruse, *Darwinism Defended* (London: Addison-Wesley, 1982), 275.
4. Arthur Allen Leff, "Unspeakable Ethics, Unnatural Law," *Duke Law Journal*, vol. 1979, no. 6 (December): 1249. Leff also said, "No person, no combination of people, no document however hallowed by time, no process, no premise, nothing is equivalent to an actual God in this central function as the unexaminable examiner of good and evil. . . . The so-called death of God turns out not to have been just His funeral, it also seems to have effected the total elimination of any coherent, or even more than momentarily convincing ethical or legal system" (1232).
5. Leff, 1230.
6. Augustine, *De Trinitate*, bk. 15, trans. Arthur West Haddan, Master Christian Library CD-ROM (Ages Software, 1999), 15. Like St. Richard and St. Hilary in their earlier works on the Trinity, William Shedd acknowledged, "Communion . . . is impossible to an essence without personal distinctions. . . . A subject without an object . . . cannot love. What is there to be loved" (232).

7. Some thinkers have tried to answer that question within the bounds of strict *a priorism* of analytical philosophy. Most notably, Richard Swinburne has launched an argument from an analysis of perfect love as subsisting not only between a divine lover, G1, and a divine lovee, G2, but a third divine individual, G3, whom G1 and G2 can "co-operatively love." *The Christian God* (Oxford: Clarendon, 1994), 177–78. When it comes to limiting the divine number to three, Swinburne admits that he must rely on his "highly fallible ethical intuitions [that] co-operating with two others is not essential to the manifestation of love so long as co-operation with one in sharing is going on" (179). Some have found Swinburne's analysis of God's goodness as analytically deducible from his omnipotent freedom and omniscience (which lay the ontological foundation for his *a priori* case for Trinitarianism) to be "notoriously less than convincing." Those considerations aside, Swinburne offers no line of evidence save his own "highly fallible ethical intuitions" that exclude a quad or quinti unity. I believe what I spell out above offers a more reliable route to the triune God of the Bible.

8. Anselm, *Proslogium*, in *Classical Readings in Christian Apologetics: A.D. 100–1800*, ed. Russ Bush (Grand Rapids: Academie, 1983), 254. See also Deut. 32:2–4; Ps. 145:3; and Isa. 46:9.

9. As John Frame puts it,

> There is little debate that the doctrine of the Trinity is unique to Christianity. There are interesting triads (threefold distinctions) in other religions, such as the Hindu gods, Brahman, Vishnu, and Siva . . . but the Hindu gods are three gods, not one God in three persons, and other alleged parallels between non-Christian deities and the Trinity collapse upon examination. Essentially rivals of Christianity ignore or deny the Trinity . . . there is nothing like it in secular philosophy. There is nothing like it in the other major religions of the world. And even in the Christian heresies there is little of the Trinity. Indeed, in these heresies the doctrine of the Trinity is often the first to go. *Apologetics to the Glory of God: An Introduction* (Philipsburg, NJ: P&R Publishing, 1994), 47.

Chapter 20: The Anti-Trinity

1. Immanuel Kant, quoted in Jürgen Moltmann, *The Trinity and the Kingdom of God*, trans. Margaret Kohl (London: SCM, 1981), 6.

2. J. Scott Horrell, "An Ontology of Mission" in *Global Missiology* 1, no. 6 (2008), 13, http://ojs.globalmissiology.org/index.php/english/article/view/31/85.

3. This image comes from the work of N. T. Wright.

4. "Devil Inside," written by Andrew Farriss and Michael Hutchence, *Kick*, Atlantic Records, 1988.

Chapter 21: First, the Bad News

1. Joel Osteen, *Becoming a Better You: 7 Keys to Improving Your Life Every Day* (New York: Free Press, 2007), 56, 87, 91.
2. Charity K, "Top Ten Fascinating Facts about Joel Osteen," *Discover Walks Blog*, January 23, 2023, https://www.discoverwalks.com/blog/world/top-10 -fascinating-facts-about-joel-osteen/.
3. Jesus spoke of the reality of eternal torment (Luke 16:23), comparing it to "Gehenna" (Matt. 10:28), "outer darkness" (Matt. 25:30), unquenchable fire where worms don't die, where people gnash their teeth in anguish and regret, and from which there is no return (Mark 9:43, 48; Matt. 13:42; Luke 16:19–31).
4. Philip Schaff, *History of the Christian Church* (Grand Rapids: Eerdmans, 1985), 3:815. For similar analysis of Pelagius's thought, see Richard Flathman, *Political Obligation* (Milton Park, Abingdon, UK: Taylor & Francis, 1973), 36.
5. Erasmus, *Diatribe Concerning Free Will*, cited in Martin Luther, *Bondage of the Will*, trans. J. I. Packer (Grand Rapids: Baker, 2002), 171.
6. Charles Finney, *Finney's Systematic Theology*, ed. Dennis Carroll (1878; repr., Minneapolis: Bethany, 1994), 307.
7. "The State of Theology," Ligonier Ministries and LifeWay Research, 2022, https://thestateoftheology.com.
8. David Meyers, "A New Look at Pride," in *Your Better Self*, ed. C. W. Ellison (San Francisco: Harper & Row, 1983), 84.
9. Meyers, 90.
10. "The End of Absolutes: America's New Moral Code," Barna, May 25, 2016, https://www.barna.com/research/the-end-of-absolutes-americas-new-moral -code/.
11. The phenomenon of widespread Christian belief that we are basically good at our core has been described accurately by R. C. Sproul as "the Pelagian captivity of the church." "The Pelagian Captivity of the Church," *Modern Reformation* 10, no. 3 (2001): 22–29.
12. Neither was God's anger motivated at Jesus on the cross. John Murray drove the point home: "It is not as if the Son of God gave himself to this undertaking while the Father turned away his face until the ordeal was ended and then received Christ into the bosom of his love again. No, the events of Gethsemane, the events of the arraignment before the High Priest and before Pilate, and the events of Golgotha, were events in which God the Father was *intensely* involved. Calvary is also the supreme exhibition of the

Father's love." *O Death, Where Is Thy Sting? Collected Sermons* (Philadelphia: Westminster Theological Seminary and Logan Murray, 2017), 73.

So said John Calvin, "Yet we do not suggest that God was ever inimical or angry toward him. How could he be angry toward his beloved Son, 'in whom his heart reposed' [cf. Matt. 3:17]? How could Christ by his intercession appease the Father toward others, if he were himself hateful to God? This is what we are saying: he bore the weight of divine severity, since he was 'stricken and afflicted' [cf. Isa. 53:5] by God's hand, and experienced all the signs of a wrathful and avenging God" (*Institutes* 1.16.11). See also Thomas McCall, *Forsaken: The Trinity and the Cross, and Why It Matters* (Downers Grove, IL: InterVarsity, 2012), 13–47.

Chapter 22: Wrath

1. John Frame notes, "Although Scripture abounds in references to God's wrath and in teaching about the final judgment, we tend to abbreviate it. In our teaching, the proportion of our references to God's love and his wrath is not nearly the same as the proportion in Scripture. I include myself in this generalization. I don't think this is necessarily wrong; we do, after all, have some biblical precedent, in the brusque references to 'the wrath.' In this usage, we can feel the writer cringe and look away. And that teaches us something about how terrible the wrath of God really is." *The Doctrine of God* (Phillipsburg, NJ: P&R, 2010), 466.
2. A. W. Pink, *The Attributes of God* (Grand Rapids: Baker, 1987), 82.
3. Barry Schwartz, *The Paradox of Choice: Why More Is Less* (New York: Ecco, 2004), 9–13.
4. C. S. Lewis, *Mere Christianity* (New York: HarperCollins, 2001), 38–39.
5. "The Shadow Proves the Sunshine," written by Jon Foreman and performed by Switchfoot, *Nothing Is Sound*, Sparrow/Columbia, 2005.
6. We can all relate to the teary-eyed joy in Gandalf's face when he beholds Sauron—manifest as a burning eye smoldering atop the tower at Barad-dûr—tumbling to smithereens while Middle-earth cracks and swallows his minions at the Black Gate. Vader hurling Emperor Palpatine into a bottomless pit, Biff turning from a lucrative casino kingpin into a bumbling car waxer, Voldemort reduced to agony and ash as Neville destroys his Horcrux snake, Nagini, and Harry smiting the Dark Lord with red-hot magic from the Elder Wand.

We delight in the sexual predator getting caught and condemned behind bars, never to abuse again. There is even joy in seeing the reckless driver weaving through traffic, grazing bumpers, tripling the speed limit, risking lives of families so he can arrive at his destination a minute or two ahead of time, then hearing the sirens whirring as justice catches up with the Vin Diesel wannabe.

7. Derek Rishmawy, "The Beauty of the Cross: 19 Objections and Answers on Penal Substitutionary Atonement," October 23, 2014, derekzrishmawy.com, emphasis added.

8. "God's Gonna Cut You Down," performed by Johnny Cash, *American V: A Hundred Highways*, American Recordings, 2006.

9. J. I. Packer, *Knowing God* (Downers Grove, IL: InterVarsity, 2018), 143.

Chapter 23: Holy Rollers

1. Chuck Shepherd, "News of the Weird," March 9, 1995, vol. 24 no. 22, accessed January 18, 2024, https://chicagoreader.com/news-politics/news-of-the-weird-612/.

2. See R. C. Sproul, *The Holiness of God* (Carol Stream, IL: Tyndale, 1998), 23–25.

3. See Philippians 3:8. For the range of meanings of *skybala* in the ancient world and why it is not the offensive swear word many well-meaning preachers claim it is, see Gary Manning Jr., "Did the Apostle Paul Use Profanity?" *The Good Book Blog*, Talbot School of Theology, October 1, 2015, https://www.biola.edu/blogs/good-book-blog/2015/did-the-apostle-paul-use-profanity; and "More Skubala: Did the Apostle Paul Use Swear Words?, *The Good Book Blog*, Talbot School of Theology, March 24, 2022, https://www.biola.edu/blogs/good-book-blog/2022/more-skubala-did-the-apostle-paul-use-swear-words.

4. Roland Bainton, *Here I Stand: A Life of Martin Luther* (New York: Abingdon, 1950), 41.

5. Bainton, 45.

6. Luther's father confessor Staupitz once told Luther, "Come in with something to forgive—parricide, blasphemy, adultery—instead of all the peccadilloes" (Bainton, 54).

7. Bainton, 65.

8. Martin Luther, "Table Talk 5537" in *D. Martin Luther's Werk: Tischreden*, 1531–1546, vol. 5, (Weimar H. Bohlaus, 1919), 222, https://archive.org/details/werketischreden10205luthuoft/page/n7/mode/2up.

9. Bainton, 65. In *Bondage of the Will*, which Luther considered his most important work, he said, "God has assuredly promised his grace to the humble [1 Peter 5:5], that is, to those who lament and despair of themselves." Martin Luther, *Bondage of the Will*, trans. J. I. Packer (Grand Rapids: Baker, 2002), 137.

Chapter 24: Healthy, Battered, Dead, or Robots?

1. To see how the Bible debunks the concept that *ought* implies "can," see Thaddeus Williams, *God Reforms Hearts: Rethinking Free Will and the Problem of Evil* (Bellingham, WA: Lexham Academic, 2021), 71–94.

2. "The End of Absolutes: America's New Moral Code," Barna, May 25, 2016, https://www.barna.com/research/the-end-of-absolutes-americas-new-moral-code/.

3. Philip Schaff, *History of the Christian Church* (Grand Rapids: Eerdmans, 1985), 3:815.

4. Reinhold Seeberg clarified Cassian's view: "The idea of Cassian is that the human will has indeed been crippled by sin, but that a certain freedom has yet remained to it. By virtue of this, [the human will] is able to turn to God, and, just as though God had first turned to it, it is able, with the assistance of divine grace, setting before it the law [i.e., Heart Persuasion] and infusing the needed power [i.e., Heart Cooperation], to will and to do that which is good. Hence the sinner is not dead, but wounded." *History of Doctrines in the Ancient Church*, trans. Charles Hay (1905; repr., Grand Rapids: Baker, 1977), 1:371–72.

5. Arminius continued, "Exactly correspondent to this Darkness of Mind and Perverseness of Heart, is the utter Weakness [*impotentia*] of all the Powers to perform that which is truly good." *The Public Disputations of James Arminius, D.D.*, in James Arminius, *The Works of James Arminius: The London Edition*, trans. James and Williams Nichols (1825–75; repr., Grand Rapids: Baker, 1986), 2:192–95.

6. John Wesley, *The Works of John Wesley*, ed. T. Jimson (Grand Rapids: Baker, 1979), 10:350.

7. This is known as "prevenient grace" in Arminian theology. In Wesley's words, "There is a measure of free will supernaturally restored to every man." John Wesley, 10:229–30. See Robert Rakestraw, "John Wesley as a Theologian of Grace," *Journal of the Evangelical Theological Society* 27 (1984): 196–99; and J. Weldon Smith III, "Some Notes on Wesley's Doctrine of Prevenient Grace," *Religion and Life* 34 (1964–65): 70–75.

8. "The Remonstrance of 1610," app. C, in *Crisis in the Reformed Churches: Essays in Commemoration of the Great Synod of Dort, 1618–1619*, ed. Peter Y. De Jong (Grand Rapids: Reformed Fellowship, 1968), 208–9.

9. "Remonstrance of 1610," 208–9.

10. Augustine believed we suffer from *liberum arbitrium captivatum* ("the captive free will"). It is not as if we are stuck in this moral captivity against our wills, trying desperately to reach up to God but cursing the chains that keep us down. Rather, we are like "[a prisoner who] kisses his chains and refuses deliverance," in the words of Francis Turretin. *Institutes of Elenctic Theology*,

vol. 1, tr. George Musgrave Giger, ed. James Dennison (Phillipsburg, NJ: P&R Publishing, 1994), 671.

11. Augustine, *On Forgiveness of Sins and Baptism*, 2.32 (cited in Francis Turretin, *Institutes of Elenctic Theology*, trans. George Musgrave Giger, ed. James Dennison (1696; repr. Phillipsburg, NJ: P&R, 1994), 2:521, 525.

12. Augustine, *On Grace and Free Will*, 32, *The Nicene and Post-Nicene Fathers*, vol. 5, ed. Philip Schaff (Grand Rapids: Eerdmans, 1980), 457.

13. Augustine, *Confessions*, Book 10, chs. 22, 32.

14. Augustinian theology has seen its population grow exponentially in the last couple of decades, in large part with the work of theologians like R. C. Sproul, John Piper, Tim Keller, James White, D. A. Carson, Wayne Grudem, and others.

15. Francis Turretin, *Institutes of Elenctic Theology*, 2:523, 521.

16. The closest possible advocate would be Benedict Spinoza in Jewish theology, given his pantheistic determinism.

17. In this heretical view, God bypasses the human will in such a way that all morally relevant human agency is lost. We are led into a strange pantheism in which God remains the only active agent in existence. This view represents a "no-man's-land" in a very literal sense of the term. There can be no "man" if God practices heart circumvention. With human desires, aversions, reasons, and intentions voided by an exercise of divine force, man reduces to the level of a machine. Every "I love you" we express to God is not qualitatively different from the soul-less "I love yous" that echo from the tiny phonograph inside a stuffed Chatty Cathy doll when a toddler pulls its string. On this view, we are merely preprogrammed dolls, devoid of power and designed for the amusement of a giant toddler.

18. For the difference between atheistic determinism and the biblical view of human agency see Thaddeus Williams, *God Reforms Hearts: Rethinking Free Will and the Problem of Evil* (Bellingham, WA: Lexham Academic, 2021).

19. Turretin, *Institutes of Elenctic Theology*, 2:523–24.

Chapter 25: A Brit, a Roman, a Dutchman, and an African Walk into a Bar

1. One could argue that universalism is another theological option in which (in its Arminian form) none can until God works then all can and all will, or (in its Augustinian form) none can until God works and then all will. While it is beyond the scope of the current work, I believe universalism, as much as I may want it to be true, cannot be faithfully squared with Jesus's teaching on the reality of an eternally occupied hell in such passages as Matthew 10:28; 13:42; 25:30; Mark 9:43; and Luke 16:19–31.

2. George Barna, "Americans' Bible Knowledge in the Ballpark, but Often Off

Base," July 7, 2011, cited on WayBackMachine, accessed August 14, 2023, https://web.archive.org/web/20110707232958/http://www.biblehistory.com /166.htm.

3. Under the old covenant—the agreement God struck with Moses at Mount Sinai—God issued ten life-giving commandments, the first tablet on how to love him and the second tablet on how to love our neighbors. Keep these commands and be blessed; break them and be cursed. As the ancient Jews moved on from Sinai on their way to the promised land, they ended up in Moab on the eastern shores of the Dead Sea. To say that on that long journey God's people did not keep up their end of the covenant would be an understatement. God made it clear in Moab why the Israelites failed under the old covenant. Their sin natures prevailed because "to this day the LORD has not given you a heart to understand or eyes to see or ears to hear" (Deut. 29:4). One factor that separates the old from the new covenant is the divine grace that transforms us so that we actually keep the commands that would be otherwise impossible given our stony hearts, blind eyes, and deaf ears.

4. I engage Pelagian, semi-Pelagian, and Arminian attempts to interpret these and other critical passages in *God Reforms Hearts: Rethinking Free Will and the Problem of Evil* (Bellingham, WA: Lexham Academic, 2021), 152–184.

5. In the context of John 6, Jesus offered himself as living bread to the crowds on the shores of Capernaum. The day before, Jesus miraculously fed thousands with literal bread, and they followed him in hopes of scoring another free meal. Jesus looked behind their felt need to their deeper existential need, their spiritual hunger. The crowd was not happy. They grumbled, refusing to feast on Christ as the Bread of Life. It was in this context, standing before a hungry, unbelieving mob, that Jesus said something both awe-inspiring and offensive all at once: "All that the Father gives me will come to me" (v. 37). This was offensive and contributed to the crowds abandoning Jesus for his "hard teaching" by the end of John 6 because the implication was that they were not coming to him because they were not given to him by his Father. Any interpretation that smooths over Jesus's teaching here to make it more palatable makes it difficult to account for the crowd's abandonment of Jesus.

6. Some interpreters advance a reading of John 6 in which those who use their libertarian free will to accept the Father's teaching (first century faithful Jews, for example), the Father, in turn, gives to the Son, and they, in turn, will come to the Son. Thus, it is claimed, the verb order and tenses of v. 37 can be read in a non-Augustinian yet exegetically faithful way.

Much could be said about this interpretation, but I will limit myself to two brief observations. First, it undermines the very libertarian free will to initially accept or reject Jesus that the interpreter is so motivated to preserve.

Yes, this interpretation preserves libertarian freedom as to whether someone will accept or reject the Father's teaching. But once he or she does so, the text is clear that the Father gives them to the Son and they will, not might, come to the Son. There is no room for someone who chooses the Father to then exercise autonomous choosing power to not come to the Son. Second, verse 44 states that "no one can come me unless the Father who sent me draws him. And I will raise him up on the last day." This text leaves no room for us to exert autonomous libertarian power to walk away from the Son once we have come to him.

Suppose the interpreter answers that these texts say nothing of the necessity of coming to the Son or being raised up, but only of their certainty. For example, I may be certain that 100 percent of my students will take their final exams, but perhaps they still took the exam by libertarian choice rather than necessity. This still raises major problems for the libertarian. The 100 percent response rate of those coming to the Son then being raised up strongly suggests something other than equiprobability or probabilistic libertarian freedom, something like compatibilistic freedom. For a full defense, see *God Reforms Hearts*.

7. In light of John 6, we may ask, "Why is election unconditional?" Because if God's choosing us is conditioned on our prior choice of him, a choice we could easily make against him, then the size of the Father's love gift to his Son could be drastically smaller than he wants it to be. Election is unconditional because the size of his intended expression of Trinitarian love is determined by the Gift Giver, not the gift. Why is the atonement effective in redeeming every sinner it is intended to redeem? Because otherwise the Son fails to fulfill his Father's will. Every autonomous human agent who says no to the cross prevents Christ from carrying out his commanded mission, impeding the full expression of God's love within the Trinity. The atonement is effective because intra-Trinitarian love is not defective. Why is grace irresistible? Because if we could shun the Father's grace as he draws us to worship his Son, then we have the power to thwart God's expression of love within the Trinity. Grace cannot be resisted because his Trinitarian love cannot be frustrated. Why are the saints preserved to their state of glory? Because otherwise the Son would fail to fulfill his Father's will that he would "lose none of all" of his love gift (v. 39 NIV), and the Father would fail to fulfill his Son's will that they would behold his glory (John 17:24). The saints are preserved because the divine persons perfectly fulfill one another's will.

8. What happens, then, to the beautiful substitution that happened at the cross? Biblically, the cross is where the Son who perfectly fulfilled his Father's will takes the place of those who fall short of such perfect

will-keeping. If, however, someone given by the Father could say no to
the Son, then we can prevent the Son from fulfilling his Father's will that
"none" of the love gift "would be lost." The cross would then become a
place where we exchange our filthy rags for another set of soiled clothes.
Imperfection is substituted for another imperfection. John's gospel does
not lead us to such a hopeless conclusion. The Son says, "I love you," to his
Father through a track record of impeccable obedience. Jesus kept every facet
of the Father's will, including losing none of his love gift, ensuring that no
stain could subtract a single iota of tearful joy as he watches his bride—the
church—march to the altar.

9. John Owen argues that Arminians "must resolve almost the sole cause of
our salvation into ourselves ultimately, it being in our own power to make all
that God and Christ do unto that end effectual, or to frustrate their utmost
endeavors for that purpose: for all that is done, whether in the Father's
loving us and sending his Son to die for us, or in the Son's offering himself
for an oblation in our stead, or for us (in our behalf) is confessedly . . . of
no value nor worth, in respect of any profitable issue, unless we believe. . . .
Whether we will believe or no, is left to ourselves. Now, whether this be not
to assign unto ourselves the cause of our own happiness, and to make us the
chief builders of our own glory, let all judge." *The Death of Death in the Death
of Christ* (Carlisle, PA: The Banner of Truth Trust, 1999), 143.

10. James Arminius, "Disputation 11: Of the Free Will of Man and Its Powers,"
The Works of James Arminius, vol. 1, https://ccel.org/ccel/arminius/works1
/works1.v.xii.html.

11. Non-Augustinians offer analogies like everyone being invited to a lavish
party. If an individual, say Jones, accepts the offer and has an epic time
at the party, we would hardly say that Jones is to thank for his epic party
experience. He simply accepted the offer that others rejected. Surely Jones
did not foot the bill for the extravagant food spread, the posh venue, the
smoke machines, the shrimp wall, the Bengal Tiger, the DJ, and so on.
Crediting Jones for his enjoyment of the party seems misguided.

Such analogies dodge the core questions. One core question is why, on a
libertarian account of free will, Jones would choose to accept the invitation to
the party/heaven rather than reject such an invitation. Libertarian freedom
requires that Jones transcends all desires, beliefs, and propensities such that
he can choose which ones to endorse and which to refrain from endorsing. If
Jones himself transcends all desires, beliefs, and propensities then he not only
bears no resemblance to the kinds of choosing agents we meet in the Bible, but
his choices become totally arbitrary and thus poor candidates for meaningful
action and moral praise or blame. For further analysis, see *God Reforms Hearts:
Rethinking Free Will and the Problem of Evil* (Lexham Academic, 2021).

Second, the Augustinian is not asking whether Jones is the reason there is a party at all. All theological perspectives would say God plans the party, foots the bill, and extends the invitations. Rather the question is why Jones chooses to attend the party while others with the identical ability to accept, let's say Smith and Winston, reject the offer and miss out on all the fun. Choosing to accept rather than reject the offer of the party/salvation is the smarter/more spiritual choice. Thus, it seems impossible to avoid the conclusion on non-Augustinian grounds that Jones made the smarter/more spiritual choice than Smith and Winston. The only reason Jones is not shivering in the cold, in darkness outside the eternal party is not on account of the Great Party Maker and Inviter—God—but because of Jones' superior use of the same power gifted to Smith and Winston. That leaves room for precisely the kind of boasting the New Testament precludes again and again.

12. Kenneth Copeland, "Praise-a-Thon" program on TBN (April 1988).
13. For deeper analysis of libertarian free will and its shortcomings, see my *God Reforms Hearts*, 3–65.
14. See Spurgeon's book by that title, *All of Grace* (Crossreach, 2019).
15. The best introduction to these difficult doctrines, if your time is limited, is Charles Spurgeon's sermon "Sovereignty and Salvation," available online at https://www.spurgeon.org/resource-library/sermons/sovereignty-and-salvation/. Other helpful resources include Jonathan Edwards, *Freedom of the Will*, vol. 1 of *The Works of Jonathan Edwards* (New Haven, CT: Yale University Press, 2016); John Owen, *The Death of Death in the Death of Christ* (Carlisle, PA: Banner of Truth, 1959); D. A. Carson, *Divine Sovereignty and Human Responsibility: Biblical Perspectives in Tension* (Eugene, OR: Wipf and Stock, 2002); D. A. Carson, *The Difficult Doctrine of the Love of God* (Wheaton, IL: Crossway, 1999); Scott Christensen, *What about Free Will? Reconciling Our Choices with God's Sovereignty* (Phillipsburg, NJ: P&R, 2016); and Matthew Barrett and Thomas Nettle, eds., *Whomever He Wills* (Cape Coral, FL: Founders Press, 2012). Specifically on the question of whether God desires all to be saved I heartily recommend John Piper's article "Are There Two Wills in God?," desiringGod, https://www.desiringgod.org/articles/are-there-two-wills-in-god. I address many of the most common philosophical and biblical objections to God's sovereign grace in *God Reforms Hearts*.
16. Some of the best works seeking to defend Arminius and refute Augustine's view of grace include Roger Olsen, *Against Calvinism: Rescuing God's Reputation from Radical Reformed Theology* (Grand Rapids: Zondervan, 2011); Robert Picirilli, *Grace, Faith, Free Will* (Nashville: Randall House, 2002); Clark Pinnock, *Grace Unlimited* (Eugene, OR: Wipf and Stock, 1999); Leroy Forlines, *Classical Arminianism* (Nashville: Randall House,

2011); and David Allen and Steve Lemke, *Calvinism: A Biblical and Theological Critique* (Nashville: B&H, 2022).

17. "The Prayer of Saint Francis," https://www.cathedralstm.org/about-our -catholic-faith/expressing-our-faith/treasury-catholic-prayers/prayer-st -francis-assisi-prayer-peace/.

18. Thomas à Kempis, *The Imitation of Christ*, trans. John Payne (Boston: Gould and Lincoln, 1856), 175–76, 177.

19. John Donne, "Holy Sonnets," no. 14, https://www.poetryfoundation.org /poems/44106/holy-sonnets-batter-my-heart-three-person-god.

20. Janette . . . Ikz, "Run Ablaze," in *His Testimonies, My Heritage: Women of Color on the Word of God*, ed. Kristie Anyabwile (Charlotte, NC: The Good Book Company, 2019), 61.

21. J. I. Packer, *Evangelism and the Sovereignty of God* (Downers Grove, IL: IVP, 1961), 15–17.

22. Augustine, *On Psalm 118*, in Thomas A. Hand, *Augustine on Prayer* (New York: Catholic Book Publishing, 1986), 35.

Chapter 26: Blind Leaps of Atheism

1. Arthur Conan Doyle, "The Naval Treaty," in *The Memoirs of Sherlock Holmes* (Moscow: Ripol Classic, 2017), 189.

2. See Robert Jastrow, *God and the Astronomers* (Kingsport, TN: Reader's Library, 2000); Hugh Ross, *The Creator and the Cosmos: How the Latest Scientific Discoveries Reveal God* (San Francisco: RTB, 2018); and William Lane Craig, *The Kalam Cosmological Argument* (Eugene, OR: Wipf and Stock, 2000).

3. See William Lane Craig, *Reasonable Faith: Christian Truth and Apologetics* (Wheaton, IL: Crossway, 2008), chs. 3–4.

4. Astronomer Hugh Ross notes, "The expansion rate of the universe determines what kinds of stars, if any, form in the universe. If the rate of expansion were slightly less, the whole universe would have recollapsed before any solar-type stars could have settled into a stable burning phase. If the universe were expanding slightly more rapidly, no galaxies (and hence no stars) would condense from the general expansion. How critical is this expansion rate? According to Alan Guth, it must be fine-tuned to an accuracy of one part in 10^{55}." "A Just Right Universe," in *Creator and the Cosmos*, ch. 14.

5. Stangl went on to explain that after the big bang, we had a universe of light elements, elements high up on the periodic table, like hydrogen and helium. For biological life to be possible, you need heavier elements (those farther down the periodic table). Heavy elements emerge in the cores of stars that are like mega-ovens smoldering hot enough to pass the Coulomb barrier

so that nuclear fusion can occur, binding together light elements to create heavy elements. This process requires amazingly fine-tuned math equations to successfully create heavy elements essential to life. Moreover, once these heavy elements emerge, there must be some way to get them out of the core of the star into the cosmos to form life-supporting planets. Lo and behold, supernovas happen—star explosions—jettisoning the heavy elements into space where they can form into planets like ours.

6. For further study, see John Lennox, *Cosmic Chemistry: Do God and Science Mix* (London: Lion, 2021).

Chapter 27: More Leaps of Atheism

1. In *Creator and the Cosmos: How the Latest Scientific Discoveries Reveal God* (San Francisco: RTB, 2018), Hugh Ross lists more than twenty variables that must be fine-tuned for life on earth to be possible. See also John D. Barrow and Frank J. Tipler, *The Anthropic Cosmological Principle* (New York: Oxford University Press, 1986); F. Bertola and U. Curi, eds., *The Anthropic Principle: The Conditions for the Existence of Mankind in the Universe* (Cambridge: Cambridge University Press, 1993); Paul Davies, *The Cosmic Blueprint: New Discoveries in Nature's Creative Ability to Order the Universe* (New York: Simon & Schuster, 1988); Michael J. Denton, *Nature's Destiny: How the Laws of Biology Reveal Purpose in the Universe* (New York: Free Press, 1998); George Greenstein, *The Symbiotic Universe: Life and Mind in the Cosmos* (New York: William Morrow, 1988); and Peter D. Ward and Donald Brownlee, *Rare Earth: Why Complex Life Is Uncommon in the Universe* (New York: Copernicus, 2003).

2. Cited by Richard Ostling in "Lifelong Atheist Changes Mind about Divine Creator," *Washington Times*, December 10, 2004, https://www.washington times.com/news/2004/dec/9/20041209-113212-2782r/.

3. Antony Flew, "Letter from Antony Flew on Darwinism and Theology," *Philosophy Now*, accessed December 14, 2023, https://philosophynow.org /issues/47/Letter_from_Antony_Flew_on_Darwinism_and_Theology.

4. For further study, see Stephen Meyer, *Return of the God Hypothesis: Three Scientific Discoveries That Reveal the Mind behind the Universe* (New York: HarperOne, 2021).

5. For a deeper analysis of naturalistic determinism and quantum indeterminism, see my *God Reforms Hearts: Rethinking Free Will and the Problem of Evil* (Bellingham, WA: Lexham Academic, 2022), 28–67.

6. For deeper analysis, see J. P. Moreland, *Scaling the Secular City: A Defense of Christianity* (Grand Rapids: Baker, 1987), 105–32.

7. Don DeLillo, *White Noise* (New York: Penguin Classics, 2016), 200.

8. For deeper analysis, see Saul Kripke, *Naming and Necessity* (Hoboken, NJ: Wiley-Blackwell, 1981).

9. Thomas Nagel, "What Is It Like to Be a Bat?" *Philosophical Review* 83, no. 4 (October 1974): 435–50.

10. Richard Dawkins, *The Blind Watchmaker* (New York: Norton, 2015), 133.

11. Alex Rosenberg, *The Atheist's Guide to Reality* (New York: Norton, 2012), 43, 281. How can atheism escape Rosenberg's nihilistic logic? In the atheistic framework, we are left either pretending our lives are objectively significant without justifying this (secular humanism), inventing subjective significance in the objectively meaningless cosmos (existentialism), or giving up hope of ever finding any significance behind our existence (nihilism).

12. Charles Darwin, "To William Graham," July 3, 1881, Darwin Correspondence Project, University of Cambridge, accessed December 14, 2023, https://www.darwinproject.ac.uk/letters/?docld=letters/DCP-LETT -13230.xml.

Chapter 28: Starmaker

1. C. S. Lewis, *Voyage of the Dawn Treader* (New York: Macmillan, 1986), 1.

2. Lewis, 175.

3. Plato, *The Dialogues of Plato*, ed. B. Jowett (Oxford: Oxford University Press, 1924), 358.

4. Aristotle, *On Philosophy*, cited in William Lane Craig, *Reasonable Faith: Christian Truth and Apologetics* (Wheaton, IL: Crossway, 2008), 101.

5. Neil DeGrasse Tyson (sonde2007), "The Beauty of the Universe," TikTok, April 21, 2007, https://www.tiktok.com/@sonde2007/video/722450318128 2266411.

Chapter 29: Shadow, Stream, and Scattered Beam Apologetics

1. Jonathan Edwards, "Sermon XII: The Christian Pilgrim," *The Works of Jonathan Edwards*, vol. 2 (Carlisle, PN: Banner of Truth, 1974), 244.

2. Jack Kerouac, *On the Road* (New York: Viking Press, 1957), 5.

3. "A Finger, Two Dots, Then Me: The Short Film," written and performed by Derrick Brown, Duality Frameworks/Write Bloody Publishing, October 11, 2012, https://www.youtube.com/watch?v=TcoMiGiDRjg, used with permission.

4. Michael Ruse, "The Evolution of Ethics," in *Religion and the Natural Sciences: The Range of Engagement*, ed. J. E. Huchingson (Orlando: Harcourt Brace, 1993), 310.

5. Commenting on Psalm 43:4, John Piper observes,

> God is the essence of our joys. God is the substance of our all our joys. He is the best part of every joy if we are enjoying things rightly. . . . He

is to be what makes all our joys most enjoyable. . . . Every joy that does not have God as the central gladness of the joy is a hollow joy and, in the end, will burst like a bubble. . . . God intends to be glorified not only by being enjoyed more than pizza and more than friendship, but by being enjoyed in the very enjoyment of pizza and in the very enjoyment of friendship. I think God intends for us to enjoy his sweetness in the sweetness of chocolate, his saltiness in the saltiness of french fries, his juiciness in the juiciness of a sizzling steak, his friendship in the company of our friends, his brightness in the sunrise, and so on. . . . let us know and enjoy God as our exceeding joy—yes, and as the gladness of all our joys ("Enjoying God in His Gifts," Ask Pastor John, Episode 2021, February 19, 2024, https://www.desiringgod.org/interviews/enjoying-god-in-his-gifts).

6. Peter Kreeft, "Twenty Arguments God's Existence," https://www.peterkreeft.com/topics-more/20_arguments-gods-existence.htm.

Chapter 30: Masterpieces

1. In the summer of 2002, I did precisely that. When I turned a corner in the Louvre and saw the swarms of tourists flocking to da Vinci's masterpiece, I deliberately kept my head down and shuffled through the crowd to the next room, not giving that enigmatic smile so much as a glance. I thought I was being cool, a nonconformist, refusing to join the herd. In reality, I was being a pretentious idiot. I resolved the error in the summer of 2015 by taking a good long look with my daughter Holland perched happily on my shoulders.

2. This number comes from the estimated 140 million babies born globally each year, plus the estimated 23 million a year God calls home before birth, plus the estimated 73 million small masterpieces aborted annually around the world.

3. Dr. Suess, *Happy Birthday to You!* (New York: Random House, 1987).

4. Bruce K. Waltke and M. O'Connor identify the use of "fearfully" in the original Hebrew as an example of "the *accusative of manner* [that] describes the way in which an action is *performed*." *An Introduction to Biblical Hebrew Syntax* (University Park, PA: Eisenbrauns, 1990), 172. If they are correct, then "fearfully" describes not the psalmist's state of mind but God's as he wonderfully makes the psalmist.

5. Dr. Suess, *Happy Birthday to You!*

6. C. S. Lewis, *The Weight of Glory* (New York: HarperCollins, 2001), 46.

7. Paul said these masterpieces are designed to do good works that God *proetoimasen*, "prepared beforehand." Far more meaning is scripted into your day than you realize. Divine appointments, meaningful moments, are planned before you even stumble off the mattress. On countless days, I

thought I was just headed to the office, joining the neighbors for barbecue, catching a flight, or chatting around a firepit. But God was up to something eternal and far more glorious than anything that could be caught on the dull video footage of the day. We only get occasional glimpses of the beautiful top of the tapestry; most of life is spent underneath the tapestry looking at a seemingly chaotic network of threads. Our pre-glory state of mind means we are usually missing the big picture. How many conversations in the new heaven and new earth will be about the glorious feats God pulled off through a forgotten conversation, shared coffee, or some other mundane encounter? There is real meaning in knowing that our days are filled with "good works prepared beforehand," especially in those inevitable seasons when life seems boring and hopeless.

Psalm 139 is a beautifully countercultural old hymn. Here the God-as-author motif is explicit: "In [God's] book were written, every one of them, the days that were formed for me, when as yet there was none of them" (v. 16).

8. Isaiah 29:16 also uses the imagery of God as potter, making humans. The Septuagint uses the same *poiema* language as Ephesians 2:10.

9. Likewise, Christ is *the* Son of God and we are to be sons of God, bearing the family resemblance (John 1:12–13; 1 John 3:1–3).

10. C. S. Lewis, *Mere Christianity* (New York: HarperCollins, 2001), 223–25.

11. If only there were another book to help us do just that. *Reflect: Becoming Yourself by Mirroring the Greatest Person in History* (Bellingham, WA: Lexham, 2021).

Epilogue: Simplicity and the Soul-Artist

1. To understand how the truth of divine simplicity is not only compatible with but essential to the doctrine of the Trinity see Matthew Barrett, *Simply Trinity: The Unmanipulated Father, Son, and Spirit* (Grand Rapids, MI: Baker, 2021).

2. Irenaeus, *Against Heresies* in Ante-Nicene Fathers, ed. Alexander Roberts (Peabody, MA: Hendrickson, 2012), 2.13.3, 374.

3. George Swinnock, *The Incomparableness of God*, in *The Works of George Swinnock* (Edinburg: Banner of Truth, 1992), 4:423-424. I found this quote in Matthew Barrett's *None Greater: The Undomesticated Attributes of God* (Grand Rapids, MI: Baker, 2019), the fifth chapter of which offers an excellent defense of divine simplicity.

4. See Thomas Aquinas, *Summa contra Gentiles, Book 1: God*, tr. Anton C. Pegis (Notre Dame, IN: University of Notre Dame Press, 1955), 1.18.3–5, 103.

INDEX